陕西师范大学“211工程”建设项目资助

跨语言文化研究

Cross-Linguistic & Cross-Cultural Studies

第十五辑

王启龙　曹　婷　主编

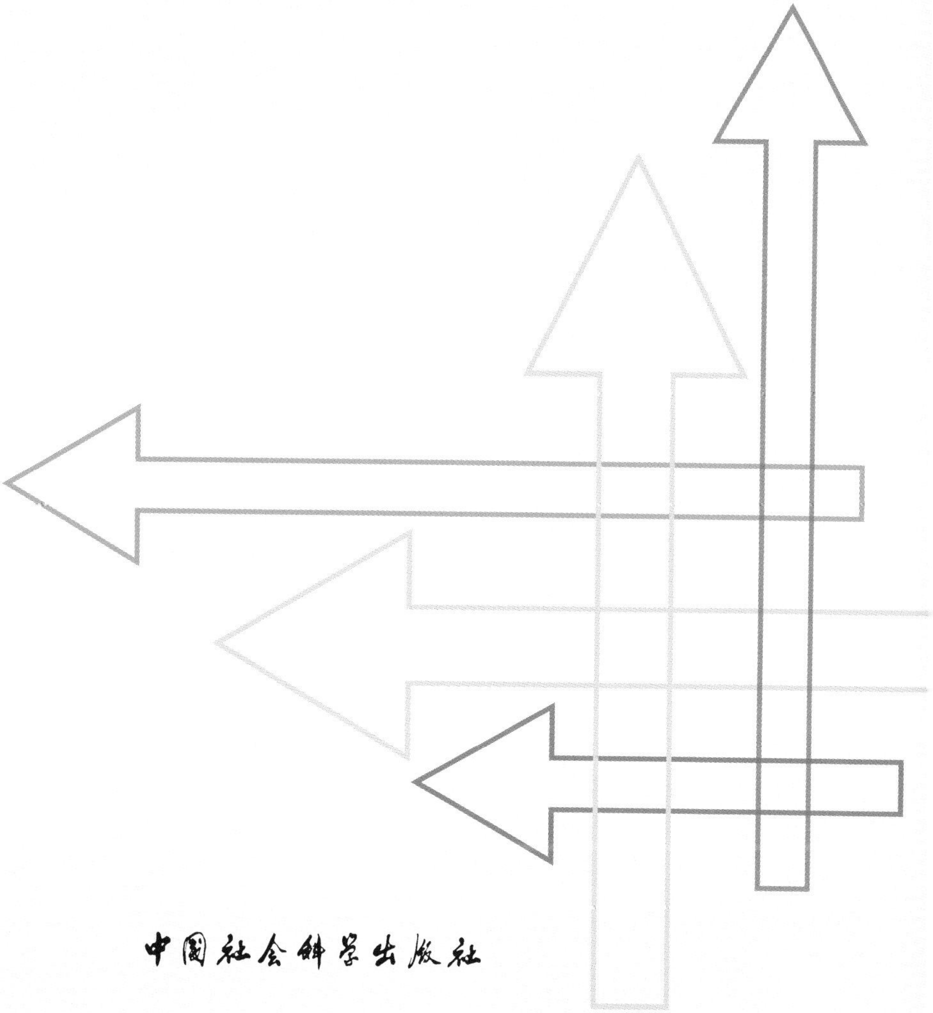

中国社会科学出版社

图书在版编目(CIP)数据

跨语言文化研究. 第15辑 / 王启龙，曹婷主编. —北京：中国社会科学出版社，2020.12

ISBN 978-7-5203-7424-8

Ⅰ.①跨…　Ⅱ.①王…②曹…　Ⅲ.①语言学—研究②世界文学—文学研究　Ⅳ.①H0②I106

中国版本图书馆CIP数据核字(2020)第205014号

出 版 人　赵剑英
责任编辑　周慧敏　任　明
责任校对　王　龙
责任印制　郝美娜

出　　版　中国社会科学出版社
社　　址　北京鼓楼西大街甲158号
邮　　编　100720
网　　址　http：//www.csspw.cn
发 行 部　010-84083685
门 市 部　010-84029450
经　　销　新华书店及其他书店

印刷装订　北京君升印刷有限公司
版　　次　2020年12月第1版
印　　次　2020年12月第1次印刷

开　　本　710×1000　1/16
印　　张　16.75
插　　页　2
字　　数　284千字
定　　价　110.00元

目　　录

特约论文

文学与文化

语言与文化

文化与教学

特约论文

Enacted signature pedagogy and becoming an academic: The case of an Applied Linguistics doctoral programme

Tae-hee Choi * and Bob Adamson

The Education University of Hong Kong

Abstract: The proposal by Shulman and his colleagues to identify the signature pedagogy of EdD degrees has led many researchers to engage in identifying the signature pedagogy of doctoral programmes of varied disciplines. Most research, however, focuses on the pedagogy in plan, leaving a research gap on implemented signature pedagogy. This paper contributes to filling the gap by analysing a PhD programme as implemented using a "successful" Applied Linguistics programme as a case. Analysing the shared, implemented pedagogy in a weekly research seminar series and PhD supervision, this paper makes a unique contribution of capturing the signature pedagogy, in particular, the subtle and intangible processes, which a doctoral programme uses to guide its peripheral members to become fully-fledged academics.

Keywords: Development of PhD students; Applied Linguistics; research seminar; PhD supervision; social constructionism

---

* Correspondence: choith@ eduhk. hk

Choi Tae-hee（崔太僖）香港教育大学教育政策与领导系副教授，博士，香港比较教育学会前任会长。研究兴趣：教育政策及改革；教师发展与变革。Bob Adamson（鲍勃·安德姆森）香港教育大学课程改革讲座教授，著作涵盖英语教学、教师教育、比较教育、课程研究和高等教育等领域，近期研究关注中国少数民族多语教育。

Introduction

How novices are inducted into a profession is a reflection of how members of that profession view themselves and their expertise. In the case of doctoral studies, pursuing a PhD or an EdD is a form of apprenticeship to academia (irrespective of whether the candidate subsequently chooses a career as an academic). In the same way that the public signage and notices of a linguistic environment tell us about the underlying role and statuses of various languages (García, Flores, & Spotti, 2016; Landry and Bourhis, 1997), the discourses to which a doctoral candidate is exposed reveal conceptualisations held by academics of their profession. In many post-secondary and tertiary institutions, a doctorate is the basic requirement for entering the academic workplace, while in other aspects of society, a doctoral degree is viewed as a mark of expertise, as evidenced by the honorific, "Doctor", which is derived from the Latin term meaning a "learned person".

Since 2005, researchers have become increasingly interested in the discipline-specific features of doctorate programmes and how they enable doctoral candidates to develop into full-fledged members of that specific academic community (Olson and Clark, 2009). Attention has been paid to ways in which the curricula of doctoral programmes can nurture competent graduates (e.g., Gurung, Chick, and Haynie, 2009). Within this research, Shulman's (2005) term "signature pedagogy" has been used to discern the key features of the practices of teaching, and to provide insights into the underlying conceptions of what characteristics the education profession considers a learned person should embody. Signature pedagogy refers to those practices of teaching and learning that characterise the education of a profession. According to Shulman (2005, p. 52), it is the "personalities, dispositions, and cultures" of specific professional fields, which are indispensable for peripheral members to be granted full membership in the professional community.

A number of researchers (e.g., Evans, 2007; Olson and Clark, 2009; Zambo, 2011), have focused on Doctor of Education (EdD) programmes, given the challenges faced by such programmes in differentiating from PhDs in the field of education and the particular professional orientations of the candidates. Evans (2007) succinctly summed up the signature pedagogy of EdD as the development of the praxis or knowledge base to guide the pedagogic practice, departing from the sole focus on the observable teaching practice. Zambo (2011) brought in a new, significant perspective by analysing the implemented signature pedagogy, using dissertations as data. Scholars from different disciplines and fields, inspired by the idea, have started to expand the investigations outside EdD programmes. Gurung et al. (2009) and Chick et al. (2012) collected the works on signature pedagogy across different disciplines including, to name but a few, fine arts, language education, and sociology, in their two edited landmark volumes. Some studies even looked beyond university education; Larrison and Korr (2013), for instance, looked into the signature pedagogy of social work.

PhD programmes, meanwhile, have received less attention, and is thus the focus of this paper. Specifically, the study analyses the signature pedagogy of a PhD programme in Applied Linguistics as implemented by faculty members and experienced by research students. The choice of Applied Linguistics is significant, given that this discipline pays attention to how languages are used in our daily lives, and the fact that they are not simply vehicles to communicate but to construct and change societies. The majority of research and publications, with a few exceptions, investigate signature pedagogy from the point of programme directors and focus on the design stage of the pedagogy, overlooking the enacted and realised version of the programmes as experienced by doctoral students. For this study, taking into account the fact that PhD students' development occurs through multiple encounters with other academics and students, the scope encompasses their individual supervisory sessions and semi-mandatory weekly research seminars in order to capture the socialisation in effect. Existing studies, furthermore, have mostly investigated the perspective of programme designers and not considered how signature pedagogy is realised in action, although there are a couple of exceptions, including Zambo (2011) who analysed the participants' learning as captured in dissertations or Amann and Knorr Cetina (1988) who discussed a discipline specific way of "seeing" in the laboratory. Applied Linguistics, despite its long history and its increasing importance in the globalising world, has been an outsider to this research expansion into PhD degrees. Ham and Schueller (2012) studied the signature pedagogy of Teaching English to Speakers of Other Languages, which is sometimes considered part of Applied Linguistics, but also limited their research to the design level. Thus, by documenting the signature pedagogy as experienced and implemented by the community members of a PhD programme in Applied Linguistics, this paper addresses several research gaps.

Data Collection and Analysis

The doctoral programme chosen for this study is offered by a university in the United Kingdom (UK). The department that runs the programme was rated in the top band in a recent national Research Excellence Framework exercise, and the staff members who belong to the research group regularly publish and are widely quoted around the world. The senior members of the group encourage the research students to aspire to become researchers of a high standard, and assist them to meet the expectation through systemised doctoral training consisting of PhD supervision meetings and regular research seminars, as well as input sessions provided by a doctoral training centre.

This exploratory study analyses the processes of socialisation of its peripheral members through the weekly research seminar and PhD supervision. The training through the graduate training centre is interdisciplinary, and therefore will not be included in the analysis. The data include observation notes from and circulars on the weekly research seminar, and an interview about the seminars with Felix (a pseudonym), a senior member of the research group (see Appendix A for the interview schedule). It also draws on data from a series of reflections, including vignettes of illustrative scenes from the seminars, by a doctoral candidate, Lee (also a pseudonym) of her experiences of being inducted into the research and teaching community of the university. These reflections were followed by an interview. Lee was an international student, coming from an Asian country, and her contribution to the study effectively captures the process of and learning from socialisation into an educational institute (and, by extension, the academic profession), by tapping into the relationship-building between a peripheral member and "collective cognition" (Samaras, 2011, p. 5; see also Hamilton, 1998).

Thematic content analysis of the data was guided by the dimensions of signature pedagogy proposed by Shulman (2005): surface structure (i. e., the operational practices of teaching and learning), and deep structure (knowledge, theory, and underlying logic) and implicit structure (professional beliefs, attitudes, and values). As the surface and deep structures are highly interrelated, they will be discussed together in reporting the findings. In the next section, the signature pedagogy of the research seminars and PhD supervision will be respectively discussed and compared, in terms of pedagogical practices and content. A brief summary and discussion of implications will conclude the paper.

Findings

Signature pedagogical practices

Surface structure of the seminars and PhD supervision

The research seminars form part of routine activities of a high profile research centre, and is held weekly and often in conjunction with other institutes and associations. The majority of the participants are MPhil/PhD students and staff of the institutes; however, several visiting scholars and visiting PhD students also regularly attend the seminar throughout the year. Though it is not mandatory officially, the doctoral students attend it regularly, especially full-time students, as the attendance is considered a sign of sincerity toward research. The typical seminar is two hours in length and is chaired either by a staff member or a senior PhD student; one or two participants make presentations. About 40% ~ 50% of the time allotted to each presenter is used for presentation while the rest is reserved for a discussion moderated by the chair. In most cases, presenters discuss their current work and receive feedback for use in their publications, conference presentations or thesis writing. Presenters are also invited from other institutes both within and outside the UK in order to keep group members up to date with recent developments in the field.

The weekly research seminar consists of four different phases: housekeeping, presentation, discussion and round-up. The pedagogy of the seminar is manifested mostly in the third phase, discussion. According to our analysis, contributions from the audience in this phase consist of three types, *clarification questions*, *observations* and *challenges*. Through clarification questions, the commenter asks about the aspects that were not presented clearly during the presentation, such as the use of a term, or methodological details. The commenter also makes observations, or general remarks on the ideas which the presentation has stimulated, such as a relevant research framework, a publication, or a similar or contrastive case in another context. It is assumed that the information may prove useful for the presenter. Finally, the commenter may challenge the knowledge claim made by the presenter, by pointing out the parts that sound illogical, unexpected, or incoherent. This leads the presenter to self-scrutinise his or her own analysis, assumptions or interpretation of the data, which contributes to increasing the rigour of their research. Comments of this nature are often picked up by other members until the issue is settled. Notably, the issues unresolved or that were perceived as important may be picked up in another presentation and, in such a case, the commenter often reminds the audience of the previous discussion.

PhD supervision is typically conducted by two supervisors. The student and the supervisors meet every three weeks on average, but depending on the stage of the student's progress, the urgency of some tasks, and styles of the participants, the schedule may vary. For each meeting, the PhD student is expected to submit a piece of writing, or PowerPoint slides if preparing for a presentation. Also, the students should write a report after these meetings, covering the main issues discussed, decisions made, and the next assignment, and the report is signed by all parties and submitted to the department. In addition to the supervisory meeting, a doctoral student has to attend mandatory input sessions which are provided by the department, the faculty and the university, most of which occur in the first year, but continue until the student is writing up the thesis.

Deep and implicit structure of the seminar and PhD supervision

The leading members of the research group regularly attend the seminar series. This shows that they consider the seminars to be seriously valuable. Reflecting this validation, Felix refers to the seminars using phrases such as "the business", "a core" and "a ritual centre of the collegial academic practice." As Felix notes, there are two major functions of the seminar, assistance with knowledge generation and continuation of the research culture. In assisting knowledge generation, members will cross-examine the knowledge claims against the discipline's collective cognition. As observed by Felix:

> [The seminar is] communion in argument and dialogue. Fundamental to academic life, academic work. It so happens that the particular types of presentation and questions emerging in a particular form are going to be coming from the discipline [of Applied Linguistics].

The discourse types and patterns induct the students into the knowledge canon of the discipline, and promote rigorous thinking and clear communication. The style of interaction is both supportive (demonstrating an inclusive attitude towards new members of the academic discipline) and critical (indicating a desire to maintain certain standards). In the seminars, the participants collectively seek to understand the use of frameworks available in the discipline, and examine whether their work is intelligible to a larger audience who may not be familiar with the focus of one's own research, though in the same discipline. Reflecting the disciplinary tradition, the participants often have a lengthy discussion on shades of meaning of a key term, or appropriateness of using a term in a certain context.

Sweeping comments or discussion on the practical value of new knowledge are often censured. The participants of a seminar jointly generate and refine new knowledge. The non-commenting audience, however, also contribute to the objective, through their regular participation, explicit appreciation for a good piece of research, and encouragement for research with room for improvement.

The second function of the seminar, that is, continuation of the research culture, is well reflected in the pattern of commenting of the members. There is no written rule about who can contribute to the open discussion after the presentation; however, in most cases members participate in the discussion only when they are "ready", to borrow Felix's term. Usually second year PhD students or more senior members contribute to the discussion and the first year students listen in. Some comments are picked up by senior members of the group, whereas others are not, and some are even cut short in the middle, which in some cases reflect these senior members' informal, negative evaluation of the comments. In order for a contribution to be appreciated, the rules on turn taking, the content and language of the comments should reflect the culture of the seminar, which can be learned only through long-term observation and gradual participation. Felix observes:

> Don't expect [the participants] to be able to [comment in the seminar] right away … Somebody who is expert has a huge stock of experience. And trying to, pretending for somebody with two years of experience to do the same is silly. [Learning to participate in the seminar appropriately] is a long hard slog.

This hierarchical distribution of turns helps the peripheral participants' socialisation, as it increases their exposure to the kind of knowledge the community values and to the way they can be collectively built and shared. Therefore, it is not rare to hear visiting scholars from other contexts remark that they are at a loss on when and how to join the discussion, regardless of their experience in academia. Difficulties of participating in the seminar reported by academics from other contexts and the remark quoted above clearly reflect previous observations that becoming a member of a professional community cannot be achieved through simply acquiring relevant skills which are transferable across contexts. It requires learning about the culture of the community including hidden assumptions and unarticulated rules through a long-term interaction (Holmes and Meyerhoff, 1999; Wenger, 1999), and the communities of higher education are not exceptions (e.g., Preece, 2009).

In addition to distribution of turns, "disciplinary" measures are also in place. The atmosphere of the seminar is collegial on the whole; however, if the presenters, either deliberately or through a lack of awareness, do not address the raised issue, they are chastised by the members collectively. The members take turns to raise the issue from varied perspectives, until the presenter acknowledges the problem in the particular knowledge claim, which is often followed by collaborative solution seeking. The following excerpt illustrates this. Here a presenter proposes the need to merge ethnography with conversation analysis (CA). The following interaction followed right after his presentation. The commenter 1 sees ethnography as a research approach that can also lead researchers to focus on patterns of interaction. (The details are omitted so that the speakers remain anonymous.)

> Commenter 1: What do you think is the difference between ethnography and qualitative research [in which the presenter positioned CA]?
>
> Presenter: Emic knowledge is important, but more is needed to explain the patterns of interaction…
>
> Commenter 2: I think it's positioning ethnography in such a narrow way that…

Here, commenter 1 tries to raise the issue that for some researchers, detailed analysis of interactional patterns as adopted by CA can also be used in ethnography, therefore, the presenter's suggestion to merge ethnography with qualitative research where he placed CA reflects a limited understanding of ethnography. The presenter does not seem to have followed the commenter's line of thinking. After the presenter's response exhibiting this lack of awareness of the raised issue, another commenter picks up the theme and argues that the presenter's way of understanding ethnography is positioning it in a narrow way, meaning that it is just one way of understanding, which may not be agreed to by all. Thus, the two commenters are challenging the assumption of the presenter on which the argument is built, that is, the two approaches are separate. At this point, the presenter acknowledged the issue. If the presenter does not understand the focal point through such indirect questions or fails to see the issue from a new perspective, the chair or a senior member explicitly but respectfully points out the problem. Such scrutiny is applied to any members: even senior academics, when they present, are subject to criticisms, and most are willing to acknowledge their oversights or need for further study, which help the peripheral members see the importance of the openness to new ideas and to criticism throughout their career.

In supervisory meetings, also the three types of comments, in particular, *observations* and *challenges*, are frequently used. In supervision, the PhD student puts forward his or her knowledge claims verbally or in writing. The supervisors listen to or read the arguments and identify areas of improvement, and use observations and challenges to draw the student's attention to the problematic area. Some are more direct and explicitly require justification of the claims, and others are rather subtle but still achieve the same function, challenging the assumptions, pointing out the incoherence in argument or questioning the interpretation of the data, as the examples below show:

> Yes–is it necessary to say why?
> So are you assuming he was already able to do this?

Lee's reflection below shows the common functions achieved by the seminars and the supervisory meetings in terms of problematising data analysis, though the different approaches between them are also noted:

> From my presentation at the research seminar, I learned that I have so many assumptions [that I do not share with the audience] and that I need to read line by line and think about each sentence if not for each word, and why the participants say something, which I dismissed as only applying to a micro level discourse analysis. However, I realised that Dr. X's [supervisor] idea of data analysis in terms of identifying themes is not much different from what Felix and others do. Of course, my supervisor does not require detailed discourse analysis, but all the same very much interested to see why the participants say each sentence, what they exactly mean, how I know it means that, and how my understanding can be justified. So in that sense, both approaches are very similar.

The culture of fostering enlightenment is also replicated in the supervision. Regular feedback on submitted drafts helps the students gradually see their writing from the supervisors' perspective. When the supervisors' views differ from that of a PhD student's on a topic or an issue, rather than claiming their expertise and making decisions for the student, the supervisors often listen to the arguments of the student, and help the student to see any gaps in the idea, or they change their own views in the light of the new knowledge brought in by the student. The supervisors' attitude has democratic qualities of openness to argument and to change. It also suggests a belief that knowledge is contestable. Supervisors' efforts not to disrupt the routine schedule of supervisory meetings also impart the attitude of sincerity and conscientiousness, which is indispensable for mutual, continuous academic growth.

There are some commonalities between this communal process of generation of new knowledge from data in the discipline of Applied Linguistics, with that of the discipline of Molecular Genetics, to view the description by Amann and Knorr Cetina (1988). The two fields share "the machinery of seeing", in a sense, though they actually differ in terms of operationalisation. Molecular Genetics adopts placing autoradiograph films against physical light, whereas the

Applied Linguistics discipline puts ideas against the light of scrutiny through verbal highlighting with challenging questions and observations. In both fields, knowledge is generated through analysing participants' speech, or talks. Through this process something which did not yet qualify as evidence is forged and refined to become a legitimate evidence of a knowledge claim, or "belief" in Amann and Knorr Cetina's (ibid.) term. Although the foci of the analysing talk are obviously different, in one field, RNA films, and in the other, verbalised ideas, in both disciplines, it is the talks which generate knowledge.

Signature pedagogical content

The previous section outlines the pedagogical practices that were prevalent in the programme; this section focuses on the pedagogical content and what it reveals about the interpretation of Applied Linguistics in the specific case. The evidence comes from Lee's reflections. As an international student on the programme, whose prior schooling had been in Asia, Lee felt that she was a peripheral member of the community because she came from different cultural and linguistic traditions. This allowed her insights from an etic (outsider) perspective, while she was being inducted into an emic (insider) perspective as part of the doctoral programme.

In an interview for this paper, Lee noted that the majority of the academics in the group adopted a post-modernist stance on studies in Applied Linguistics.

> There is a strong preference for authors such as Foucault and Bourdieu among the members and I felt that it was almost compulsory to cite their work or to adopt their analytical lenses in our studies. I thought the works by students who adopted post-modernist views were more valued.

This preference led Lee to feel rather marginalised in the group. Lee, who had long been an educational practitioner, would sometimes ask what practical implications the shared research would have, which received a rather lukewarm response, and, on one occasion, was openly censured.

> I felt as if I was out of the place because my contributions to the discussion, which often asked about the practical implications were not as enthusiastically responded to by the leading members. We were advised that we should be wary of prescriptions out of the context. In one discussion, an academic said that, while focusing on practical values of research, I was perhaps evaluating the research from a neoliberal perspective, which the person had been fighting against. I felt ashamed.

The post-modern orientation of the research group created a hierarchy in terms of research perspectives, with critical, post-modernist studies being placed at the top rung, while for instance, investigative studies of practice were viewed as low status, and of inconsequential topics.

> Overall, I felt my proposed research was seen as not really valuable. Other topics which had a strong post-modernist orientation attracted far more discussion and positive comments. I think throughout all the years I was studying, I had to fight the internalised sense of self-doubt.

Discussion and Conclusion

The signature pedagogy of the focal PhD programme in Applied Linguistics suggests that members of the academy sought to induct new researchers into a culture of rigour, criticality and collegiality, while valuing work that favoured a post-modernist orientation. While it seems quite natural that groups of academics with a similar research perspective will tend to work together, they also need to be aware of how this orientation might impact upon the induction of new academics. They may like to consider whether alternative perspectives are acknowledged and presented through the doctoral programme in a way that does not promote a preferred school of thought as orthodoxy. Analysing the signature pedagogy could help programme leaders to become aware of such orientations and allow them to consider the merits and demerits of adopting them. To what extent do the pedagogical practices and content reflect the traditions of a particular culture and the beliefs of a particular school of thought within the broader field of Applied Linguistics? How inclusive and tolerant are the choices of pedagogical practices and content, or is the programme deliberately designed to induct the students into a particular way of thinking about and conducting research?

The findings reported in this paper are based on a small-scale study. For reasons of space and accessibility, the manifestations of the signature pedagogy were restricted to some key events; obviously the whole student experience was much more comprehensive, encompassing informal and formal, explicit and hidden curricular phenomena, and it should be taken into account that reflections and recounts of those experiences are necessarily subjective. Also, the number of respondents was restricted due to the sensitivity of the subject matter. Nonetheless, despite these limitations, studies such as this one, of the deep and implicit structure of the signature pedagogy as experienced and implemented, as well as describing its surface structure, would appear to have great potential in capturing the subtle processes that full members in the field of Applied Linguistics deploy to socialise peripheral members into becoming fully-fledged academics. As a consequence, such studies can contribute to concerted efforts to ensure the quality of doctoral programmes and theorise students' learning in higher education.

References

Amann, K., & Knorr Cetina, K. (1988). The fixation of (visual) evidence. *Human Studies*, 11, 133-169.

Chick, N. L., Haynie, A., & Gurung, R. A. R. (Eds.) (2012). *Exploring more signature pedagogies: Approaches to teaching disciplinary habits of mind*. Sterling, Va.: Stylus Pub., LLC.

Evans, R. (2007). Comments on Shulman, Golde, Bueschel, and Garabedian: Existing practice is not the template. *Educational Researcher*, 36 (9), 553-559.

García, O., Flores, N. & Spotti, M. (2016) Introduction - Language and society: A critical poststructuralist perspective, In O. García, N. Flores, & M. Spotti (Eds.), *The Oxford Handbook of Language and Society* (pp. 1 - 16). Oxford: Oxford University

Press.

Gurung, R. A. R., Chick, N. L., & Haynie, A. (Eds.) (2009). *Exploring signature pedagogies: Approaches to teaching disciplinary habits of mind.* Sterling, Va.: Stylus Pub., LLC.

Ham, J., & Schueller, J. (2012). Traditions and transformations: Signature pedagogies in the language curriculum. In N. L. Chick, A. Haynie & R. A. R. Gurung (Eds), *Exploring more signature pedagogies: Approaches to teaching disciplinary habits of mind* (pp. 27-41). Sterling, Va.: Stylus Pub., LLC.

Hamilton, M. L. (Ed.). (1998). *Reconceptualizing teaching practice: Self - study in teacher education.* London: Falmer Press.

Holmes, J., & Meyerhoff, M. (1999). The community of practice: Theories and methodologies in language and gender research. *Language in Society*, 28, 173-183.

Landry, R. & Bourhis, R. Y. (1997). Linguistic landscape and ethnolinguistic vitality: An empirical study. *Journal of Language and Social Psychology*, 16 (1): 23-49.

Larrison, T. E., & Korr, W. S. (2013). Does social work have a signature pedagogy?, *Journal of Social Work Education*, 49 (2), 14-206.

Olson, K., & Clark, C. M. (2009). A signature pedagogy in doctoral education: The leader-scholar community. *Educational Researcher*, 38 (3), 216-221.

Preece, S. (2009). *Posh talk: Language and identity in higher education.* Basingstoke: Palgrave Macmillan.

Samaras, A. P. (2011). *Self-study teacher research: Improving your practice through collaborative inquiry.* London: Sage.

Shulman, L. S. (2005). Signature pedagogies in the professions. *Daedalus* 134 (3), 52-59.

Wenger, E. (1999). *Communities of practice: Learning, meaning, and identity.* New York: Cambridge University Press.

Zambo, D. (2011). Action research as signature pedagogy in an educational doctorate program: The reality and hope. *Innovative Higher Education*, 36 (4), 261-271.

标志性教学与博士研究生科研成长：基于应用语言学专业的个案

崔太信　鲍勃·安德姆森

摘要： 自舒尔曼教授及其团队提出标志性教学法（the signature

pedagogy）以来，这一方法被广泛应用在诸多学科的博士培养中，相关研究也日益增多，但大都集中在对这一方法的教学应用的探索上，相比之下，对标志性教学法应用成效的研究相对不足。本文以应用语言学专业博士培养为个案，分析了标志性教学在博士生每周科研例会中的应用，探究了这一方法在博士生从初级科研者成长为成熟的研究人员过程中复杂、隐性的建构作用。

关键词：博士生专业发展；应用语言学；科研例会；博士生培养；社会建构理论

日语敬语史的历史走向及其日语史上的意义*

李长波**

摘　要：本文回顾了迄今为止有关日语敬语的理论以及有关敬语体系的主要研究，对一些旨在学校教育以及普及敬语知识等的通俗分类提出了质疑。指出渡边实的敬语体系以及敬语史的研究在理论框架和对日语敬语史的有效性上值得我们充分认识。同时从日语敬语史研究要以“上下的原则”与“内外的原则”二者之间的优先程度的历史变化的角度出发，提出了以下几个观点。

一，在日语史上，从来不曾存在过一个“絶対敬語”的时代。金田一京助提出的日语敬语史是由“絶対敬語”到“相対敬語”变化的历史的说法是不能成立的。

二，我们从“上下的原则”与“内外的原则”二者之间的优先程度的历史变化的角度考察日语敬语的历史，“聞手敬語”的发生及其发展是敬语体系重视听话人即重视二人称的视点的体现。这一倾向大约在江户后期文化与文政年间（1804—1929）在日语史上得以确立。

三，日语敬语对听话人即二人称视点的重视与日语二人称人称词在历史上频发交替，指示体系对二人称的重视，日语终助词的历史演变等语言

---

* 文献的引证标准和范围如下：日语敬语的研究论文可谓汗牛充栋，即使最粗线条地把敬语研究的先行文献整理一下，也远非一两篇文章所能容纳的。本文中仅就日语敬语的分类中对日语敬语史的描述最有效的和最为人知的几个分类作出评介，见仁见智、遗珠之憾在所难免。鉴于日语语法的学术词汇与汉语语法术语间在翻译不具备完全的对应关系，本文对日语语法术语采用直接使用日语词汇的方法，以求理解准确。日语语法术语加「」括号以示区别。

** 作者简介：李长波，男，1962 年生，1982 年大连外国语学院日语系毕业。1999 年获京都大学博士学位。研究方向：普通语言学，语言哲学，日语史，中日比较文体史，中日比较语法史，东亚语言思想史。1997—2011 年任京都大学助手，讲师。2011—2017 年任同志社大学日语暨日本文化教育中心准教授。现任同志社大学日语暨日本文化教育中心教授。

现象如出一辙。就日语敬语以及日语与人际关系，人称体系之间关系而言的，这是除了日语史变化是从非分析性到分析性的变化的大方向以外的，日语史变化的另一个大方向。

关键词：敬语体系；敬语分类；绝对敬语与相对敬语指示体系；终助词；听话人

引言

有关日语敬语的体系、分类以及历史的研究已经很难以汗牛充栋来形容了。众说纷纭、莫衷一是之程度亦远非指示词指示体系可比。有鉴于此，笔者在本文的前半部分花费大量的笔墨对描写敬语体系的几种主要的观点做了梳理，旨在从这个乱象之中找出一个既可以对现代日语敬语体系作出清晰的描写，同时又为日语敬语史的变化提供强有力的理论框架。日语敬语体系分为「尊敬語」、「謙譲語」、「丁寧語」三类的传统分类以及以无原则地增加分类来描述现代日语敬语体系的说法至今还在学校语法中视为定论的现象，虽然有有利初学等功利性的效果，但就揭示日语敬语体系的本质，阐释日语敬语史变化的本质性的动态而言，自然不无绠短汲深之憾。本文综合敬语体系的历史、指示体系的历史以及其他相关的语法范畴的历史等语言事实，除了对日语史变化中较为人知的，即从非分析性的表达方式到分析性即近代日语①的逻辑性倾向（分析化倾向）的变化以外，逐步重视听话人的视点的方向即强化交际功能的方向作出初步探讨。

1　日语敬语的分类及有关敬语体系的研究

1.1　传统的敬语三分法以及对三分法的批判

日语敬语的传统分类为「尊敬語」、「謙譲語」、「丁寧語」三类。对于传统的三分法，时枝诚记最先系统地提出了批判②。时枝诚记将敬语分为：

・素材の表現（詞）に現れた敬語法

① 传统日语史中的近代，一般以室町时代为起点涵盖近世即江户时代与狭义的近代即历史学领域的近代即明治时代衔接。

② 此外，岗村和江（1963）和根来司（1963）也是以时枝诚记的「词」「辞」二分法批判三分法的。

・主体的表現（辞）に現れた敬語法

时枝诚记敬语分类与传统的敬语分类的对应关系为：

話手と素材との関係の規定……（尊敬）
詞的敬語
敬語　　素材と素材との関係の規定……（謙譲）
辞的敬語——聴手への敬意の直接的表現……（丁寧）

时枝诚记的敬语分类是从他的「言語過程説」也就是把日语词汇分为「詞」「辞」两类的语法体系演绎出来的。事实上，「詞」「辞」本身已经是不能截然分开的两个词类①，时枝诚记把二者的关系对立起来的学说，在敬语分类上更是走上了极端。他无视了两个基本事实：一是敬语不同于通常所说的任何词类，它的使用不单纯取决于「素材と素材との関係」，即话题中人物的地位高低等因素并非敬语使用的唯一决定因素；一是敬语本身都是说话人对听话人以及话题中的人物作出的，旨在表达敬意或表示自身修养和品味的表现。这说明，在敬语分类中，把「話手と素材との関係」与「素材と素材との関係」一分为二的做法既违背了语言的逻辑分析必须缜密的原则，也违背了研究对象的分类不能交叉的原则。

1.2　渡边实的敬语研究

渡边实对日语敬语的研究主要有三篇论文，各有侧重。渡边实（1971）在敬语分类上独树一帜，系统阐述自己的敬语体系，重在理论研究；渡边实（1973）在此基础上对日语敬语史作出了描述，重在历史研究；渡边实（1981）虽属短篇，但在理论上对渡边实（1971）有所补充。

首先，渡边实（1971）的敬语研究基本清算了时枝诚记和传统的敬语分类的敬语学说（即把敬语分为「尊敬」「謙譲」「丁寧」的三分法。传统的敬语三分法的问题主要在以下三点：(1) 违反了多项分类必须有层次性的原则；(2) 三分之间如「尊敬」「謙譲」与「丁寧」互有交叉；(3) 忽视了「丁寧」乃至所有敬语表现都有为人为己两个目的。事实上，渡边实敬语研究的

① 尽管以渡边实为首的学者对时枝诚记的「詞」「辞」两分法提出质疑，但时枝诚记本人自始至终对「詞」「辞」的关系持「非連続的」观点，参见时枝诚记 1954。

基本框架早在玉上琢弥（1955）的敬语分类中已经形成了。[1]

渡边实（1971）从准确描述实际的敬语现象的角度出发，对日语敬语的体系作出了独创性的研究。渡边实的敬语分类，既不同于以敬意的属性即敬意的实际内容为分类标准的传统三分法，也不同于时枝诚记的简单的二分法。他的独创性在于按说话人表示敬意的对象的不同进行分类，也就是说是以敬意的指向作为分类原则的。

渡边实（1971）的敬语体系第一次提出在理论上应该区分「話題の世界」、「対話の場面」[2]，他以此确立了「話題の世界」中的「受手敬語」（受事敬语）、「為手敬語」（施事敬语），二者均为间接尊敬听话人的手段，即二者的使用是以对听话人不失礼为条件的。其结构如下图所示：

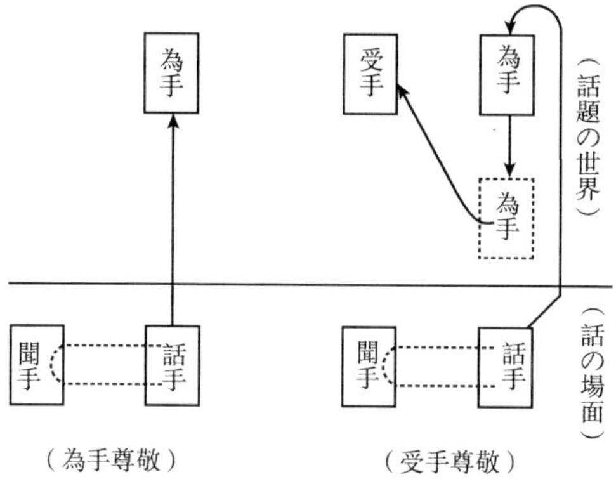

① 玉上琢弥（1955）的敬语分类出自渡边实之手。玉上（1955）「終りに」敬語については国語学者が扱うことが多く、源氏物語の敬語についても、吉沢義則、島津久基、宮田和一郎、時枝誠記、伊奈恒一、松尾捨次郎、中村添、北山谿太、和田利政氏らによって研究が進められて来たのである。わたくしの研究会のメムバーである伊藤和子も調査研究を続けていられ、本稿も氏に負う所が多い。なおわたくしは国語学に対しては門外漢であるので、本書の目的に副うようにと思い、渡辺実氏に協力を乞うた。記して謝意を表する。（见玉上琢弥（1955：97页）除小松寿雄（1963）以外，根来司（1963）和辻村敏树（1963）也根据玉上琢弥（1955），误以为是玉上琢弥的观点。

② 「日本語の敬語の体系を記述するに当って、是非とも準備しておかねばならないのは、話題の世界と対話の場面との峻別である。（中略）」「あなた」と聞き手、「わたし」と話し手は、人間としては同一だが、言語へのかかわり方では、一方は話される話題の世界の人物、他方は向き合って話し聞く対話の場面の人物、として明瞭に区別されねばならないのである。」渡辺実（1981：13页）

其次，渡边实（1971）还廓清了一直混淆在一起的两种敬语，一是「受手敬語」（受事敬语）」，一是间接对听话人表示敬意的「謙遜」(「話手が自分を為手とする話題を話す時に、為手としての自分の行動を殊更に低く待遇して表現し、それによって間接に聞手への敬意を表わす敬語」(渡边实，1971：435）)。

渡边实（1971）指出，将二者混为一谈是日语敬语研究的最大缺陷(渡边实（1971：435-436)。他所描述的「謙遜」敬语的结构为：

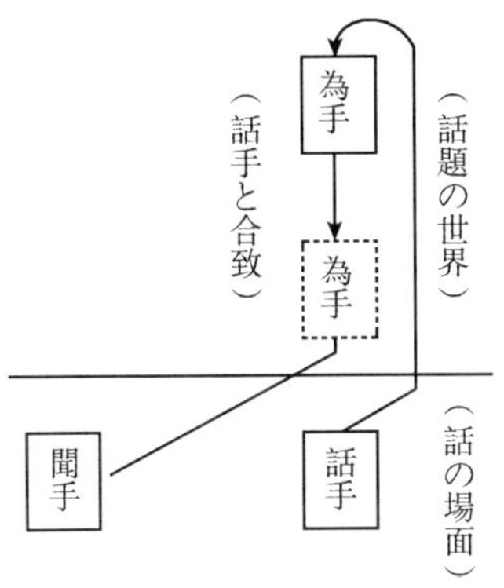

（謙　　遜）

渡边实（1971）还指出，以往的敬语研究，把「受手尊敬」(尊敬受事）」的敬语中对施事者的冷遇这一手段误认为「受手尊敬」（尊敬受事）」的敬语的本质；同时，尽管在「謙遜」敬语中就对施事者的冷遇这一手段有所认识，但是对这一手段的目的即借以间接地尊敬听话人这一点却没能作出充分的解释。二者的手段均被误解为本质，致使二者均被误认为「謙遜」(渡边实，1971：436—437)。

以说话人为施事、以听话人为受事的情况下，例如，

わたくしが（あなたを）御案内申し上げましょう。

使用尊重受事的敬语，直接表达对听话人的敬意。下个例句，

わたくしが（あなたを）御案内致しましょう。

则以使用「謙遜」敬语为手段表达对听话人的敬意。前者的受事者不限于听话人，还可以是听话人以外的人，并不一定就是与听话人同属一个势力范围的人；后者不论有无受事者，施事者仅限于说话人自己或其自然延伸即家属、同辈等，二者性质不同（渡边实，1971：437）。

最后，渡边实（1971）把现代日语的敬语体系描写如下图所示：

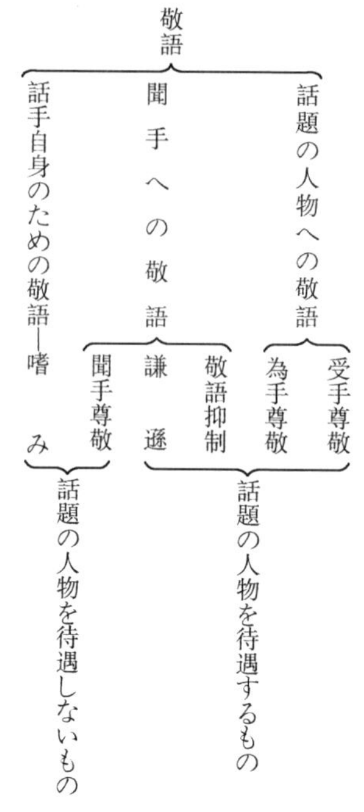

这个分类，既明确了敬语体系的核心部分「受手尊敬」（尊敬受事者）、「受手尊敬」（尊敬受事者）、「聞手尊敬」（尊敬听话者）三者间的结构关系，同时也明确了日语敬语史变化的大方向，即「聞手尊敬」从无到有这一事实。①

① 就渡边实与时枝诚记在日语语言研究史上的关系而言，渡边实对时枝诚记的语法体系集中体现在语法体系的构建上。对于时枝诚记敬语研究本身评价不高。尤其是对时枝诚记提出的「関係認識」没有充分注意。但从学术史的角度看，我们可以认为，渡边实的敬语研究是对时枝诚记敬语研究的发展。但是，就体系的完整性、有效性和解释性而言，后者大大优于前者。渡边实的语法体系是由「構文論」和「敬語体系」构成的有机的整体。渡边实的「敬語体系」附于『国語構文論』卷末的意义就在于此。

渡边实（1973）为探讨日语敬语史的专文的具体内容留在下节评介，下面介绍除渡边实以外的几个有代表性的观点。

1.3 宫地裕与辻村敏树的敬语分类

除渡边实以外，从时枝诚记到20世纪80年代，宫地裕和辻村敏树两人的敬语研究影响最大。

宫地裕（1971）把敬语分为「尊敬語」、「謙譲語」、「丁重語」、「丁寧語」、「美化語」五类。辻村敏树（1964）的敬语分类如下所示：

- 素材敬語
  - （1）上位主体語（＝敬称）
  - （2）下位主体語（＝謙称）
- 対者敬語（＝謙称）
- 美化語

简言之，二者的分类的问题与传统的敬语三分法一样，既违反了分类的层次性原则，而且各分类之间互有交叉。二者不同的是，辻村敏树（1963）的敬语分类是以行为主体为核心的分类原则。之所以称之为“核心”的分类原则，是因为他把所谓「美化語＝美称」定义为「表現素材を美化する言い方」[辻村敏树（1963：11）]。事实上，即使辻村敏树（1963）所说的「美化語」也不是美化「表現素材」的。它属于指向听话人或者表示说话人的修养，维持说话人品味的敬语，与渡边实（1971）提出的「たしなみの敬語」相关连的。由此可见，辻村敏树（1964）的敬语分类是交叉使用了两个以上的分类标准得来的。[①] 敬意的指向只有话题中的「為手」「受手」和属于话语场的「聞手」三者，这也是渡边实（1971）所反复强调的。

以上主要介绍了两个较为人知的敬语分类。此外，在渡边实（1971）发表以前，还有森野宗明（1968）的敬语分类值得一提，他把「尊敬」「謙譲」作为指向听话人的敬意合为一类与「丁寧」分属两个层次。森野宗明（1968）首次对传统的敬语分类「尊敬」「謙譲」「丁寧」

① 辻村敏树（1963）的敬语分类里，所谓「素材敬語」，实质上与除掉「丁寧語」中属于「辞」的部分后的剩余部分相当。（辻村敏树，1963：13）

三项并列的问题。区别了「発言の素材への敬語」和「聞き手に対する敬語」，力图把「尊敬」「謙譲」「丁寧」之间的层次廓清。他的分类如下所示：

敬語 { 丁寧
　　　{ □ { 尊敬
　　　　　　{ 謙譲

敬語 { 丁寧（聞き手に対する敬意の表現）
　　　{ 尊敬（話題の人物に関する敬意の表現） { 動作状態主尊敬（いわゆる尊敬）
　　　　　　　　　　　　　　　　　　　　　　　 { 被影響主尊敬（いわゆる謙譲）

但是，森野宗明（1968）的敬语分类实际上旨在调和传统的敬语三分法与时枝诚记的敬语分类，他的分类原则事实上是在吸收了玉上琢弥（1955）中渡边实的敬语分类的合理内核之后提出的。前者的努力实属徒劳，而后者按敬意的指向分类，「動作状態主尊敬」「被影響主尊敬」与玉上琢弥（1955）的「為手敬語」「受手敬語」是对应的，不过是渡边实敬语分类的翻版而已。同时他的分类里还把「被影響主尊敬（いわゆる謙譲）」与「謙譲」画了等号，这个问题直到渡边实（1971）才得到解决。

1.4　其他的分类法：敬语与人称的关系——山田孝雄和石坂正藏的敬语研究

有关日语敬语与人称之间的关系，早在江户时代就有西方传教士提及，近代以后，任东京帝国大学语言学教授的张伯伦也曾在他的『日本口語文典』一书中做过简述①。但真正系统性的研究是从山田孝雄的『敬語法の研究』（1924）开始的。他首先把日语的「敬語法」作为语法研究

① 原作为英文，有关部分日译文如下：393。敬語の使用は、4つの主な考慮すべき点によって示される。i. 敬語は，その人の話し相手の行為や所有のことを話すときに使い，一方卑下または謙遜は，その人自身のことを話すときに使う。言いかえると，私たちは一人称は自己を卑下し，2人称では，敬意を表する。ii. 他の人を指すとき（3人称をどう呼ぶか），敬語は，話題となる人間が話し相手より上位にある場合，または同席している場合，また，その人が上位か，少なくとも同等であったり，礼儀上において当然の場合にのみ使われる。iii. 敬語の使用には段階があり，話し相手や話題となる人間に払うべき敬意の大小によって決まる。（チャンブレン1999：244頁）

的一部分，力图通过与人称（person，山田孝雄使用「称格」一词）的关系来证明这一点。然而，正如石坂正藏（1952）所指出的，他的敬语研究明显存在以下两个缺陷。

> 山田博士はかような組織に於いて人称（博士の所謂「称格」）との関聯から敬語法の法たる所以を説かれたのであるが、此の点から言って大きく次のような批判の余地が残されている。(1) 博士は敬語を敬称と謙称とに大別されて、謹称を立てられなかった。口語の助動詞「ます」について、その重要性を認め、極めて汎い用法に立つ「補助動詞」とされたが、「ます」が謙称の動詞にも敬称の動詞にも、敬意をあらわす複語尾のついたものにも、又存在詞の敬語にも附いて、一層の敬意をあらわすものとしながら、なおこれを謙称の中に包含せしめられたのであって、そのため体系内部に大きな無理を生じたのである。(中略) (2) 敬語と人称との関聯を考えたのは正しいが、それはあくまで人称に拠って敬語を見たもの、乃至は人称の枠に当てはめた敬語の様相であって、そこに無理も起り、煩雑さも加わっている。(石坂正藏 1952：3-4 页)

针对第一点，石坂正藏指出，

> 尊卑上下の関係に於いて、一人称者的ものと、二人称三人称的なものとがある。前者を「自称」とし、後者を「他称」とすれば、自称は卑位下位に置かれ、他称は尊位上位に置かれる。(中略) 一般に話手の素材に対する距離と角度によって素材は話手及び話手側にあるものと、聞手若くは第三者側にあるもの、即ちこちら側にあるものとあちら側にあるものとの二つに分別して把えるのが、国語の敬語的把握である。いわば「敬語的自称」と「敬語的他称」である。謙称と敬称とは此の立場から見直されねばならない。この敬語に於ける人称的なものの把へ方、在り方が即ち「敬語的人称」である。(石坂正藏 1952：18 页)

针对第二点，石坂正藏指出，

それでは敬語的人称の体系の中に、謹称は如何に位置づけられるか。謹称とは聞手に対する敬意表現であろうか。或は漠然と、又話手の品位を高めるための、丁寧な表現であろうか。私は時枝博士の所謂詞と辞との区別をそう決定的なものとは見ないから、謹称を敬辞として割り切ることは出来ないし、又丁寧な表現は必ずしも謹称のみに限らず、敬語の充分な全般的使用を意味しているから、謹称を丁寧な表現と言うことも適当ではない。しかし謹称が敬称や謙称と異なった敬語表現の方向であり、形態であることは、例えば「おっしゃいます」「申し上げます」「言います」の「ます」のように、敬称—他称にも、謙称—自称にも、又敬語的無記（「敬語的不定称」とも言うべきであるが敬語系列に於いては敬語的自称の表現価値を持つことが多い）にも、同じ語線上で附くことからも言える。これは尊敬・謙譲の昇華した敬意表現一般と言うべきものである。謙称から「侍り」「候う」「ます」等が、敬称から「ござる」などが、脱化した。「お野菜」「お舟」などの「お」の用法から見ても、このことが言える。謹称はいわば無人称的な人称と言ってよい。私は暫くこれを「敬語的汎称」と呼ぶ。（石坂正藏 1952：23 页）

关于敬语是否是语法问题，石坂正藏和山田孝雄持同样的观点。

国語の敬語表現は、文法・語彙・修辞の各面にわたることながら、その中心はやはり文法的なものであり、従って敬語法というべきである。而してそれが文法的である所以は、敬語法が敬語的人称の体系であるからである。（石坂正藏 1952：23 页）

不管石坂正藏把「謹称」作为「敬語的不定称」还是「無人称的な人称」，他和山田孝雄都忽视了一个基本事实，那就是，所谓敬语的人称问题并不是人称本身的问题。因为话题中出现的三人称不但可以作为第三人称使用敬语，还可以有根据地或人为地被说话人“内外”两分，即要么与第一人称同等对待为“内”，要么与听话人同等对待为“外”。那么敬语的人称问题，是人称体系在敬语中的反映呢，还是与人称体系的平行的另一个自成体系的人称范畴呢？这个结论我们暂时还没法作出，有待进一步探讨。

2 渡边实的敬语分类与敬语史研究的关系

从上面对几种主要的敬语分类作出的批判性的介绍可以看出，每一种敬语分类都可以对日语敬语史作出一番描述，这是不争的事实。但是，哪一种敬语分类对敬语史具有最有效的解释性，则是各不相同的。前节提到的敬语分类中，传统的三分法和时枝诚记的分类既然在逻辑分析和分类原则上存在严重问题，那用它来描述日语敬语史的有效性必然值得怀疑。辻村敏树和宫地裕的敬语分类也不例外，因为缺乏层次性的分类自然不具备对语言事实描写的体系性。例如，宫地裕对敬语史的描述是否既揭示日语敬语史的本质性属性，同时又能与其他日语史的现象，比如人称词的体系、指示词与人称体系的关系等语法范畴保持相关性，都不能令人满意。

	上代	中古	中世	近世	現代
尊敬語	○	○	○	○	○
謙譲語	○	○	○	○	○
丁重語	×	○	○	○	○
丁寧語	×	△	○	○	○
美化語	×	×	△	○	○

＊引自宫地裕（1981）

以如此的敬语分类，我们就「丁重語」「丁寧語」「美化語」三者在敬语史上的意义就会迷失日语敬语史是以「聞手尊敬」（尊敬听话者）从无到有为其历史变化为主流的大方向。

有关日语敬语史的主要先行研究

有关日语敬语史的研究中，金田一京助的「絶対敬語」「相対敬語」的观点曾普遍被人接受。所谓「絶対敬語」「相対敬語」，就是，是否使用敬语和使用哪一类敬语取决于表示敬意的对象的地位和身份等因素。所谓「絶対敬語」，就是使用敬语和使用哪一类敬语并不取决于表示敬意的对象的地位和身份等因素。日语敬语史的历史走向是从上代日语的「絶対敬語」到现代日语的「相対敬語」的演变。

这一观点有几个问题值得探讨。一是，所谓「絶対敬語」「相対敬語」二者的内涵也有失简单化。二是，这个观点尽管对上代日语和现代日语两个对比鲜明跨度逾一千三四百年之久的两个敬语体系间的差异具有很强的说服力，但是无法解释两个体系间的中间形态即保证二者之间连续性的环节。下面我们就逐一探讨这两点。就第一点而言，现代日语的敬语体系是否为「相対敬語」姑且不论，上代日语的敬语体系是否可以「絶対敬語」一言蔽之，是值得我们注意的。

但是，上代日语的敬语体系是"绝对敬语"吗？上代日语的敬语中，「給ふ」「います」等典型的与敬意的对象的身份地位相应的敬语动词是只用于女子对男人之间，没有相反的例子。请看《万叶集》第一首和歌的例子：

籠もよみ籠持ちふくしもよみぶくし持ちこの岡に菜摘ます児家告らせ名告らさねそらみつ大和の国は押しなべて我こそ居れしきなべて我こそいませ我こそば告らめ家をも名をも（万・巻一・0001）

尽管「す」一般认为敬意较轻，而且有时还用在天皇的「自敬表現」。但是，这里出现在天皇对素不相识的民间少女的和歌里。这不能不令我们对上代日语的敬语是「絶対敬語」这一观点产生怀疑。那么，日语史上，确实曾经有过一个「絶対敬語」的时代吗？

还有另外一个现象也同样说明问题之所在也在「絶対敬語」上。下面的两个例子是女性对男性用的，这里就没有用敬语形式。

卯の花の咲き散る岡ゆほととぎす鳴きてさ渡る君は聞きつや（万・10・1976）

人言を繁みと君に玉づさの使ひも遣らず忘ると思ふな（万・11・2586）

而下面的例子是对天皇也没有使用敬语的例子。

久方の天行く月を網にさし我が大君はきぬがさにせり（万・3・240）

大君は神にましませば赤駒の腹這ふ田居を都となしつ（万・19・4260）

不论和歌的作者地位有多高，如果对天皇这样尊贵的人，也可以不用敬语的话，这无疑说明，上代日语敬语并非属于「絶对敬語」①。

以上的简单分析就可以说明，在上代日语里，敬语的使用一方面与敬意指向的对象的地位身份紧密相连，同时也有一定的灵活性。这种灵活性基本上是说话人可以根据自己与对方之间的关系事实上是否密切，或者根据双方关系的密切程度在敬语使用上作出调整。就是说，即使我们把上代日语的敬语体系用「絶对敬語」来描述，也不能排除上代日语的敬语里有「絶对敬語」的成分，二者是交织在一起的，我们只能说它们有主次之分。②

由此可见，所谓「絶对敬語」「相对敬語」，其实就是说话人在敬语使用上的自主性从上代日语的相对的「小」变为现代日语的相对的「大」之间的两个极点。二者之间存在一个漫长的连续的过程。为了把这个中间的过程描述清晰，我们还有必要把我们上面提到的，「絶对敬語」「相对敬語」以及渡边实的上述观点进一步具体化。

渡边实的敬语史研究论文有两篇，一篇是「日本語の変化」（渡辺実 1958），一篇是「上代・中古敬語の概観」（渡辺実 1973）。

渡边实（1958）里，渡边实把敬语分为「受け手尊敬」「仕手尊敬」「聞き手尊敬」和「上品敬語」四大类。这既是玉上琢弥（1955）（实为渡边实 1955，参见注 2）的延续，也是渡边实（1971）的前身。在这里，渡边实指出：

（中古語では）Cの敬語抑制の習慣が現在ほどに強くはないの

① 关于上代日语的敬语体系，笔者将以专文论述，本文从简。

② 西宫一民（1991）的敬语史研究就是根据宫地裕（1971）的分类作出的。

である。あまり身分の高くもない者の侍女が、高貴の人を聞き手として、自分の主人のことを話題にするとき、必ずしも神経質に敬語抑制をしないのである。(中略) おそらくそれは敬語使用の規準である人間関係が、客観的な身分関係によって枠づけられていて、その枠を聞き手次第ではずしたり、はめたりすることは、思いもおよばぬ社会機構だったからではあるまいか。聞き手がだれであるかによって敬語規準を変えることは、ひとえに話し手自身の判断にまつが、話し手自身の自主的判断よりは客観的身分関係の束縛のほうが強い、という時代だったかと思われるのである。(渡辺実 1958: 245 页)

中古の敬語規準は話し手の外にあった。現代はそれが話し手の内にあり、話す行為における話し手の自主性はきわめて高いものになってきたのだ、と考えてよさそうに思われる。それはおそらく徐々にであろうが、人間が社会機構に従属的であった時代から、個人の自主性の強い時代への移り変わりがあって、それがこういう敬語体系の変化に反映しているのにちがいない。(渡辺実 1958: 246 页)

渡边实（1973）里还指出：

上代の敬語が、現代のような対象に話手が加える敬意であるよりは、対象の側に含まれるべきものであったのではないか、ということを考えさせる一つの手がかりは、聞手尊敬の敬語の未発達の事実であろう。(渡辺実 1973: 21 頁)

聞手敬語は実際問題として、対象の側の敬語から話手の側の敬語へ変ずることによって発達し、それとともに対象のためのことばの出現位置から離れて、それからより遠い文末付近へと、その出現位置を移す傾向があるように思われる。(渡辺実 1973: 22 頁)

敬語は元来は、対象に属するものとして発生し、次第に話手に属するものとして、対象から分離する方向で発達してきたのではあるまいか。(渡辺実 1973: 22 頁)

要するに対象から離れた聞手尊敬は、その出現位置もが対象に関する叙述の場所から離れようとし、敬意というものを、対象に属するものではなくて、本来話手に属するものであったのだと気づかせる、導火線となるもののように思われる。裏をかえせば、対象から離れた聞手尊敬の未発達な上代は、敬意がなお多分に対象の側に属するものであった時代だったのではなかったか。(渡辺実 1973：23 頁)

尽管渡边实没有承认也没有否定日语史上，不论是上代还是中古，都曾经存在过一个「絶対敬語」的时代，但是，他把语义分为「対象の側の意義」和「話手の側の意義」，并试图从宏观上解释日语敬语史的历史变化的尝试的积极意义是不容质疑的。同时，我们还必须承认，上代日语的敬语体系既然不是一个「絶対敬語」的体系，那么，渡边实所说的日语史发展的大方向，即从「対象の側の意義」向「話手の側の意義」发展的大方向虽然不容否认，但是就敬语史而言，我们就要大打折扣。因为，就是上代日语，敬语也并非纯属「対象の側の意義」，这可以通过《万叶集》中大量从地位和关系上都该用而不用敬语的实例证明。可见，上代日语中敬语使用的原则是相对性的，其相对性的程度与现代日语相比，我们很难确定哪一个更相对。我们知道，现代日语敬语的使用以对听话人不失礼这个原则对说话人是否使用敬语、如何使用、使用那一类敬语所具有的约束性是很强的，这一点体现了日语是对听话人的立场，感情以及对信息的占有与否高度重视的语言。

3　有关日语敬语体系的思考

首先，就日语史的基本事实而言，自从有文献记载以来，日语史上并不曾存在过一个「絶対敬語」的时代。然而，现代日语的敬语是「相対敬語」的说法似乎不容置疑。那么，我们如何描述日语敬语史的历史进程呢？

事实上，所谓「絶対敬語」「相対敬語」，我们完全可以把它们的实质概括为“上・下的原则”与“内外的原则”。同时我们还要回避迄今为止的敬语史研究方法的误区，即不把某一时代的敬语体系单纯界定为某一单一的特征。

3.1 “上·下的原则”与“内外的原则”

我们首先应该明确，我们这里提出的“上·下的原则”与“内外的原则”并不是仅仅为了取代「絶対敬語」「相対敬語」而引进的。通过上面的分析，我们发现，上代日语并不是仅一个「絶対敬語」可以描述的。我们只能把它描述成“上·下的原则”相对优势的敬语体系。从日语史发展的结果看，我们可以把现代日语的敬语体系概括为“内外的原则”优势的敬语体系。同时，考虑到日语敬语史发展的历史方向，我们就可以把它表述得更加周密。那就是，上代日语的敬语体系是“上·下的原则”相对优先于“内外的原则”的，而现代日语则是相反，是“内外的原则”绝对优先于“上·下的原则”的。①

那么，日语敬语中的「聞手尊敬」从无到有，其意义何在呢？

3.2 「聞手尊敬」即指向听话人的敬语发生的意义及其相关现象

这个问题有两个方面，一是日语敬语中的「聞手尊敬」从无到有，其意义何在？一是这一类敬语何时发生，不只在日语敬语里听话人被重视的程度，在相关的语言现象里的同类项是何时形成的呢？我们现在可以就其第一个方面提出一个观点。

首先「聞手尊敬」从无到有，意味着日语敬语中对听话人的重视程度是一个标志性起点。它是日语对听话人开始重视的一个体现。而现代日语中，综合几个主要的相关语言现象，如人称体系，指示体系，助动词体系化的方向等来看，这个过程的方向都是一致的。随之，我们可以就这个问题提出一个基本的想法。

日语史上对听话人的关注和重视的起点在平安时代中叶，有关指示体系方面的论证请参见拙著 2002，有关敬语史中「聞手尊敬」即指向听话人的敬语表现的出现早有定论，主要文献可以参看石坂正藏（1944）、阪仓笃义（1952）、渡边实（1973）以及有关平安时代敬语史的研究。就第二点中，日语史上，对听话人的重视程度何时得以与现代日语基本相去不远②这一点，笔者根据拙文（2000）、拙著（2002）以及有关的先行研究，综合几个相关的语言现象的出现，初步把这个时间设定在江户后期文化以

① 关于“上·下的原则”与“内外的原则”以及各自比重的变量和二者之间的平衡关系在日语敬语史研究上的有效性，尚有待笔者进一步论证。因此，本观点尚处于假说的阶段。

② 此处仅以相去不远表达基本框架上的基本相同，事实上，其间距离是远是近，有待于进一步深入细致的研究。

及文政年间，日语史通称「化政期」，相当于公元 1804—1829 年。

其主要根据为，除敬语以外的表示「待遇」的表现中，人称词中的「对称」即第二人称词在近世分化以及复杂化。[①] 还有动词活用形中命令形以及其他的命令表现的发展在近世最为突出。表示打招呼和应答的词汇在近世不但数量增加而且功能也越来越多样化，以及感动助词也是如此。[②]

最后，有一点需要说明，以上的观点对我们如何界定现代日语的视点类型这个问题是否有参考价值，笔者尚不敢断言。日语敬语史的发展方向与现代日语视点之间关系的问题有待进一步研究。[③]

3.3 有关日语史发展方向的先行研究的探讨

迄今为止，有关日语史变化的发展方向的论述，除前文提到的渡边实（1973）独树一帜外，大多以龟井孝（1955）为出发点，即把日语史的发展方向概括为从非分析性的表达方式到分析性即近代日语逻辑性倾向（分析化倾向）的变化。阪仓笃义（1993）也不例外。

> 日本語が、本来持っていた未分化な表現の方法から、次第に分析的な、論理の明晰な表現の方法を獲得する方向へと時代とともに進んできたことは、いずれにせよ、たしかに言えるだろう。それがまず、日本人自身の知的・情的成熟という内発的要因によることはもちろんであるが、たとえば右に見たように漢文訓読文が早くその変化の方向を示しているというような事実からすれば、この進展を援ける外的要因として、漢語・漢文の翻訳ということがあったことが十分に考えられる。漢語は、日本語に対して、文字・音韻・語彙

① 佐久间鼎（1937）揭示了对人称词的历史演变的意义。其后的主要研究有山崎久之（1963）、小島俊夫（1974）、山崎久之（1990）等可供参考。

② 有关室町时代以及江户时代的终助词，江户后期的助动词的演变，笔者将专文论述，此处恕不详论。现阶段可以参考的主要文献有六笠寿子（1957）、山崎久之（1963）、小松寿雄（1971）、小松寿雄（1977）、中野伸彦（1986）、中村香生里（2017）等。其中中村香生里（2017）的研究把「~するつもりだ」、「~（よ）うと+思考動詞」的用法确立的时间也定在了「化政期」，这为我们推断现代日语所谓的不可冒犯的听话人的势力范围的成立时期提供了一个有力的证据。

③ 有关日语和汉语视点类型的研究，请参阅彭广陆（2008）、彭广陆（2014）和彭广陆（2016）等论文.

などの面で直接的な影響を与えたことと並んで、あるいは、むしろそれ以上に、こういう表現の面、ないしは発想の面で深い影響を与えたと考えるべきではなかろうか。それは『万葉集』の歌が漢籍の影響のもとに作られたり、あるいはまた、文体としての和漢混淆文が一般化したりするといった事態以前の、もっと深刻な意味においての文化的影響であったと思われるのである」（阪倉篤義 1993：272–273 页）

对此，早在20世纪60年代，小松寿雄（1963）就已经指出了日语史变化的另一个倾向。

しからば、古代語から近代語への歴史的展開として、なにが数えられるか。これには、新しい文体としての近代日本語の成立と、表現に関する選択の自由の増大とが指摘できる。近代日本語の諸相の成立は、それが音韻現象であれ、文法現象であれ、すべて古代語に近代語が取って代ってゆく。新しい口語的表現の確立過程なのである。選択には、価値判断が伴う。時間の流れに沿って起る個々の現象の変化に対して、社会が積極的な取捨選択を加えるとき、そこに、規範の交替が起る。したがって、国語史は、文体史として把えられる。口語の文体として、近代日本語の諸相が社会的に成立したのは、概括的にいえば、結局のところ、室町時代末期から江戸時代初期へかけてであろう。

表現に関する選択の自由には、いろいろの問題がある。たとえば、敬語表現の発達や漢語の浸透のごときは、すべて、日本語に文体論的な表現のはばを賦与するもととなっている。

さらに、また、視野を変えれば、格助詞の体系の整備や種々の接続助詞の発達は論理の明晰を主とする文体の確立として把えられる。［亀井孝（1955：4–5 页）］

小松寿雄（1963）认为，指向听话人的「待遇表现」和敬语的发达归结为与逻辑性并列的，旨在强化交际性的倾向（小松寿雄 1963：7 页）。有关这个倾向的研究非一日之功可成，需要综合相关的语言事实，逐一甄别，统一整合，自然也非一人之力所能。对笔者而言，能否发现以上提到的几个相关的语言事实之外的相关现象是下一步研究的重要课题。

四　几点初步的结论

最后、我们把本文的几个主要结论整理如下：

一、尽管现代日语的敬语属于「相対敬語」即说话人享有根据话题中的人物属于“内”还是“外”来选择是否使用敬语的“自由”，但是，选择敬语使用的所谓“自由”都是相对的。日语史上根本不曾存在过一个「絶対敬語」的时代。因此，所谓日语敬语史是从「絶対敬語」到「相対敬語」的变化的历史的说法是不成立的①。

二、现代日语敬语体系以及日语敬语史可以运用“上・下”“内・外”两个原则之间的优先顺序不同作出解释，即日语敬语史的变化方向是从一个“上・下”的原则相对优先于“内・外”的原则的敬语体系到一个“内・外”的原则相对优先于“上・下”原则的体系的变化。推动这一变化的动力则是对听话人的视点的重视程度逐渐加强的语言意识，其结果为日语的交际功能逐渐得以强化。

三、日语敬语史发展的大趋势，即「聞手尊敬」（指向听话人的敬语）从无到有，与日语二人称词在历史上交替频繁等现象都应该作为日语是朝着重视听话人的存在这个方向发展的类似的语言现象来解释。日语是重视听话人存在和立场的语言，这与日语指示体系的历史变化的方向是一致的。

四、根据现在掌握的资料，日语史上的历史变化中逐步重视听话人的视点的方向即强化交际功能的方向的倾向基本可以确定在江户后期文化文政年间（1804—1829）基本形成了与现代日语大体相近的态势。

五、如何解释日语敬语史发展的方向与日语史发展的大趋势之间的关系，除了从非分析性的表达方式到分析性即近代日语的逻辑性倾向（分析化倾向）的变化以外，逐步重视听话人的视点的方向即强化交际功能

① 福島直恭（2010）、福島直恭（2011）对「絶対敬語」的批判虽然有混淆学术研究与意识形态之嫌，其结论与笔者偶同。任何语言体系的历时性延续即体系化是没有止境的，不论是就整体而言，还是就局部而言，我们都无法期待历史上的任何时期的语言体系是铁板一块，一成不变的. 就敬语体系的体系化而言，其历史进程是有一定的方向性的，这一点毋庸置疑。问题在于我们无法就日语史的某一时期的敬语体系作出单一性的描述。

的方向的研究也值得重视。有关强化交际功能的方向的研究，在诸多先行研究的基础上如何展开，如何解释二者间的关系等问题则有待进一步研究。

> 补笔泷浦真人 2005 的敬语研究
>
> 这里着重提及两个较新的敬语研究：一是菊地康人 1994，一是泷浦真人 2005。不仅为了对敬语研究先行者的公允，更为了对笔者不学的反省。
>
> 菊地康人 1994 是上个世纪 90 年代后的敬语研究中值得瞩目的研究成果之一。该书重点在于敬语的使用上的分类整理，其实用价值自不待言。只是对敬语体系方面的研究着力不多，处于本稿兴趣之外。在这一点上，泷浦真人 2005 与菊地康人 1994 适成互补。

泷浦真人 2005 的研究最值得瞩目之处有两点。一是对敬语研究史做了详细的梳理。发掘了时枝诚记的「関係認識」在学术史上的历史意义。二是高度评价了三上章的敬语研究（三上章，1955、1972），提出了「“上下” の関係」和「“ウチ/ソト” 」两种关系是日语敬语的相对性的核心的观点。尤其后者在敬语研究史上值得大书特书，高度评价。引文如下。

> タテの関係は“上下”の関係であり、ヨコの関係は“ウチ/ソト”の関係である。<視点>と<距離>の表現である共感度の不等式は、それらを一元的に書き表す。このことは、日本語敬語の相対敬語性を担う“上下”の軸と“ウチ/ソト”の軸が一つに還元可能であり、それらがじつは一つの関係の二つの表れであることを強く示唆している。泷浦真人 2005：252 页

泷浦真人 2005 对三上章的「敬語法のA 線」的图示见下图。

这个图示标志着泷浦真人 2005 对三上章的敬语研究发展的深度，也标志着日语敬语史研究的新的高度。如果能将其与渡边实的敬语研究结合起来，其体系性以及对日语敬语史的解释性都可以令人叹为观止。

笔者对泷浦真人 2005 所论述的，「“上下” の軸」与「“ウチ/ソト”

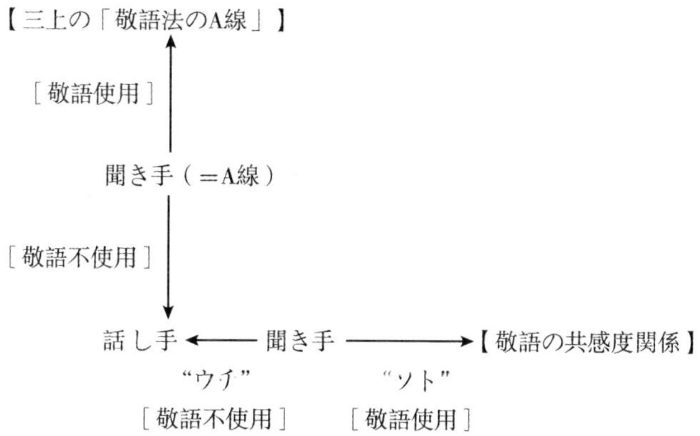

本图引自，泷浦真人 2005：252 页

の軸」为日语敬语的相对性的核心的观点十分赞同。但对二者可以还原为一的观点不敢苟同。笔者认为，所谓的还原为一是一个人为的抽象而已。二者之间的比重的变量和二者之间的平衡关系，对揭示日语敬语史的历史变化的动态则更为有效。惜乎笔者是在最后修改本稿时才看到泷浦真人 2005 的研究，否则本稿也许不作了。

毋庸置疑，日语敬语研究史上渡边实的学说与时枝诚记的学说之间的关系既有继承也有发展。笔者认为，渡边实在敬语体系研究上的贡献就在于他提出的体系不论与时枝诚记的「関係認識」相比，还是与三上章的「敬語法のA 線」相比都较为完善较为系统。泷浦真人 2005 对渡边实的批判不无求全责备之嫌，对时枝诚记的评价则有厚古薄今之憾。泷浦真人 2005 对渡边实的批判详见泷浦真人（2005：58—60）。

此外，泷浦真人 2005 一书中「Ⅲ　敬語の語用論のために」（泷浦真人，2005：207—256 页）最为精彩值得一读、其中「［Ⅲ - 2］<視点>と<距離>の敬語論」（泷浦真人，2005：233—256 页）一节探讨了敬语与<視点>和<距離>的关联性，窃以为，有待研究<視点>的学者参考。

感谢陈力卫教授百忙之中校阅拙稿。没有陈教授的指教，笔者对 20 世纪 90 年代以后的敬语研究将依然一无所知，这个补笔也不会写出来。

参考文献

石坂正藏（1944）『敬語史論考』、文進堂。

石坂正藏（1951）「敬語的人称の概念」、『熊本大学法文論叢』第二号、1—26 頁。

岡村和江（1963）「尊敬・謙譲・丁寧」、『国文学言語と文芸』昭和 38 年 3 月号「敬語問題特輯」、23—28 頁。

春日和男（1976）「敬語の変遷（1）」、『岩波講座日本語』、95—134 頁。

亀井孝（1955）「近代日本語の諸相の成立」、『国語学』第 22 輯、1—5 頁。

菊池康人（1994）『敬語』、角川書店。

木下正俊（1968）「敬語の変遷のとらえ方・上代」、『月刊文法』昭和 43 年 12 月号、83—88 頁。

金田一京助（1942）『国語研究』、八雲書林。

金田一京助（1948）「女性語と敬語」、『増補国語研究』、八雲書林、1948 年増補版、293—315 頁。

金田一京助（1955）「万葉集の敬語」、『万葉集大成・言語篇』、平凡社、215—239 頁。

小島俊夫（1974）『後期江戸ことばの敬語体系』、笠間書院。

小松寿雄（1963）「待遇表現の分類」、『国文学言語と文芸』昭和 38 年 3 月号「敬語問題特輯」、2—7 頁。

小松寿雄（1971）「近代の敬語Ⅱ」、辻村敏樹編『講座国語史』第五巻『敬語史』、大修館書店、283—365 頁。阪倉篤義（1952）「『侍り』の性格」、『国語国文』第二一巻一〇号、41—45 頁。

小松寿雄（1977）「江戸語の形成」、『松村明教授古稀記念国語学と国語史』、505—523 頁。

阪倉篤義（1952）「『侍り』の性格」、『国語国文』第二一巻一〇号、41—45 頁。

阪倉篤義（1983）「時代区分」、川端善明・森岡健二他編『講座日本語学Ⅰ総論』、明治書院、1—19 頁。

阪倉篤義（1993）『日本語表現の流れ』、岩波書店。

佐久間鼎（1937）「言語における水準転移——特に日本語における人代名詞の変遷について——」、『速水博士還暦記念心理学哲学論文集』、岩波書店、143—164 頁。

時枝誠記（1941）『国語学原論』、岩波書店。

滝浦真人（2005）『日本の敬語——ポライトネス理論からの再検討』、三水社。

玉上琢弥（1952）「敬語の文学的考察——源氏物語の本性（其二）——」、『国語国文』第二十一巻第二号、40—63 頁。

玉上琢弥（1955）「源氏物語の解釈文法（敬語）」、大野晋他（1955）『時代別作品別解釈文法』、至文堂、69—97 頁。

チャンブレン1999『「日本口語文典」全訳』、丸山和雄・岩崎攝子訳、おうふう。

辻村敏树（1958a）「ことばの使い方——敬語——」、『日本文法講座 5 表現文法』、明治書院、248—285 頁。

辻村敏树（1958b）「待遇語法」、『続日本文法講座 1 文法各論編』、明治書院、323—344 頁。

辻村敏树（1963）「敬語の分類について」、『国文学言語と文芸』昭和 38 年 3 月号「敬語問題特輯」、8—13 頁。

辻村敏樹（1971）「敬語史の方法と問題」、『講座国語史 5 敬語史』、大修館、1—32 頁。

辻村敏树（1981）「敬語意識史——敬語史における敬と卑、親と疎、公と私——」、『講座日本語学 9 敬語史』、明治書院、26—42 頁。

時枝誠記（1954）「詞と辞の連続・非連続の問題」、『国語学』第 19 輯、1954 年。

中野伸彦（1986）「洒落本における終助詞『の』」、『松村明教授古稀記念国語研究論集』、明治書院、489—500 頁。

中村香生里（2017）「『~するつもりだ』『~（よ）うと+思考動詞』の歴史的変遷」、『同志社大学日本語・日本文化研究』第 15 号、1—51 頁。

西宮一民（1981）「上代敬語と現代敬語」、『講座日本語学 9 敬語史』、明治書院、1981、114—139 頁。

根来司（1963）「敬語の分類」、『国文学言語と文芸』昭和 38 年 3 月号「敬語問題特輯」、29—32 頁。

福島直恭（2010）「自敬表現と絶対敬語」、『学習院女子大学紀要』第 12 号、115—132 頁。

福島直恭（2011）「身内尊敬表現と絶対敬語—進歩史観的敬語論批判—」、『日本語と日本文学』筑波大学国語国文学会、第 52 号、L1—L12 頁。

彭広陸（2008）「从翻译看日汉移动动词「来る/行く」和“来/去”的差异」、《日语学习与研究》2008 年第 4 期、7—14 頁。

彭広陸（2014）「日本語の場所指示名詞に関する一考察——中国語との比較を通して」《外语教育研究》2014 年第 4 期、6—15 頁。

彭広陸（2016）「日中両語のヴォイスに見られる視点のあり方」『言語の主観性——認知とポライトネスの接点』くろしお出版、35—51 頁。

三上章（1955［1972］）「中編　敬語の問題」、『現代語法新説』、刀江書院［くろしお出版］，191—238 頁。

宫地裕（1971）「現代の敬語」、『講座国語史 5 敬語史』、大修館書店、367—425 頁。

宫地裕（1981）「敬語史論」、『講座日本語学 9 敬語史』、明治書院、1—25 頁。

六笠寿子（1957）「『浮世風呂』における間投助詞『な・なあ』『の・のう』『ね・ねえ』の使い分けについて」、『国文』（お茶の水女子大学国語国文学会）、第八号、64—72 頁。

森重敏（1958）「つれづれ草の『侍り』をめぐって」、『女子大国文』第八号、1—19 頁。

森野宗明（1968）「敬語の分類」、『月刊文法』昭和 43 年 12 月号、27—34 頁。

山崎久之（1955）「国語の待遇表現体系とその歴史」『国語学』第 21 輯、17—29 頁。

山崎久之（1961）「敬語・丁寧語『おまへ』『あなた』の発生は待遇表現体系にどんな影響を与えたか」『国語学』第 45 輯、1—14 頁。

山崎久之（1963）『国語待遇表現体系の研究』、武蔵野書院。

山崎久之（1990）『続国語待遇表現体系の研究』、武蔵野書院。

山田孝雄（1924）『敬語法の研究』、東京宝文館。

李長波（1999）「古代中国語の指示詞とその文法化について」、『デュナミス』、Vol. 3，45—72 頁。

李長波（2000）「『カレ』の語史とその周辺——三人称代名詞が成立するまでのみちすじ——」、『デュナミス』、Vol. 4，1—33 頁。

李長波（2001）「古代日本語の人称体系における「自・他」の問題——古代中国語の人称代名詞と上代語との関連を中心に——」文部科学省科学研究費補助金特定領域研究（A）「古典学の再構築」（平成 10 年度～平成 14 年度）『公募研究論文集』、427—446 頁。

李長波（2002）『日本語指示体系の歴史』、京都大学学術出版会。

渡辺実（1958）「日本語の変化」、『コトバの科学 2 コトバと社会』、中山書店、232—252 頁。

渡辺実（1971）「敬語体系」、『国語構文論』附説、421—442 頁。

渡辺実（1973）「上代・中古敬語の概観」、林四郎・南不二男編『敬語講座第 2 巻上代・中古の敬語』、明治書院、7—27 頁。

渡辺実（1981）「敬語の言語学」、『国文学』第二十六巻二号（昭和五十六年一月臨時増刊号）、學燈社、13—19 頁。

Inquiry into the Meaning of the Historical Development of Japanese Honorific Language through a Review of the History of its Research

Li Changbo (Doshisha University)

Abstract: In this paper I examine the main theories of existing research on honorific language and discuss the strengths and weaknesses of each theory. Specifically, I point out the conceptual framework of Watanabe Minoru's research on honorific language as being the most effective not only for theoretical research, but also for historical research on honorific systems. Additionally, regarding the history of Japanese honorific language, in this paper I will discuss the following three points.

1. The descriptive framework of the honorific language system and history of honorifics should be conceived according to whether "the principle of upper and lower" or "the principle of inside and outside" has relative priority over the other. In the history of Japanese honorifics there has never been a time of "absolute honorifics," therefore it is not possible to conceive of the history of honorific language as a development from "absolute honorifics" to "relative honorifics."

2. If the history of Japanese honorifics is understood according to whether "the principle of upper and lower" or "the principle of inside and outside" has relative priority, the honorifics expressing "respect for the listener" have developed as a manifestation of the "listener - orientedness" of the honorifics system. This tendency is estimated to have come about in late Edo culture, during the Bunsei period (1804-1929).

3. Honorifics' "listener - orientedness" is consistent with, among other phenomena, the frequent historical change of second person pronouns, the hist-

orical development of "listener-orientedness" in the history of the system of demonstratives, as well as the historical development of sentence-ending particles. From the viewpoint of interpersonal relations in Japanese language, this "listener-oriented" tendency can be regarded as one of the major trends in the historical development of Japanese language.

Keywords: the principle of upper and lower; the principle of inside and outside; listener-orientedness

文学与文化

试论中西诗歌起源的趋同性

冯红变*

摘　要：中国诗歌的产生要早于西方2000多年，中西思维方式、社会意识形态的差异很大，对诗歌起源的认识也不相同。"诗言志"和"摹仿说"分别代表了中西对诗歌起源的认识，二者有着很大的区别。然中西对诗歌起源的不同认识中也存在着许多共同的因素，这些因素对诗歌而言是至关重要的。主要有：都对诗歌提出了情感的要求；对诗歌与现实的关系认识也是相同的；都强调诗歌的创造性。中西诗歌起源趋同性的研究，有助于人们更好地认识诗歌的本质规律。

关键词：中西诗歌；起源；趋同性

一　引言

我国第一部诗歌总集《诗经》收录了西周初年（约公元前11世纪）至春秋中叶（约公元前6世纪）的诗歌305篇，这是我国有确切文字记载的、较为成熟的文学的开始。然而近年来在西安半坡遗址和临潼姜寨等遗址出土的陶器上刻有简单的刻画符号，这可能就是中国最早的文字，是公元前5000—前3000年时候的事了。如果这些文物能够得到进一步证实的话，就说明在公元前50世纪的时候，中华民族已经有了自己幼稚的文学，距今已经有5000多年的悠久历史了。而在西方，埃及金字塔中的《亡灵书》产生于公元前3000年，是西方最早的诗歌；印度现存最古老的诗歌总集《梨俱吠陀》是公元前15世纪前编成的；希伯来文学遗产《旧约》中最深无的诗歌集《诗篇》收录150首诗歌，最早的是公元前11世纪大卫的作品；完成于公元前9—前8世纪的《荷马史诗》则是

---

* 作者简介：冯红变（1970—　），女，陕西师范大学外国语学院副教授，研究方向：英汉对比；英语教学。

西方较早的、成就最大、对后世影响最深远的诗作，这都说明西方文学也有悠久的历史。当东方的中国人正忙碌于为“饥者歌其食，劳者歌其事”而吟诵的时候，西方人也在引吭高歌。可以说中西方人的始祖用其嘹亮的歌喉，为世界诗歌史上留下了最为宝贵的、辉煌灿烂的文明。在中西文学中最早出现并发展成熟的是诗歌，但是在诗歌的起源问题上，中西方人的看法则不尽相同。本文拟对中西方的诗歌起源理论进行对比研究，以便我们更好地了解中西方人思维的不同特点和把握诗歌的本质。

二　中西诗歌起源的差异

中国人认为诗歌起源于人们情感的表达。这一认识产生得早，而且贯穿于中国古代诗歌史的始终。具体来说就是“诗言志”理论的提出以及不断地被修正。

《尚书·尧典》中的“诗言志，歌永言”是目前所知对这一理论的最早阐述。此后《左传》开创了“赋诗言志”的传统。但这里的“志”主要指的是政治上的理想和抱负，与后世所说的情感是有区别的。屈原在其作品中一再地说“发愤以抒情”（《九章·惜诵》）、“苟余情其信姱以练要兮，长颇颔亦何伤?”“荃不察余之中情兮，反信谗而斎怒”“不吾知其亦已兮，苟余情其信芳”（《离骚》）、“结微情以陈词”（《九章·抽思》）、“抚情效志”（《九章·怀沙》）、“申旦以舒中情兮，志沉菀而莫达”（《九章·思美人》）等，诸如此类的例子不胜枚举。同时屈原也不忽略“志”，他说：“屈心而抑志”（《离骚》）、“有志极而无旁”（《九章·惜诵》）、“易初而屈志”（《九章·思美人》），即屈原认为他的作品是由于“志”不得施展、受到压抑而作的。屈原这种通过抒情来达到“言志”目的的认识，较之荀子的认识又前进了一步。汉代的《毛诗大序》云：“诗者，志之所之也，在心为志，发言为诗。情动于中而形于言，言之不足故嗟叹之，嗟叹之不足故永歌之，永歌之不足，不知手之舞之、足之蹈之也。”（郭绍虞、王文生，1979：30）这一段话明确地提出诗是抒情的，并进一步指出“诗者志之所之也”的“志”与“动于中而形于言”的“情”是相统一的。这种“情”“志”统一的认识，较之在此之前对诗歌起源理论又有所进步，比较接近诗歌的实际。但又提出了“发乎情，止乎礼义”的要求，要求诗歌所抒之情必须受儒家礼义的约束。这无形又给诗歌情感的抒发设置了障碍，使人们对诗歌的认识难免穿凿附会。

西晋时的陆机在《文赋》中对古代的“言志”理论做了进一步的发挥，他说：

> 诗缘情而绮靡，赋体物而浏亮。碑披文以相质，诔缠绵而凄怆。铭博约而温润，箴顿挫而清壮。颂优游以彬蔚，论精微而朗畅。奏平彻以闲雅，说炜晔而谲诳（郭绍虞、王文生，1979：67—68）。

陆机将文体分为诗、赋、碑、诔、铭、箴、颂、论、奏、说十类，并对各类文体的风格特征逐一进行了概括。他对文体的分类是否正确尚且不论，对除了诗之外其他九种风格的把握是否准确也不想涉及。在此，我们主要分析一下他对诗的认识。陆机论诗只讲“缘情”而不讲“言志”客观上已经要求诗歌能够摆脱儒家礼义规范的要求，基本上接触到诗歌的本质。但却遭到后人的指责，比如沈德潜在《说诗晬语》中说：“言诗章教，惟资涂泽，先失诗人之旨”（张少康、刘三富，1995：190），纪昀在《云林诗钞序》中也说：“知‘发乎情’而不必‘止乎礼义’，自陆平原‘缘情’一语，引入歧途”（张少康、刘三富，1995：190）。沈氏、纪氏的指责，恰恰不是陆机理论的缺陷，而是其理论的进步性之所在，是能够体现诗歌本质的东西。

从以上的分析论述来看，中国的“诗言志”理论，由最初《左传》的只重思想，强调用诗来表现人的政治理想抱负；到荀子的《乐论》在“志”之外提出了“情”的要求；到屈原在“志”的基础上很注重“情”的因素；再到《毛诗大序》“志”“情”并重，并要求情感的抒发要受儒家礼义规范的限制；最后到陆机《文赋》要求诗歌不受儒家礼义规范约束地去抒情，至此，中国理论家把握了诗歌的本质，完成了对诗歌起源的正确认识。

西方理论家认为诗歌起源于摹仿。较早提出摹仿理论，并对其进行分析，而且对后世产生巨大影响的是一些古希腊、罗马的思想家、哲学家和文艺理论家。

古希腊的思想家赫拉克利特（Heraclitus）最早提出摹仿理论，他认为艺术是摹仿自然的。紧接着希腊的又一思想家德谟克利特（Democritus）说：“在许多重要的事情上，我们是摹仿禽兽，作禽兽的小学生的。从蜘蛛我们学会了织布和缝补；从燕子学会了造房子；从天鹅和黄莺等歌唱的鸟学会了歌唱。”（伍蠡甫、蒋孔阳，1979：4—5）德谟克利特的理论很明显是对赫拉克利特的继承。古希腊的另一思想家柏拉图（Plato）在《理想国》卷三中将诗歌分为三种：“头一种是从头到尾都用摹仿，像你所提到的悲剧和喜剧；第二种是只有诗人在说话，最好的例子也许是合唱队的颂歌；第三种摹仿和单纯叙述掺在一起，史诗和另外几种诗都是如此。”（转引自缪朗山，1985：28）。在这三种诗中，他攻击史诗和剧诗两种所谓“摹仿的艺术”，唯独肯定“非摹仿的艺术”的歌功颂德的颂诗。在该书卷十中又说：“摹仿和真实体隔得很远，它在表面上像能制造一切事物，是因为它只取每件事物的一小部分，而那一小部分还只是一个影象。”（转引自胡经之，1986：38）。也就是说，文艺只是摹仿的摹仿、影子的影子，是“和真理隔着两层”。和希腊其他摹仿理论的倡导者相比，柏拉图可以说是一种倒退。前代注重反映现实的诗歌摹仿理论在他这儿荡然无存，柏拉图的摹仿理论使诗歌与现实的距离越来越远。针对柏拉图的这种认识，亚里士多德（Aristotle）做了适当的弥补和发挥。亚氏认为史诗、颂诗和剧诗都是摹仿的艺术。与柏拉图相比，他拓展了范围。在摹仿的诗与现实的关系上也表现出与柏拉图迥然不同的认识，他在《诗学》第二十五章中说：

> 衡量诗和衡量其他艺术正确与否，标准也不一样。在诗里，错误分两种：艺术本身的错误和偶然的错误。如果诗人挑选某一件事物来摹仿……而缺乏表现力，这是艺术本身的错误。但是，如果他挑选的事物不正确，例如写马的两只右腿同时并进，或者在科学（例如医学或其他科学）上犯了错误，或者把某种不可能发生的事写在他的诗里，这些都不是艺术本身的错误。（罗念生、杨周翰，1962：154）

也正如以上所述，亚里士多德认为艺术的真实与自然科学的真实是有区别的。认为艺术不仅仅要摹仿现实的事物，而且要用一种适宜的方式来表现，实际上指的是创造。亚里士多德对诗歌起源问题的认识更接近诗的实际，也抓住了其本质。公元前1世纪左右，罗马奥古斯丁时期的诗人和文学批评家贺拉斯（Quintus Horatius Flaccus）对亚里士多德的摹仿理论进行了补充。在诗所摹仿的对象上，他认为除了像亚里士多德所说的那样摹仿现实外，还可以向艺术摹仿。他在《诗艺》中说，“不是每个批评家都能指出（这样的）诗的音律是和谐还是不和谐，因此过分地放纵了罗马诗人。难道因此我也就可以毫无拘束地乱跑，随便乱写么？但即使我的错误人人可以看到，难道我就应该只求安全，小心翼翼地希望别人原谅我么？我最多不过是避免了（别人的）赞许。你们应当日日夜夜把玩希腊的范例？”（罗念生、杨周翰，1962：151），明确地提出要摹仿古希腊的艺术。

三 中西诗歌起源的共同之处

诗歌的言志说和摹仿说分别代表了中西方人对诗歌起源问题的认识，正如上所述，它们之间存在着巨大的差异。尽管如此，中西方人对诗歌的认识却有些是相同的，现分述如下。

（一）二者都提出了情感的要求

诗歌是否要抒发情感，这实际上涉及诗歌的本质。中西理论家对诗歌的起源认识各异，但对其本质的认识是清晰的，即认为诗歌创作中必须有情感的参与。

中国的“诗言志”说是主情的，前述已甚详。此外，“诗言志”说非常重视心灵在诗歌创作中的作用。汉代的扬雄在《法言・问神》中首次将“心”作为文学的本源凸显了出来，但这与“诗言志”说强调诗起源于情感并不矛盾。因为“情”本身就源于“心”，《毛诗序》就曾说过“情动于中而形言”的话。文学本是一种精神活动，是凭借语言来抒发内心感情的。扬雄在论述了文学源于心后，并对文学提出了所谓“动情”的原则。这一原则的提出，更进一步说明他的“心声书画”论是与“诗言志”说殊途同归了。扬雄在这里论述的是文学，当然亦包括诗歌在内。扬雄这种认识是符合诗歌实际的，因而对后世产生了深远的影响。明代的李贽提出了著名的“童心”说，他说：“夫童心者，绝假纯真，最初一念本也。”“童心既障，于是发而为言语，则言语不由衷；见而为政事，则政事无根柢；著而为文辞，则文辞不能达。非内含以章美也，非笃实生辉光也，欲求一句有德之言，卒不可得。所以者何？以童心既障，而以从外入者闻见道理为之心也。”“天下之至文，未有不出于童心焉者也。”（郭绍虞、王文生，1980：117—118），他认为“童心”即真心，是与人生之俱来的，是人的自然本性。简而言之，“童心”说要求文学抒发人的真情感。继李贽的“童心”说后，明代的袁宏道提出了著名的“性灵”说，他说：“大都独抒性灵，不拘格套，非从自己胸臆出不肯下笔。有时情与境会，顷刻千言，如水东注，令人夺魂。其间有佳处，亦有疵处，佳处自不必言，即疵处亦多本色独造语。然予则极喜其疵处；而所谓佳者，尚不能不以粉饰蹈饰为恨，以为未能尽脱近代文人气习故也。”（郭绍虞、王文生，1980：211），要求文学是真性灵、真感情的自然流露。在诗歌创作中要求对心灵高度重视的论述，实际上是对“诗言志”中“志”的含义的进一步修正。

西方的摹仿说虽然不像中国的“诗言志”理论那样十分强调诗歌的抒情色彩，但从其论述中也可以发现，他们并没有忽视诗歌的情感因素。古希腊的德谟克利特在《著作残篇》说：“摹仿坏人而甚至不愿摹仿好人，是很恶劣”，这里虽未提及情感，但诗人在摹仿的过程中情感显然参与其中。柏拉图在《斐德若篇》中说：

> 此外还有第三种迷狂，是由诗神凭附而来的。她凭附到一个温柔贞洁的心灵，感发它，引它到兴高采烈神飞色舞的境界，流露于各种诗歌，颂赞古代英雄的丰功伟绩，垂为后世的教训。如果没有这种诗神的迷狂，无论谁去敲诗歌的门，他和他的作品都永远站在诗歌的门外，尽管他自己妄想单凭诗的艺术就可以成为一个诗人。他的神志清醒的诗遇到迷狂的诗就黯然无光（张少康、刘三富 1995：190）。

他认为诗人一旦具有了诗兴迷狂（在本篇中，柏拉图分析了四种迷狂，即预言的迷狂、宗教的迷狂、诗兴的迷狂和爱美的迷狂），可以创造出垂为后世典范的作品；如果没有这种迷狂，无论诗人如何具有高超的才情却难窥诗歌之门。柏拉图这里所谓的“迷狂”实际上是指诗歌创作的情感达到高潮、诗如泉涌的一种境界。如前所述，柏拉图在论述的摹仿理论虽然有一定的偏颇，但这里强调情感参与创作的“迷狂”的说法却是很准确的，基本上抓住了诗歌的本质。令人遗憾的是，他将这种“迷狂”归结为神的“凭附”，则不免堕入形而上学的泥坑。亚里士多德说：“人对于模仿的作品总是感到快感。经验证明了这样一点：事物本身看上去尽管引起痛感，但惟妙惟肖的图像看上去却能引起我们的快感，例如尸首或最可鄙的动物形象。”（伍蠡甫、蒋孔阳，1979：53）他将摹拟与快感联系起来，认为尽管有些东西很丑恶，但经过艺术的摹仿后可以给人以快感。由此我们看出，亚里士多德也非常注重诗歌的抒情性。

与中国的“诗言志”理论相似，西方的摹仿理论亦重视诗歌创作中心灵的作用。希腊的历史学家色诺芬认为艺术不仅要摹仿外行，而且要摹仿心理。柏拉图在《伊安篇》中说：

> 抒情诗人们在作诗的时也是如此。他们一旦受到音乐和韵节力量的支配，就感到酒神的狂欢，由于这种灵感的影响，他们正如酒神的女信徒们受酒神凭附，可以从河水中汲取乳蜜，这是她们在神志清醒时所不能做的事。抒情诗人的心灵也正像这样，他们自己也说他们像酿蜜，飞到诗神的园里。从流蜜的泉源吸取精英，来酿成他们的诗歌。(伍蠡甫、蒋孔阳，1979：78—79)

在这里，柏拉图用蜜蜂酿蜜的过程来比喻心灵在诗歌创作过程中的作用，形象而贴切，在此基础上发展成为他的著名理论——灵感。他在《伊安篇》中对灵感做了详细的描述：

> 磁石不仅能吸引铁环本身，而且把吸引力传给那些铁环，使它们也像磁石一样，能吸引其他铁环。有时你看到许多个铁环互相吸引着，挂成一条长锁链，这些全从一块磁石得到悬在一起的力量。诗神就像这块磁石，她首先给人灵感，得到这灵感的人们又把她传递给旁人，让旁人接上他们，悬成一条锁链。凡是高明的诗人，无论在史诗或诗歌方面，都不是凭技艺来作成他们的优美的诗歌，而是因为他们得到灵感，有神力凭附着。(伍蠡甫、蒋孔阳，1979：18)

柏拉图用了非常形象的比喻，将灵感比喻为磁石。一块磁石凭借自身的力量可以吸收铁环并使之与其他铁环衔接在一起，同样诗神将灵感传递给朗诵者，朗诵者再传递给听众。柏拉图的灵感说基本上接近今人所谓“诗的感染力”，因此其认识是非常准确而且是难能可贵的。但他乞灵于神的说法则是完全错误的。

(二) 二者都探讨了诗歌与现实的关系问题

诗歌与现实的关系问题，是任何一位诗人都不能回避的、必须作出正面回答的论题。中西理论家对此都做了各自的阐释，而且其认识都基本接近。

中国的“诗言志”理论认为情感的抒发是受外物的触发而引起的。南朝齐梁之际的刘勰在《文心雕龙》中说：“人禀七情，应物斯感，感物吟志，莫非自然”（《明诗》），“文变染乎世情，而兴废系时序”（《时序》），已经认识到外物是触发情感的媒介。此后钟嵘在《诗品》中做了更进一步的详细分析，他说：

> 若乃春风春鸟，秋月秋蝉，夏云暑雨，冬月祁寒，斯四候之感诸诗者也。嘉会寄诗以来，离群托诗以怨，至于楚臣去境，汉妾辞宫，或骨横朔野，魂逐飞蓬；或负戈外戍，杀气雄边；塞客衣单，孀闺泪尽；或士有解佩出朝，一去忘返；女有扬蛾入宠，再盼倾国。凡斯种种，感荡心灵，非陈诗何以展其义，非长歌何以骋其情。（徐达，1990：21）

钟嵘从分析《楚辞》、《汉乐府民歌》、《古诗十九首》、建安文学入手，阐明了外物对人心灵施加影响而生情感的道理。这种因物感情的提法，实际上就是后代诗歌创作中所强调的触景生情。此后清代的王夫之继承了钟嵘的这种认识并有所发展，提出了诗歌情景交融的创作境界：

> 情景名为二，而实不可离。神于诗者，妙合无垠，巧者则有情中景，景中情。景中情者，如“长安一片月”，自然是孤栖忆远之情；“影静千官里”，自然是喜达行在之情。情中景尤难曲写，如“诗成珠玉在挥毫”，写出才人翰墨淋漓、自心欣赏之景。凡此类，知者遇之，非然，亦鹘突看过，作等闲语耳。（张少康、刘三富，1995：307）

情景交融是中国古代诗歌创作的最高境界，而且也是诗人们孜孜以求的。王夫之在此将它分成“景中情”和“情中景”两类，并分别用李白《子夜吴歌》、杜甫《喜达行在所》和杜甫《奉和贾至舍人早朝大明宫》为例来做一分析说明。无论是“景中情”还是“情中景”都达到了情景交融的境界。上述钟嵘的因物感情和王夫之的情景交融，实际上已经初步涉及文学与现实的关系问题，而且这种看法非常符合文学创作的实际，中国的理论家在此基础上生发出一系列诗歌反映现实的理论。《诗经》“饥者歌其食，劳者歌其事”，汉代的乐府诗“感于哀乐，缘事而发”，曹操诸人“用乐府旧题写时事”，杜甫“即事名篇，无复依傍”的新题乐府诗，白居易的新乐府运动倡导“文章合为时而著，歌诗合为事而作”……这些诗歌创作理论成为中国古代诗歌的主导，无论哪一个朝代的哪一位作家都会自觉地按照这一原则正确处理诗歌与现实的关系问题。

西方的摹仿说在诗歌与现实的关系问题上比较复杂，经历了一个曲折的过程。柏拉图认为包括诗在内的一切艺术只不过是摹本的摹本、影子的影子，是和真理隔了两层。很明显是说诗不是反映现实的，是不真实的。亚里士多德对柏拉图这种偏颇的认识进行了纠正，亚里士多德认为，人们在进行艺术摹仿的同时也在认识事物。这种看法和柏拉图是相反的，他承认艺术的真实性，认为艺术可以反映现实事物。在同书的第九章强调艺术不必墨守成规，可以进行虚构，他说：

> 但也有些悲剧只有一二人名是家喻户晓的，其余则是虚构；有些甚至全篇是虚构，例如，阿伽同的《安条斯》，剧情和人名皆是虚构，但仍然为人所喜爱。因此，诗人不必务求墨守悲剧所惯用的传统的野史，这样拘泥，实属可笑……（转引自缪朗山，1985：75）

亚里士多德肯定诗歌的真实性，认为它可以反映现实的认识。在不妨碍认识真实的前提下，可以虚构。这些认识与柏拉图相比较，可以说是基本上正确地理解了诗歌与现实的关系。古罗马的贺拉斯第一次明确地提出了诗人应该向现实学习的看法，他说：“我劝告已经懂得写什么的作家到生活中到风俗习惯中去寻找模型，从那里汲取活生生的语言吧。”（罗念生、杨周翰，1962：154），向生活汲取营养，反映现实生活，这里所昭示的诗与现实的关系，则与中国“诗言志”理论的认识是一致的。

（三）二者都强调诗歌的创造性

摹仿（或复古）与创造是一对孪生姐妹，如何正确处理二者的关系对诗歌的创作是非常重要的。虽然中西理论家对诗歌的起源认识不一，但他们都不约而同地强调诗歌的独创性。

汉代的王充在《论衡·超奇》中说：“故夫能说一经者为儒生；博览

古今者为通人；采掇传书，以上是奏记者为文人；能精思著文，连接篇章者为鸿儒。故儒生过俗人，通人胜儒生，文人逾通人，鸿儒超文人。”（郭绍虞、王文生，1979：42—43）王充是针对汉代解经之学越来越精细、烦琐而说的这一番话的，虽然他在论经学，但同时也涉及诗歌。他将一般的文人分为儒生、通人、文人、鸿儒四类，而他最赞美的是鸿儒。“夫鸿儒希有，而文人比然，将相长吏，安可不贵？岂徒用其才力游文于牒牍哉？州郡有忧，能治章上奏，解理结烦，使州郡连事”，认为鸿儒有独立的见解，能创造性地写文章，故被他称之为“超而又超”“奇而又奇”，是“世之金玉也”。王充在这篇文章中还将屈原归入鸿儒，很明显他在要求经学独创性的同时又强调诗歌的创造性。明代的袁宏道说：

> 至于诗，则不肖聊戏笔耳，信心而出，信口而谈。世人喜唐，仆则曰唐无诗；世人喜秦、汉，仆则曰秦、汉无文；世人卑宋黜元，仆则曰诗文在宋元诸大家。昔老子欲死圣人，庄生讥毁孔子，然至今其书不废；荀卿言性恶，亦得与孟子同传。何者？见从已出，不曾依傍半个古人，所以他顶天立地，今人虽讥讪得，却是废他不得。不然粪裹爵查，顺口接屁，倚势欺良，如今苏州投靠家人一般。记得几个烂熟故事，便曰博识；用得几个见成字眼，亦曰骚人；计骗杜工部，囤扎李空同，一个八寸三分帽子，人人戴得。以是言诗，安在而不诗哉！不肖恶之深，所以立言亦自有矫枉之过。（郭绍虞、王文生，1980：211）

袁宏道是针对前后七子的剽窃模拟之风而发的，由于他对这种风气深恶痛绝，故不乏偏颇之词，但其核心部分则是极为正确的。他极力赞赏孔子、荀子“见从已出，不曾依傍半个古人”的创造精神。他在这里论文，实际上也在言诗，在《叙梅子马王程稿》中强调诗歌要“独抒己见，信心而言，寄口于腕”就是力证。清代的赵翼一反韩愈“李杜文章长，光焰万丈长”（《调张籍》）的歌颂李白、杜甫的看法，说“李杜诗篇万口传，至今已觉不新鲜。江山代有才人出，各领风骚数百年”（《论诗》其二），同样是强调诗歌要有独创性。

西方的摹仿说同样强调诗歌的创造性。亚里士多德在《诗学》第二章中说：

> 摹仿者所摹仿的对象既然是在行动中的人，而这种人又必然是好人或坏人——只有这种人才具有品格，一切人的品格都只有善与恶的差别——因此他们所摹仿的人物不是一般人好，就是一般人坏，或是跟一般人一样 。恰像画家描绘的人物，波吕格诺托斯笔下的肖像比一般人坏，……悲剧和喜剧也有同样的差别：喜剧总是摹仿比我们今天的人坏的人，悲剧总是摹仿比我们今天的人好的人。（伍蠡甫、蒋孔阳，1979：52）

亚里士多德是柏拉图的弟子，然正如他自己所表述的那样：吾爱吾师，吾更爱真理。亚里士多德针对柏拉图认为诗是摹本的摹本、影子的影子理论，提出艺术形象应该比现实较优或较劣。这种看法可以说是一种创造性的摹仿。希腊的卡利马科斯（Callimachus）说："诗人且莫在车马挤拥的路上徘徊，且莫步他人的后尘，应该独辟蹊径，采摘鲜花。"（转引自缪朗山，1985：106），也强调诗歌的独创。西方的摹仿说之所以没有沦为中国明代前后七子那样的剽窃风气，其原因在于要求诗歌摹仿的同时又强调其独创性。

参考文献

郭绍虞、王文生：《中国历代文论选》（一卷本），上海古籍出版社 1979 年版。

郭绍虞、王文生：《中国历代文论选》（第三册），上海古籍出版社 1980 年版。

胡经之：《西方文艺理论名著教程》，北京大学出版社 1986 年版。

罗念生、杨周翰：《亚里斯多德〈诗学〉贺拉斯〈诗艺〉》，人民文学出版社 1962 年版。

缪朗山：《西方文艺理论史纲》，中国人民大学出版社 1985 年版。

伍蠡甫、蒋孔阳：《西方文论选》（上），上海译文出版社 1979 年版。

徐达：《诗品全译》，贵州人民出版社 1990 年版。

张少康、刘三富：《中国文学理论批评发展史》（上、下），北京大学出版社 1995 年版。

On the Convergence of the Origin of Chinese and Western Poetry

Feng Hongbian

Abstract: The emergence of Chinese poetry is more than 2000 years earlier than that of the West. There are great differences between Chinese and Western ways of thinking and social ideology, and their understanding of the origin of poetry is also different. "Poetry expresses ambition" and "imitation theory" respectively represent Chinese and Western understanding of the origin of poetry, and they are quite different. However, there are many common factors in the different understanding of the origin of poetry between China and the West, which are very important for poetry. The main points are as follows: they all put forward emotional requirements for poetry; they all share the same understanding of the relationship between poetry and reality; they all emphasize the creativity of poetry. The study of the convergence of the origins of Chinese and Western poetry will help people better understand the essential law of poetry.

Key words: Chinese and Western poetry; origin; convergence

俄苏侨民文学两次浪潮之比较研究*

李　琳　杨苗苗**

摘　要：20世纪的侨民文学在俄苏文学史中具有独一无二、不可取代的地位。俄苏侨民文学第一浪潮与第三浪潮规模庞大、作家众多、作品丰富、影响广泛。侨民文学的两次浪潮在形成背景、文学成就、作品风格方面有明显差异，而在政治主题、家国情怀和国际声誉上有共通之处，"本土文学"与"侨民文学"相得益彰，促进了俄苏多元格局的文学史形成。

关键词：俄苏文学；侨民文学；两次浪潮

一　俄苏侨民文学①

20世纪的俄罗斯文学史中曾经先后出现过三次侨民文学浪潮，分别为1917—1923年，即十月革命前后的第一次浪潮；30年代"二战"与"大清洗"后的第二次浪潮；60—80年代"解冻"与"停滞"期间的第三次浪潮，俄苏文学家集体迁离故土、国外定居，并形成了相对稳定的文化活动圈，得到国际文化界的瞩目，成为世界文学史上的一簇奇葩。1991年苏联解体后，侨民文学再次掀起回归浪潮，俄罗斯学界开始重新审视20世纪侨民文学，"流亡中的俄国文学"现象亦成为文学评论与文学史研究的焦点。

---

* 2018年国家社科基金一般项目"俄罗斯重塑'苏联记忆'与重建国家认同的历史鉴戒研究"（项目号18BKS048）的阶段性成果。

** 作者简：李琳，陕西师范大学副教授，主要从事俄罗斯社会与文化研究。杨苗苗，陕西师范大学俄语语言文学硕士研究生。

① 苏维埃政权成立之前的俄罗斯称为"俄国"，十月革命到苏联解体称为"苏联"，侨民文学第一次浪潮起于十月革命之前，第三次浪潮终于苏联解体之前，因此称之为俄苏侨民文学。

俄苏侨民文学家的出走、流亡、定居、回归，都与20世纪的俄苏历史密切关联。20世纪俄罗斯经历了许多重大历史事件：二月革命、第一次世界大战、十月革命、国内战争、大清洗、伟大的卫国战争、阿富汗战争、苏联解体等，每个历史事件都有“持不同政见”的知识分子或主动、或被动地“出走”他国，漂泊在外的作家继续创作，重新审视自己的国家和民族，重塑祖国历史和人物。俄苏侨民文学三次浪潮中，第一浪潮与第三浪潮规模庞大，文学经典显著，其中三位侨民作家获得了诺贝尔文学奖，对世界文坛造成了强烈而新鲜的冲击。相对而言，第二浪潮的侨民队伍中精英知识分子比例较低，文学作品数量和质量均有所不及，广度和深度有所欠缺。

相较于俄罗斯的本土文学，侨民文学集俄罗斯文学与世界文学于一身，兼收并蓄、博采众长，它独特的诞生背景和特有的文化气息决定了自身的多元化和综合性。作为“境外文学”“非官方文学”的侨民文学见证了20世纪的俄苏历史，从作家的笔下我们看到了俄语的优美和丰富、看到了俄罗斯文学的高度、体会到了俄罗斯知识分子对祖国的深沉的爱。俄苏侨民文学作为曾经“被封锁”“被驱逐”“被批判”的文学，理应“重建”与“回归”，构建20世纪俄罗斯文学史的完整图像。

二 俄苏侨民文学两次浪潮的差异性

1. 历史背景

侨民文学的第一次浪潮发生在1917年二月革命后，沙皇俄国即将崩溃，而苏维埃社会主义革命尚未成功。俄国社会面临前所未有之大变局：政治上，知识分子阶层普遍存有对资本主义社会的向往和对社会主义革命的不理解，知识界并不认同、不接受布尔什维克主义；社会上，国内战争的爆发和“红色恐怖”行动的实施，社会局势动荡，阶级矛盾激化，冲突动乱不断，随之而来的饥荒遍地、饿殍遍野使人们的崩溃情绪达到顶峰，许多知识分子纷纷逃离俄国；文化上，苏维埃政权建立后，在文化领域推行了一系列不合理的政策和措施，早期的“无产阶级文化派”以及后期的“РАПП”（俄罗斯无产阶级作家协会）对业已存在的人类文化遗产持全盘否定的态度，借力打压和排挤党外知识分子，许多愿意为苏维埃服务的人才精英频频遭受不公正的待遇（冯玉律，1992）。为避免人心动乱，维护新政权稳定，1922年夏秋之际，俄共发起知识分子驱逐运动，许多知识分子乘坐从德国租来的船离开俄罗斯，史称“哲学之舟”（философский пароход）。在这种历史背景下，大批文学家或主动或被迫地离开俄罗斯迁往国外定居，形成了俄国侨民文学的第一次浪潮。

第三次浪潮源于20世纪50年代赫鲁晓夫时期的“解冻”，终于80年代勃列日涅夫“停滞”时期。赫鲁晓夫“解冻思潮”盛行一时，一些揭露社会阴暗现象的批判文学流行起来，官方文学与地下文学冲突不断，文学出现了新旧交替的局面。20世纪70年代起，在美苏冷战的背景下，苏联受到西方世界各方面的打压，社会开始出现经济停滞，社会矛盾不断加剧；与此同时，由于“地下文学”的风靡，官方“害怕引起洪水泛滥，无法控制……”（马家骏，1988），再加上以美国为首的资本主义阵营利用这些“地下出版物”来攻击苏联的意识形态和价值观，苏维埃政府进一步加强了对文艺界的意识形态干预，对文化领域的一系列举措将矛盾推至顶峰。在这种情况下，一些“持不同政见者”（диссиденты）纷纷出现，政府对这些作家进行了不同程度的迫害：他们或受到猛烈批判，或被逮捕、判刑，或被驱逐出境。

与第一次浪潮相比，第三次浪潮持续时间久、作家群体规模大，且大多作家采取了主动出走、离开苏联，无论是被动还是主动，第三次浪潮侨民作家的出走亦带有强烈的政治色彩。第一次浪潮的产生尽管存在一定政治因素的影响，但更多的是人们对战争的畏惧、对新制度的不理解和对未知的恐惧，而第三次浪潮则是知识分子对现存的经济、政治体制的不满以及对苏维埃政府的失望。如果说“第一浪潮”是“白银时代”的延续，那么，“第三浪潮”就是“解冻时期”的延伸（周启超，1995）。

2. 文学成就

侨民文学“第一浪潮”与1917年的历史文化变动有着密切的联系，这次浪潮也是俄侨文学最辉煌的时期。自1918年起，大量“白银时代”的作家离开祖国侨居国外，成为俄苏侨民文学第一浪潮的主要构成群体，例如阿克梅派的作家阿达莫维奇（А. М. Адамович）、格·伊凡诺夫（Г. В. Иванов）等，未来派的诗人谢维里亚宁（И. В. северянин）等，象征派的主要代表巴尔蒙特（К. Д. Бальмонт）、梅列日柯夫斯基（Д. С. Мережковский）等，现实主义作家什梅廖夫（И. С. Шмелев）、扎伊采夫（Б. К. Зайцев）、库普林（А. И. Куприн），不属于任何流派的诗人茨维塔耶娃（М. И. Цветаева）、霍达谢维奇（В. Ф. Ходасевич）等，他们均在第一次侨民文学浪潮中创作了大量经典优秀的作品，使之得以流芳百世。其中，最著名的当属作家伊凡·蒲宁（И. А. Бунин）。侨居法国后，蒲宁创作了数百篇短篇小说，完成了享誉世界的长篇小说《阿尔谢尼耶夫的一生》（《Жизнь Арсеньева》）。1933 年，蒲宁由于其严谨的艺术才能、生动优美的语言以及完美继承了俄国古典文学现实主义传统的优秀作品被授予诺贝尔文学奖，也是俄罗斯第一位获得诺贝尔文学奖的作家。

第一浪潮中侨民作家的活动范围主要在西欧，1921—1923 年间俄罗斯侨民的主要活动中心是柏林和布拉格，后来渐渐转移到巴黎，"二战"后逐渐转移到纽约。侨民作家出版了一百多种报纸和几十种刊物，还创办了数十家出版社。其中报纸最著名的有柏林的《舵轮报》，巴黎的《最后消息报》《共同的事业报》《复兴报》，华沙的《争取自由报》等；周刊有巴黎出版的《时代》《俄罗斯》《俄罗斯与斯拉夫人》等；文学杂志则有巴黎的《俄罗斯未来》《当代纪事》等，1942 年纽约开始出版名为"新杂志"的俄罗斯侨民文艺刊物，流传至今。俄国侨民创办的大型出版社有：柏林的"言辞"出版社、"黑里康"出版社、"思想"出版社、"彼得罗波里斯"出版社、布拉格的"火焰"出版社、巴黎的"俄罗斯土地"出版社、"当代纪事"出版社、"复兴"出版社；斯德哥尔摩的"北方的火焰"出版社；索菲亚的"俄国—保加利亚"出版社，里加的"格拉玛多—特劳克斯"出版社，等等（冯玉律，1992）。显然，"第一浪潮"为俄苏侨民文学最为辉煌的时期。

"第三浪潮"侨民作家大都侨居在巴黎、慕尼黑、维也纳和美国。正如第一代侨民作家们十分重视出版社和文学刊物的创办一样，"第三浪潮"的作家们同样将俄罗斯文化和文学的传播当作其主要使命。他们创办了《大陆》《时代与我们》《回声》等杂志，并建立了一些出版机构。这一代侨民作家在出国之前一般已有作品在国外发表，到国外后继续推出新作，其总体文学成就尽管略逊于第一次浪潮，但也不容小觑。第三次浪潮的代表性人物是作家索尔仁尼琴（А. И. Солженицын）和诗人布罗茨基（И. А. Бродский）。1962 年，索尔仁尼琴发表成名作《伊凡·杰尼索维奇的一天》（《Один день Ивана Денисовича》）后，又发表了长篇小说《癌病房》（《Раковый корпус》）和《第一圈》（《В круге первом》），在欧美各国产生了强烈的政治影响。1970 年，他因"在追求俄罗斯文学不可或缺的传统时所具有的道义力量”获得诺贝尔文学奖。1973 年，他的《古拉格群岛》（《Архипелаг Гулаг》）在国外出版，引起极大反响，次年 2 月被驱逐出境。他在国外创作的长篇小说《红轮》（《Красное косело》）勾画出从第一次世界大战到十月革命前俄国历史的曲线，享誉海外。

约·布罗茨基（1940—1996）则是一位“联结起传统与现代、俄语文学世界与英语文学世界的个性独特的诗人”（朱红琼，2010）。他于 1972 年被驱逐出境，当时已有诗集多种在国外出版。定居美国后，他同时用俄语和英语写作，逐渐成为一名具有世界性影响的伟大诗人。在《荒野中的停留》（《Остановка в пустыне》）、《美好时代的终结》（《Конец прекрасной эпохи》）和《罗马哀歌》（《Римские элегии》）等诗作中，诗人围绕人的“生命”这一基本主题，写时间与空间，存在与虚无，别离与孤独，地狱与天堂，表现自由、爱情、疾病、衰老、死亡以及对死亡的超越。诗人于 1987 年被授予诺贝尔文学奖。除此之外，涅克拉索夫（В. П. Некрасов）、马克西莫夫（В. Е. Максимов）、阿克肖诺夫（В. П. Аксенов）、加利奇（А. А. Галич）、科彼列夫（Л. З. Копелев）、弗拉基莫夫（Г. Н. Владимов）、库布拉诺夫斯基（Ю. М. Кублановский）、沃伊诺维奇（В. Н. Войнович）等作家均在海外创作了大量的文学作品，并取得了不菲的成绩。

3. 作品风格

（1）传统文化的传承

俄苏侨民文学第一次浪潮中的大部分作家，是来自“白银时代”的文学精英，他们不满于十月革命的必要性，对苏维埃政权产生怀疑而迁居国外。作为俄罗斯传统文学的传承者和发扬者，这些侨民作家即使到了国外，仍然坚定地捍卫普希金、托尔斯泰和陀思妥耶夫斯基的人道主义传统，仍然认同俄罗斯传统的集体主义、国家主义和宗教观，俄罗斯传统理念的核心思想在他们的作品中从未缺失。第一代侨民作家大多数都是遵从 19 世纪文学传统的现实主义作家，以及从前的象征主义者和阿克梅派诗人。因此，第一浪潮是 20 世纪俄侨文学最辉煌的时期，名家无数，成就显赫，可以看作为“白银时代”作家的延续，其作品风格也是俄罗斯传统文学的继承。

而在第三次侨民浪潮中，总体上看，大多数作家更为推崇西方先进的现代主义思潮，认同现代西方世界的基本价值观。如果说“第一浪潮”中的侨民作家为了保全俄罗斯传统文化而成为文学观念上的保守派，那么第三代侨民作家中的多数人则是颠覆现存文学传统中的异端（单之旭，1999）。第三浪潮的代表人物都出生在苏维埃时代，没有“白银时代”作家的宗教教育背景，也缺乏对斯拉夫传统文化的热爱，他们没有怀旧情绪，并不尊崇古典主义文学。在对待传统俄罗斯文化的态度上，有的作家保留了对本民族文化的尊重和继承，而有的作家对其持全盘否定的态度，对西方社会流行的文化思潮则全盘肯定。

（2）苏联文化的态度

由于所处历史背景不同，第一浪潮和第三浪潮的侨民作家对苏维埃政权的态度、对苏联文化的态度有所不同。侨民文学第一次浪潮中，知识分子不接受社会主义革命、不理解苏维埃政权的政治和文化政策而选择主动离开或者是遭到驱逐，其呈现的作品主要是对 1917 年革命事件和国内战争的回顾，由此引发对个人命运乃至民族和国家前途的探索，以及对祖国的眷恋之情，抒发自己的去国之苦、思乡之情也成为一个重要主题。因此，第一代侨民作家中的多数人对苏维埃政权、对苏联社会主义建设并不明晓，其作品以保守和发扬俄罗斯文化传统为己任，传承俄罗斯经典主义文学，缺少苏维埃语言与文化特质。

第三浪潮的代表人物出生在苏维埃时代，他们见证了社会主义建设的成就，也体会到了伟大卫国战争的胜利，他们曾经为祖国自豪，也为国家的多灾多难而痛心。第三浪潮的很多作家是在赫鲁晓夫“解冻”时期开始文学创作，在美苏冷战后的“停滞”时期离开苏联，同时把苏维埃的语言和文化带到了国外。大部分第三代侨民文学家的“流亡作品”大多延续苏联时期的文学体裁与风格，具有强烈的政治化倾向，作品中既有对社会的压抑、政权的不合理以及制度、政策的专制的描写，也有对苏联祖国和人民的深深眷恋和自豪。

（3）异域文化的接受

侨民作家的身份具有“双重性”与“混杂性”，其民族身份与文化身份不断发生冲突，对居住国异域文化的认可和对民族文化的身份认同造成矛盾，其作品的“民族性”和“异域性”也构成了侨民文学的重要特征。

第一浪潮中的“白银时代”作家，具有俄罗斯族裔身份，并历经俄罗斯文化教育，怀有深深的俄罗斯民族记忆，这种俄罗斯文化认同感是根深蒂固的，难以迅速融入异域文化。而较为年轻的第一代侨民作家，则善于吸取西方现代主义文学经验，投身于欧美文学的新潮流中。

第三浪潮侨民作家深受意识形态的影响，对西方价值观和语言文化怀有好感，往往在国外主动学习英语，甚至用外语写作，其文学活动具有“边缘性”，其创作主题与文学品格也具有独特的艺术魅力。如，诺贝尔奖得主布罗茨基广泛吸收英美等国的文化精华，把俄罗斯传统与西方现代主义结合起来，取得辉煌成绩。

三　俄苏侨民文学两次浪潮的共通性

1. 共通的政治主题

两次侨民文学浪潮中文学作品的政治主题有着许多共通之处。两次浪潮中的作家都存在对现有社会制度或文化政策的不满。无论知识分子们是主动还是被迫出走，都具有浓郁的政治色彩，归根结底是对当时的政治体制和社会制度的不满。

两次侨民文学浪潮中充斥着对布尔什维克统治的不满，对苏维埃当局举措的不理解，但同时也表达了对理想社会的希冀。这些特点在什梅廖夫（И. С. Шмелев）和索尔仁尼琴的作品中有所体现。1923 年，什梅廖夫发表了中篇小说《死者的太阳》（《Солнце мертвых》）。文中深刻再现了战争的残忍，反映出社会变革对个人命运的影响。全文充斥着作家对战争和革命的不解，表达了作者的人道主义情怀，带有强烈的政治抨击色彩。

侨民作家索尔仁尼琴兼文学家、政治学家、历史学家、文化学家于一身，其作品被称为“我们的固化的眼泪”和“俄罗斯的安魂曲”。索尔仁尼琴是苏联“集中营文学”的开创者，长篇小说《古拉格群岛》反映了苏联“大清洗”的政治主题，以纪实手法描绘了 20 世纪 30 年代的苏联公民无辜被捕，受到侦查、关押、服劳役的历史命运。中篇小说《癌病房》影射了苏联的政治问题，“癌——这是所有沉浸在难以忍受的、焦灼的、屈辱的、受压抑的情绪中的人无法逃脱的必然命运。人在黑暗中生活，在屈辱中死亡”。通过深刻的政治隐喻，显现了一个患有绝症而且“癌瘤细胞”正在四处转移扩散的国家机体。

2. 共同的家国情怀

俄苏侨民作家普遍不满当时国家的社会制度或文化政策，但对故国有深深眷恋之情、浓重的思乡情绪，他们尊重斯拉夫传统文化，并善于接受异域文化。流亡海外的侨民作家都怀有对故土的家国情怀和深深思念。生活在异国他乡，语言上的障碍、生活习惯的不同、异国文化的不适应以及他民族的排斥对他们而言都是巨大的挑战，这也使侨民作家们更为怀恋故国，想念广袤的祖国大地。因此，侨民作家的作品中总是蕴含着深厚的离国之苦和思乡之情。

被誉为“二十世纪第一诗人”的茨维塔耶娃的作品中，祖国这一主题有着很重的分量。著名的怀乡诗《祖国》（《Родина》）中，茨维塔耶娃深情地讴歌魂萦梦绕的国家：“俄罗斯呀——令我肝肠寸断的土地——我的骄傲啊，我的祖国!”诗人极其直率地表明了自己对俄罗斯炽热的爱，用至真至纯的语言抒发了自己回归祖国的渴望。尽管因遭到驱逐而侨居他乡，约瑟夫·布罗茨基对祖国的依恋却不曾改变。诗歌《明代书简》（《Письма династии Минь》）通过对明朝残酷的描写，影射了自己去国怀乡的伤感情绪，作家对祖国的怀念跃然纸上：“还不知要走多少千里。一千里也好，两千里也好，都意味着此刻你与故乡远离。”蒲宁在中篇小说《苏霍多尔》（《Суходол》）、《阿尔谢尼耶夫的一生》和《米佳的爱情》（《Митина любовь》）中，都以俄罗斯生活为背景，对俄罗斯、俄罗斯人民、俄罗斯性格进行了深入挖掘和思考，表达对遥远故园的思念、对俄罗斯大自然的迷恋和对俄罗斯乡村风情的眷恋。

侨民作家对于流亡的态度是不同的，他们或自愿、或被迫；或把流亡视为解救、或视为死亡，但对祖国的眷念和亲人的思念是相同的，他们渴望回到祖国，渴望祖国的召唤。三代侨民文学家索尔仁尼琴虽然被迫流亡美国，但他始终否认自己是个侨民，自始至终都认为自己是俄罗斯文化的传播者，并期待着再次回归家园。

3. 相同的国际盛誉

20世纪的俄罗斯文学有两部并行发展的文学史，一部是“本土文学”、一部是“侨民文学”，一部在国内、一部在境外。侨民文学家在“流亡”中坚持对文学的忠诚与热爱，不仅对俄罗斯文化，而且对世界文化的丰富和发展都作出了卓越的贡献，有着深远的国际影响。

两次浪潮中众多杰出的作家及其作品在海内外享有很高的声誉。如第一浪潮作家蒲宁的短篇小说集《幽暗的林荫道》（《Темные аллеи》）和中篇小说《阿尔谢尼耶夫的一生》（《Жизнь Арсеньева》）、什梅廖夫（И. С. Шмелев）的《朝圣》（《Богомолье》），扎伊采夫

（Б. К. Зайцев）的自传性四部曲、纳博科夫（В. В. Набоков）的《洛丽塔》（《Лолита》）等，第三浪潮作家索尔仁尼琴的《第一圈》和《伊万·杰尼索维奇的一天》、布罗茨基的《小于一》（《Меньше единицы》）、西尼亚夫斯基（А. Д. Синявский）的《来自合唱队的声音》（《Голос из хора》）等优秀作品都享誉世界。其中蒲宁（И. А. Бунин）、索尔仁尼琴（А. И. Солженицын）和布罗茨基（И. А. Бро́дский）三位文坛大家更是获得了诺贝尔文学奖，两次浪潮的国际影响可见一斑。

侨民生活实质上就是俄罗斯社会在海外的缩影（王亚民，郭颖颖，2005），在侨民作家们的不懈努力下，俄罗斯文学才得以在异国他乡扎根并繁茂生长，最终发展成为俄罗斯乃至世界文学史上不可或缺的一页。一方面，俄侨文学继承了俄罗斯本土文学的传统。伟大的俄罗斯母亲尽管已“不尽如人意”，流亡海外的作家们毕竟无法割舍与俄罗斯的血脉联系，这就导致了他们的作品永远无法脱离祖国而独立存在，处处体现着“俄罗斯声音”；另一方面，侨民文学不可避免地受到了侨居国文化的影响。身处异国，侨民们或主动或被动地接受到侨居国文化、风俗、宗教等方面的熏陶。特别是在第三浪潮中，大多数作家们能够对西方流行的社会思潮以及价值观产生共鸣和认可。正是以上两方面特性造就了俄苏侨民文学能够在世界文坛独树一帜。俄罗斯侨民文学在推动世界文学多样化的同时，也为他国侨民文学的发展提供了借鉴性的参考。

四 余论

普京总统认为：“世界并不存在像俄罗斯这样的被称为文学之国的国家，可以毫不夸张地说，我们对整个世界文明富有保存并维护俄罗斯文学，及其巨大人文潜力的责任。我们的任务是引起社会对本国文学的关注，使俄罗斯文学和俄语成为俄罗斯从思想上影响世界的强大力量。”① 俄苏侨民文学是俄罗斯文学丰富而宝贵的文化遗产，从多个角度对俄侨文学的“第一浪潮”与“第三浪潮”进行比较，可以更为全面、深入地认识俄语与俄罗斯文化，深刻理解俄苏多元格局的文化发展史，了解俄罗斯丰富的民族性格和民族精神。

---

① 2013 年 11 月 21 日，俄罗斯总统普京在俄罗斯人民友谊大学举办的俄罗斯文学大会上的发言。

参考文献

Сост. П. Басинский и С. Федякин. Современное русское зарубежье. изд. АСТ, М, 1998: 5.

冯玉律:《俄国侨民文学的第一浪潮》,《苏联文学连刊》1992 年第 5 期。

马家骏:《当代苏联文学》, 河南大学出版社 1988 年版。

周启超:《二十世纪俄语文学: 侨民文学风景》,《国外文学》1995 年第 2 期。

朱红琼:《20 世纪俄罗斯侨民文学观照》,《社会科学家》1995 年第 6 期。

王亚民、郭颖颖:《哈尔滨俄罗斯侨民文学在中国》,《中国俄语教学》第 2 期。

A comparative study between Two Movements of Russia-Soviet Emigrant Literature

Li Lin, Yang Miaomiao

Abstract: The emigrant literature of the 20th century plays a unique and irreplaceable role in the history of Russia-Soviet literature. The first and the third movements feature wide scale, numerous writers, sophisticated works, having a profound influence. The emigrant literature has witnessed obvious differences in its background, achievements and work styles during two movements, however, they have something in common including political themes, emotions of "Family-country" and international reputation. Besides, native literature and emigrant literature have made the old and new contrast and complemented each other, promoting the pluralistic structure of history of Russia-Soviet literature.

Key words: Russia-Soviet literature; emigrant literature; two movements

《诗章》对维多利亚诗歌传统的颠覆*

郭英杰

摘　要：作为一位倡导"日日新"的美国先锋派诗人，庞德通过《诗章》对曾经辉煌的维多利亚诗歌传统进行背叛和颠覆，取得了非凡的艺术成就。其中有四个方面表现最为突出：（1）摈弃烦琐冗长的句式，主张使用铿锵有力、意象鲜明的短句；（2）避免使用华丽、花哨的书面语，倡导口语和日常用语；（3）打破传统的句式书写，根据感情宣泄的程度和意识流，呈现与众不同、标新立异的表达；（4）少用或尽量不用标点符号。庞德通过上述特立独行的作诗方式，彰显了他的现代主义风格。

关键词：庞德；《诗章》；维多利亚诗歌传统；颠覆

一　引言

埃兹拉·庞德（Ezra Pound，1885—1972）既是美国公认的先锋派诗人兼诗歌评论家，又是美国意象派诗歌领袖及其重要代表人物。他花费54年（1915—1969）时间（Nadel，2006：1）撰写的长诗《诗章》（*The Cantos*）不仅被誉为"一部记录着西方文化的史诗"，而且也被学界称作"一部满载着个体经验的抒情诗"（王晶石，2019：108—115）。作为一个特色鲜明的文本存在，《诗章》充满开放性的话语，字里行间洋溢着丰富的表述以及能够不断被读者阐释和解读的意义。俄国著名文艺理论家、批评家巴赫金（1998：176—177）在《对话、文本与人文》一书中指出："每一个表述……都充满他人话语的回声和余音"，该表述"首先应该视

* 本文为陕西省社会科学基金项目（项目号：2019K035）、中央高校社科项目（项目号：17SZYB12）、基于学生发展核心素养的《大学英语》英美文学选读课程教学模式与创新（项目号：校20180002）以及基于OBE教育模式和思维型课堂教学理论的美国文学选读教学模式创新与实践研究（项目号：JSJX2019Z24）的阶段性成果，同时受到国家留学基金资助。

为对该领域中此前表述的应答……它或反驳此前的表述，或肯定它，或补充它，或依靠它，或以它为已知的前提，或以某种方式考虑它”。《诗章》作为庞德在特殊的年代和语境下书写的诗歌表述，自然而然具有上述文本的特点：不仅“充满他人话语的回声和余音”，而且包含“对该领域中此前表述的应答”。这其中一个不容忽视的“应答”，就是对维多利亚诗歌传统的颠覆。按照巴赫金（1998：177）的说法，这是一种“反驳此前的表述”。

二 遭遇现代主义语境的维多利亚诗歌传统

维多利亚诗歌传统特指1836—1901年间英国维多利亚女王执政时期所形成的诗歌创作理念、语言表达风格及其诗学建构体系。该时期的诗歌艺术在英国文学史上享有盛誉，曾经被视为“成就最辉煌、传播范围最广、影响也非常久远”的历史时期之一，可与英国文艺复兴时期和浪漫主义时期媲美（张伯香，2005：233）。其前期的文风特点拥有显而易见的优势，具体表现为：气势磅礴，场面恢宏；措辞优雅，格调清新；聚焦生活，活力四射。但是发展到后来，维多利亚诗风的这些优势和特点逐渐成为阻碍欧美诗坛向前发展的重要因素（Altick，1973）。

在这纷繁复杂的因素当中，除了社会的、政治的和历史的成分在潜移默化地发挥着作用，实际上还有一个十分重要的因素在强劲地影响着当时西方文学艺术发展的趋势，那就是：现代主义（modernism）思潮的风起云涌和希望破旧立新的新生代诗人群体的摇旗呐喊。这些具有鲜明的现代主义特色、敢作敢为、喜欢标新立异的先锋派诗人，如庞德、艾米·洛厄尔（Amy Lowell，1874—1925）、瓦谢尔·林赛（Vachel Lindsay，1879—1931）、T. E. 休谟（T. E. Hulme，1883—1917）、威特·宾纳（Witter Bynner，1881—1968）、F. S. 弗林特（F. S. Flint，1885—1960）、约翰·G. 弗莱契（John G. Fletcher，1886—1950）、H. D.（Hilda Doolittle，1886—1961）、理查德·阿尔丁顿（Richard Aldington，1892—1962）等，针对英国维多利亚后期普遍存在的无病呻吟、颓废俗套的诗歌风气，感到不满和厌倦，开始以“前无古人后无来者”的姿态大胆尝试新形式，书写新内容，以扭转19世纪末20世纪初欧美诗坛逐渐衰微、毫无生机的“荒原”景象，并最终开创民族诗歌以及个人创意写作的新时代。

在此过程中，为了做到对维多利亚诗歌传统的颠覆，不少新诗诗人有意识地转换思维方式。一方面，他们把欧洲新兴的时尚艺术，如雕塑、音乐、绘画、舞蹈等领域的最新成果纳入文字系统，实现诗歌文本内容和形式的革新或者翻新；另一方面，他们还注意改造已有的民族诗歌传统，同时将视野聚焦于其他民族诗歌，有的放矢地把其他民族诗歌的艺术风格与自己的艺术风格融会贯通，实现诗歌文本的升级和换代（Gray，1992：29—38）。比如，庞德等一批有胆识、有魄力的现代派诗人，充分借鉴和吸收中国古典诗歌意象鲜明、语言精练、意境宏远等文风特点，积极把这些特点转化为自己诗歌风格的重要组成部分，书写出清新、坚硬和富有异国情调的美丽诗篇。从根本上讲，中国古典诗歌的确为美国诗歌摆脱维多利亚晚期颓废的诗风起到了推波助澜的作用。正如庞德于1915年在美国新诗运动核心刊物《诗刊：一本诗文杂志》（*Poetry*：*A Magazine of Verse*）① 上断言的那样，中国诗"是一个宝库，今后一个世纪将从中寻找推动力，正如文艺复兴从希腊人那里寻找推动力"。而且"很可能本世纪会在中国找到新的希腊"（赵毅衡，2003：17—18）。

三 《诗章》对维多利亚诗歌传统的颠覆及其表现

庞德的诗歌，尤其是中晚期诗歌，带有明显的颠覆维多利亚诗歌传统的印记。无论是他的语言表达、抒情方式，还是排版印刷、标点符号，无不彰显了他的现代主义话语风格及其艺术特色。尤其是在史诗《诗章》里，随处可见庞德对维多利亚诗歌传统的背叛和革新。

为了便于讨论，这里归纳并概述为四个主要方面，同时予以阐释：

第一，摈弃烦琐冗长的句式，主张使用铿锵有力、意象鲜明的短句。维多利亚诗歌充满复杂句式，有些还非常夸张，这与当时所处的时代背景和社会环境息息相关。一般认为，只有接受正规或良好教育的人才能写出长篇且文绉绉的句式；反之，能够写出冗长、文绉绉句式的人应该是接受

① 该刊物是美国著名社会活动家哈丽特·门罗（Harriet Monroe，1880—1936）在1912年创办的，学界通常把该刊物简写为 *Poetry*（《诗刊》）。《诗刊》是当时喜欢破旧立新的现代主义诗人们发表作品的主要阵地和舞台，也是意象派和自由体诗辩论的重要论坛，曾经为20世纪美国现代主义诗歌的发展立下汗马功劳。作为《诗刊》创始人，门罗声称："我们特别关注具有现代意义的作品，但与此同时，我们也乐于接受高水平的古典主题作品。"她还引用惠特曼的一句名言"要有伟大的诗人，必须要有伟大的读者"作为该杂志的箴言。参见 Schulze，R. G. "Harriet Monroe's Pioneer Modernism：Nature，National Identity，and Poetry，A Magazine of Verse，" *Legacy*，2004，21（1）：50-67.

了良好教育的人。而这些人多数被认为来自上流社会。为了表现或者附和这一点，很多作家自觉不自觉地使用复杂句。当然，不排除有些作家使用复杂句和冗长句是为了表情达意的需要。但是，庞德比较讨厌这一点。他认为，“我们渴望那种清晰而硬朗的诗”，我们要为“避免了新象征主义运动的软绵绵与多愁善感，避开了更加娘娘腔的新现实主义派”而欢欣鼓舞（Eliot，1954：410—416）。庞德所说的“清晰而硬朗的诗”，不是充满烦琐冗长句式的诗，而是铿锵有力、意象鲜明、以短句形式写成的诗。比如在《诗章》第2章中，庞德有这样的表达：

船桨上沉重的葡萄藤，
生于无，一声呼吸……
野兽们像镜中的阴影，
长着长毛的尾巴拖在虚空
(Pound 8)①

再如《诗章》第52章末尾：

鱼汛期开始
河流和湖泊冻得坚实
现在把冰放进汝之冰室
各种风的大型音乐会
辨明善恶
(Pound 261)

还有《诗章》第83章：

在泰山下看不见根基
但水明亮　　　水

① 本文所有翻译和引用的《诗章》原文均出自 Pound，E. The Cantos of Ezra Pound，New York：New Directions Publishing Corporation，1971. 本文标注时，以“（Pound 8）”的形式出现，不另作注。

杨树梢在亮光中漂浮
唯有栏柱不移
此刻蚁群似乎摇晃不安
(Pound 531) (黄运特 译)①

第二，避免使用华丽、花哨的书面语，倡导口语和日常用语。维多利亚诗歌因为要迎合上层统治阶级的需要，其语言要求华丽、优雅、高贵。口语和日常用语不被提倡写进诗歌，因为显得俗气和不庄重。但是，在庞德所处的时代，因为各种文风激流勇进，不少有远见卓识的诗人认识到，真正鲜活的语言和具有不朽历史价值的语言，是那些存活在普通老百姓中间，体现老百姓思想，展现老百姓风格，直白、爽朗、不做作、不虚伪的语言。庞德通过《诗章》试图复活和再现特定时代和特定语境中普通老百姓的口语和日常用语，一方面体现他作为一名语言学习者和研究者对语言的高度敏感性和求索精神，另一方面使《诗章》充满"人情味"和"趣味"，拉近高雅诗歌艺术与普通老百姓之间的审美距离。比如在《诗章》第46章，庞德使用了非常口语化的语言表达和喧哗的日常用语，表现"骆驼队长"(Camel driver)与"我"(I)的对话：

"他屁主意都没有!"
……"他也生不出个屁主意
问题出在你这儿，你压根儿不是打探消息的料儿。"
……
"希腊人!"……"就会要些花把戏!"
"还能干啥？一个国家都折腾不好!"
"甭想改造我，也改造不了我，"
"说'我晓得我没有问过你，你爹把你送到这儿
受锻炼。我晓得我的感觉。
送儿子去英国，让他回来变成基督耶稣!'"

① 关于庞德《诗章》的翻译及其引用，黄运特先生的译文均出自［美］庞德《庞德诗选·比萨诗章》，黄运特译，张子清校，漓江出版社1998年版。本文引用时，标识为"(黄运特译)"；其余未标注者，均为笔者自译，不另作注。

“我还能有嘛感觉？”……
（Pound 232）

再比如在《诗章》第 76 章，出现了监狱中“黑鬼杀人犯”（the nigger murderer）对“牢笼之友”（cage-mate）所说的话，以及“小黑个儿”（the smaller black lad）对“大黑个儿”（the larger）说的话：

罪犯不爱动脑筋？
“嘿，无齿的，神经有哪几本书？”
“说说看，有啥？”
“拉丁文？我学过拉丁文。”
那黑鬼杀人犯对牢笼之友说
（弄不清楚他们中谁在说话）
“算了吧，小薯条，”小黑个儿对
大黑个儿说。
“玩玩而已，”在死亡前没有妓女
（“那是进步，我的你的，”说/管它叫进步）
（Pound 454—455）（黄运特 译）

第三，打破传统的句式书写，根据感情宣泄的程度和意识流，呈现与众不同、标新立异的表达。典型的维多利亚诗歌句式工整，格律性强，每个小节的诗歌之间联系紧密，逻辑清晰。即使像阿尔弗雷德·丁尼生（Alfred Tennyson，1809—1892）的《尤利西斯》（*Ulysses*）和罗伯特·布朗宁（Robert Browning，1812—1889）的《我已故的公爵夫人》（*My Last Duchess*）那样具有开拓性的作品，也不过是传统史诗主题的遗风（比如《尤利西斯》是对荷马史诗《奥德赛》主题的吸收和改编）或者是对传统史诗风格的继承和延续（比如《我已故的公爵夫人》是用古老的英雄双行体完成的独白体）。而庞德等标新立异的诗人，不拘泥于传统诗行的格律束缚和书写规范，故意违反语法规则和大小写，甚至违背句法规则，使文风特点和句式表达符合他本人情感起伏的实际。尤其是在表达方式方面，庞德有非常另类和他者的一面。比如，在《诗章》第 28 章，庞德写到：

“我……
(走过比利牛斯山一间餐厅里的光滑木板)
　　　　　……比活佛……
　　　　　　　　　　……更强壮!”
(毋庸置疑)
“我……
　　　　　……比基督……
　　　　　　　　　　……更强壮!”
(毋庸置疑)
“我早该……
　　　　　减轻……
　　　　　　　　　　体重!”①
(寂静，有点儿让人不舒服)
(Pound 137)

类似别具匠心的宣泄表达越是在《诗章》的后期写作中，越显得频繁、密集和技艺娴熟。如《诗章》第100章中，庞德写到：

“那东西粘
　　　　　在
　　　　　　　　我的
　　　　　　　　　　喉咙。”
A. G. 加德纳②
　　　　　　　1914年8月1日
也是个确切的记录
(Pound 721)

再比如《诗章》第110章：

---

① 引号里的话原文是法语。

② 原文为“Gardner，A. G.”。他是庞德在欧洲自我放逐时认识的一位友人。

你见过小船在海堤上醒来，
　　　　　　　　如何到了浪尖吗？
有什么夸耀的呢？
　　　　　　　　船身拍打着波浪，波浪拍打着船身，
　　　　　　　　　　　那就是快乐，
鸟羽僧正觉犹[①]，
　　　　　　　　走向清澈透明
(Pound 777)

第四，少用或尽量不用标点符号。维多利亚诗歌有较为严格的标点符号用来支撑语言表达，因为标点符号是一种规范、文雅和正统诗歌形式的象征。但是庞德在《诗章》中，很少像传统诗人那样一丝不苟地运用标点符号，而是少用或者尽量不用标点符号。该特点在《诗章》文本的前期创作中不明显，到了《诗章》创作的中后期，跟他带有叛逆风格的诗行一样，愈发显得清晰。至于这是否因为庞德后来受到《论语》《中庸》《诗经》等中国古典著作不用标点照样能够表情达意的呈现手法的影响，还是庞德在《诗章》里故意彰显个性，同时不断试验和创新的结果？答案不得而知。但是，有一点应该引起读者们的注意，那就是：庞德在《诗章》中频繁引用《大学》里的话："MAKE IT NEW"，"Day by day make it new"（Pound 265），并附汉语表达"新，日日新"[②] ——由此，庞德少用或尽量不用标点符号，是否可以视为庞德写作《诗章》时力求"日日新"并试图打破维多利亚诗歌传统的一种特殊表达方式呢？对此可以作出这样的讨论：这种可能性不仅存在，或许就是事实。

一个明显的依据就是：庞德在《诗章》中少用或尽量不用标点符号的现象，随处可见。这里试举几例。比如，在《诗章》第 74 章，庞德回忆一幅油画留给他的深刻印象时，语句中没有一个标点符号：

而孩子的面孔像在

---

① 原文为"Toba Sojo"。鸟羽僧正觉犹（1053—1140）是 12 世纪日本艺术家，因绘制《鸟兽戏画》而出名。该作品后来被视为日本漫画的原型。

② 庞德在《诗章》写作中，还喜欢直接把"日日新"的汉语发音——"jih hsin"，"jih hsin renew"（Pound 571，629）入诗，表明他对"日日新"的特殊喜好和个人感悟。

卡波夸德里①门口上方方形的壁画里
中央背景
形体在日神下抵达岸滩
柔光倾泻下来
某些意象在脑中形成
留在那里
(Pound 446)（黄运特 译）

在《诗章》第83章，庞德呈现他眼中静谧、安详的自然世界，同时暗示那是一种美的享受时，也不用任何标点符号：

此刻新月照临泰山
我们应以晨星计时
护树女神啊
你平静如水
池上有九月的阳光
(Pound 530)（黄运特 译）

在《诗章》第104章，庞德描述“黄金”（gold）对人来说是“宝”（treasure），对“蚂蚁”而言什么也不是时，也不用任何标点符号：

曾经黄金
　　被蚂蚁
　　　　带出洞穴
　　　　　　不是
Pao[3] **寶**
　　它不是宝
(Pound 740)

再比如在《诗章》最后一章，即第117章的开始部分，庞德以特别

① 原文为“Capoquadri”。这是庞德在意大利锡耶纳曾经租住过的房子。

的方式"记录"(mark)他落寞寂寥的心态时，也不用任何标点符号：

布朗库西之鸟
　　　　在松树树干的空心处
或者当雪看起来像是大海的泡沫
微明的天空用榆树枝开道
(Pound 801)

四 结语

庞德是一位喜欢破旧立新的诗人，他也是一位自觉把中国儒学经典——比如《大学》及其名句"日日新"——作为自己的创作理念并不断开拓创新的诗人。在20世纪那个彰显艺术家创作个性及其张力的时代，庞德通过《诗章》对曾经辉煌的维多利亚诗歌传统进行背叛和颠覆，取得了非凡的艺术成就。无论是在摈弃烦琐冗长的句式，主张使用铿锵有力、意象鲜明的短句方面，还是在避免使用华丽、花哨的书面语，倡导口语和日常用语方面；无论是在打破传统的句式书写，根据感情宣泄的程度和意识流，呈现与众不同、标新立异的表达方面，还是在少用或尽量不用标点符号等方面，庞德都以他特立独行的方式，彰显了他的现代主义作诗风格。当然，上述探讨还只是管中窥豹，关于《诗章》对维多利亚诗歌传统的颠覆，还存在可以深入挖掘和拓展的内容，因为《诗章》作为一个开放的文本，充满着各种被读者阐述和解读的可能性。

参考文献

Altick, R. D. Victorian *People and Ideas: A Companion for the Modern Reader of Victorian Literature*, New York: Norton, 1973.

Eliot, T. S. *Literary Essays of Ezra Pound*, London: Faber and Faber, 1954.

Gray, R. *American Poetry of the Twentieth Century*, London and New York: Longman, 1992.

Nadel, I. B. *The Cambridge Companion to Ezra Pound*, Shanghai: Shanghai Foreign Language Education Press, 2006.

Pound, E. *The Cantos of Ezra Pound*, New York: New Directions Publishing Corporation, 1971.

[俄] M. 巴赫金：《对话、文本与人文》，钱中文译，河北教育出版社1998年版。

[美] 庞德:《庞德诗选·比萨诗章》, 黄运特译, 张子清校, 漓江出版社 1998 年版。

王晶石:《主体性、历史性、视觉性——论艾兹拉·庞德〈三十章草〉中"我"的多重性》,《国外文学》2019 年第 3 期。

张伯香:《英美文学选读》, 外语教学与研究出版社 2005 年版。

赵毅衡:《诗神远游》, 上海译文出版社 2003 年版。

On the Subversion of Ezra Pound's *The Cantos* upon the Victorian Poetry Tradition

Guo Yingjie

Abstract: As an American avant-garde poet who advocated "Day by day, make it new", Ezra Pound betrayed and subverted the once brilliant Victorian poetry tradition through *The Cantos*, and made remarkable artistic achievements. Among them, four aspects are fairly prominent: (1) abandoning tedious and lengthy sentence patterns and calling on using short sentences with strong and clear images; (2) avoiding the use of gorgeous and fancy written language and advocating oral and daily language; (3) breaking the traditional forms of writing sentence patterns and presenting different and innovative expressions by referring to the degree of emotional catharsis and the stream of consciousness; (4) using less or not even using punctuations. Ezra Pound showed his modernist style through the above unique ways of writing poems.

Key words: Ezra Pound; *The Cantos*; Victorian poetry tradition; subversion

《青梅竹马》中的“信如”与明治时代的国家意识*

韩春红**

摘　要：小说家樋口一叶在其代表作《青梅竹马》中成功地塑造了信如、美登利、正太郎等经典少年群像。其中，男主人公信如是一个孤独的存在，但也有着独特的个人魅力，即他是有学问之人。一叶虽是批判现实主义文学开拓者之一，但是她也是一位执着于学问的女性，信如身上正好折射出一叶的这一人生阅历。本文通过文本分析方法，旨在解析信如这一人物形象所再现的明治时代的近代价值观——“学历”论、“学问”论，同时阐明信如人物形象中所隐含的明治时代的国家意识。

关键词：“学问”论；“学历”论；明治国家意识；信如人物形象

引言

2004 年 11 月 1 日起，樋口一叶的肖像被印在了 5000 日元纸币上，成为有史以来第一位出现在纸币正面的女性肖像人物，这足以说明一叶的文学成就之高。一叶堪称日本近代第一位真正意义上的职业女性作家，也是近代批判现实主义文学的早期开拓者之一。虽然其文学创作生涯短暂，但却留下了一系列不朽之作，如《大年夜》《青梅竹马》《浊流》和《十三夜》等。其中，《青梅竹马》是 1895—1896 年间发表于《文学界》的一部短篇小说，中村稔（2012：17）评价说：“《青梅竹马》描写了青春期少男少女之间无果的清纯之爱，作为爱情小说它无疑是一部无与伦比的绝佳之作。”这里的男女指的是藤本信如和大黑屋美登利。本论文拟通过分

* 本文系教育部人文社会科学研究规划基金项目“战后日本文学对近代日本国家主义的认知研究”（18YJA752020）、黑龙江省哲学社会科学研究规划项目“日本明治文学女性伦理构建的国家主义倾向”（17WWD225）的阶段性成果。同时，本文得到中国国家留学基金资助。

** 作者简介：韩春红（1980—　），女，黑龙江大学东语学院讲师，研究方向：日本文学。

析信如的人物形象进而挖掘出该人物形象所蕴含的内涵。

1.《青梅竹马》中的信如：孤独的存在

在《青梅竹马》中，男主人公15岁的藤本信如是第一个出现的，他是龙华寺方丈的儿子，个子不高不矮。小说中有一句话令人印象深刻：“这孩子是注定要换穿黑纱法衣的，他的头发还不知能留到几时哩。”（萧萧译，2005：11。下略，只标注页码。）这就为信如的人生之路埋下了伏笔。正如小说中旁白所言：“难道这孩子是自愿的吗？”那么，处于少年期的信如单单是因为他的出身而选择求佛之道吗？答案是否定的。

1.1 信如的性格特征

信如自小在寺院长大，将来也是要继承父亲衣钵的。他不屑于父母亲不顾寺院及个人名声发展副业赚钱之事，甚至极力劝阻父亲。一方面“担心四邻的人会怎样想”，另一方面“又怕小伴们谈天时讥笑自己”（76页）。可见，信如是一个正直、敏感、重名誉的人。正因为如此，他会在买鳗鱼时疑心孩子们的谈笑是在讥笑自己。然而，美登利口中的信如却是“乖僻的性子，阴阳怪气的别扭人”（91页）、“表面上摆着一副温和相，古里古怪的脾气”（93页）。也许信如外表看起来会让人觉得“阴沉”“脾气古怪”，但诚如文中所述，“因为他生来忠厚，而一家人都不听他的劝告，就不由得遇事感到乏味”（77页）。同时，他也是一个“又忧郁又懦弱”的孩子，比如说，“听见别人说他一点坏话时，他从来没有立刻出来同人家打架争论的勇气，只是躲在自己的屋子里”（78页）。

尽管如此，信如毕竟是一个15岁少年，当答应长吉之邀决定加入“小胡同组”时，亦发出了豪言壮语：“像田中正太郎那种小子，我把他像摆弄小指一样摆弄摆弄给你看看。”（20页）此处樋口一叶不禁感叹：“信如竟忘记了自己的软弱。”可以说，正直、敏感、重名誉、忠厚、忧郁又懦弱的信如也有少年所特有的鲁莽与义气之处。由此可见，信如的性格是多重的。关于这一点，徐琼（2012：124）也论述到：“樋口一叶的后期小说更多地体现了一种写实和批判现实主义的精神，人物性格也更加丰满复杂，并具有多义性。”

另外，小说中提到恨他的孩子如此评价信如：“龙华寺的藤本像没蒸透的年糕一样，外面软，里面硬。”（78页）确实如此，信如是一个外柔内刚的少年。在信如身上，多少能让人找到一种“举世混沌我独清，众人皆醉我独醒”的寂寞与清高。在小说所描绘的这个灯红酒绿、物欲横流的世界里，信如堪比出淤泥而不染的莲花，他与这世道格格不入，与周围的少男少女们也不嬉笑打闹，难以与大家融为一体。所以，这样的信如，看破红尘出家为僧也不足为奇。

1.2 信如因家人而产生的孤独感

信如的性格形成固然有天生的因素，但是来自家庭的影响也不容忽视。信如生活在一个四口之家。父亲是龙华寺方丈，生活富足，又有社会地位；母亲比父亲小了 20 岁，利落勤快，心地不坏；姐姐阿花长得可爱，又正值妙龄，人缘好，替父亲经营茶店。总之，“老和尚一家嫡亲骨肉，和和睦睦”（77 页）。

1.2.1 父亲：痴迷于金钱的老和尚

说到信如的父亲，便先谈谈龙华寺。龙华寺本是佛门清修之地，却充斥着凡尘俗世的气息，以至于“如果把他们当作木石的人看见了，一定会嫌恶得掉过脸去的”（71 页）。之所以会如此，皆因龙华寺方丈本人的所作所为。

龙华寺方丈不同于一般佛门弟子，他是一个“通达世故人情”（75 页）的老和尚，每天过着“早上念经，晚上查账”（77 页）的日子。对于这样的生活，樋口一叶都不禁感叹“这怎么叫人受得了呢”（74 页）。但是，老和尚却甘之若饴，特别是查账时“乐得合不拢嘴”的财迷像，令人印象深刻。如果说龙华寺香火不旺倒是可以说迫于生计而无奈选择的。但是，老和尚经管各种法事，每月还有固定的讲经日，方丈太太对待香客殷勤周到，按理说寺院的香火应该不错，从美登利曾说过的“龙华寺有好多有钱有势的施主”（56 页）也可窥见一斑，甚至于“有人说他过于贪心”（75 页）。因此说，信如的父亲可谓是一位痴迷于金钱的老和尚。其实，关于这一点，在家人身上可举之例便有一二。老和尚之所以娶了信如的母亲，就是因为她利落勤快，于是“心中打个算盘”（73 页），觉得“有这么个女人倒也合算”，后来老和尚确实也让妻子卖簪子赚钱；老和尚给女儿安排在自家开设的茶店账房里应酬买主。可以说，老和尚在妻女身上都挖掘出了生财之道。

1.2.2 母亲：以家人为中心的传统妇人

信如的母亲在小说中被称为“方丈太太”（日语为“御新造”），刚过 40 岁，模样儿不太难看。说起来，她也是苦命之人，由于第一任丈夫早逝而无家可归，只得暂住寺院，甚至为了赚到一口饭吃，每天都忙忙碌碌的，洗衣做饭、照管香火、打扫坟地。后来，又迫于生计委身于比自己大 20 岁的老和尚，不顾众人非议。怀了女儿阿花时才与老和尚结为正式夫妻，又生下儿子信如。对于曾孤苦伶仃的她来说，现今衣食无忧、儿女双全的生活应是惬意的。

小说中关于方丈太太的叙述较少，一共出现了三次。初次登场是介绍信如一家人的第九章，在此介绍了方丈太太的自然情况以及与老和尚结为夫妻之事。对于丈夫，她是言听计从的，毕竟现今的生活完全得益于老和尚，所以，即便害羞也按照老和尚要求卖簪子，最终“贪心使她忘了羞耻”（76 页）扯着嗓子叫卖；第二次出场是吩咐信如去给他姐姐送小袄的第十二章，从小说中“做娘的心里就愿意赶快让姑娘穿上”（98 页）这句话即可看出方丈太太对子女的疼爱；第三次出场是三五郎转述给正太郎提及方丈太太跟他爹说信如要进和尚学校的第十六章，不难想象方丈太太在同他人谈论儿子信如时脸上的喜悦与骄傲。

总之，方丈太太的出场全部是围绕家人来叙述的，可以说她是一个以家人为中心的传统妇人。虽无主见，但重视家人，称得上贤妻良母。

1.2.3 姐姐：“吉原”的特殊存在

信如的姐姐名叫阿花，在“家家都把女孩子当成宝贝”（59 页）的吉原，佛门出身的阿花似乎是一个特殊存在的姑娘，毕竟佛门姑娘做艺伎过于匪夷所思，而吉原的女孩子之所以被当成宝贝正是因为可以通过自身原始本钱来赚取大量金钱。老和尚也顾虑他人非议，于是开了一家雅致的茶店。对于痴迷于金钱的老和尚来说，这是一举两得之事，一是女儿有门营生免了赋闲在家，二是发挥了女儿人缘好这一优点赚足了金钱。如此，在阿花身上也反衬出了老和尚痴迷于金钱的本性。

通过上述介绍，显而易见，生活在如此家庭之中的信如并不快乐，因为家人的作风与他正直、敏感、重名誉、忠厚的性格特征格格不入。对于父亲，信如看不惯他痴迷于金钱的作风，觉得“他太下贱了”（77 页），不配佛门弟子的身份；对于母亲，信如虽是“万事顺从娘的温顺孩子”（98 页），却也看不惯母亲听命于父亲卖簪子的行为；对于姐姐，信如觉得她所受的教育是不正当的，从侧面也反映出他对父亲的不满。总之，商业气息浓厚的家人的种种行为使他感到灰心，“把郁闷藏在自己的心里”（77 页），在心灵上就滋生了孤独感，从而“变成一个阴沉的人”。

2. 信如形象隐含的明治国家意识

樋口一叶于明治二十七年（1894）十二月下旬开始撰写《青梅竹马》，明治二十九 年（1896）一月二十日左右完稿，同年三月十日左右完成原稿的修改。在一叶文学创作生涯中，该小说耗时最长，又是少见的以少男少女为主人公的作品。除了男女主人公信如和美登利之外，还有正太郎、长吉、三五郎等各具特色的少年。其中，关于信如这一人物，松坂俊夫（1982：183）指出："信如不仅仅在藤本家是异质的存在，在围绕着美登利的少年们中也是唯一一个例外的存在。"关于文学作品与作家的关系问题，曹顺庆（2015：72）如是解释："文学是人学，任何文学作品都是作家精神的投射与心灵的产物。而作家的思想与精神，最集中地凝聚在自己所创造的文学作品中。"那么，一叶所设定的这一例外的存在的信如形象，到底有什么内涵呢？笔者从挖掘该人物形象的独特之处和个人魅力着手试以分析。

2.1 信如的独特之处

虽然信如与周围格格不入，又因家人而滋生了孤独感，但是作为《青梅竹马》这篇小说的主人公，他仍有自己的独特之处，不容小觑。

在《青梅竹马》中，曾如此描述过："虽然信如的名字是用训音，但那剃平的头顶总觉不同凡俗，从他的风度上看来，他倒蛮像个佛门弟子了。"（12 页）在日本，出家人的称呼通常为日语汉字中的音读。这简短的一句话便展现给读者一个与众不同的信如形象。因为大音寺前巷被居民说成"红尘闹市"（2 页），只有绕过它才能走到吉原这个花街柳巷的大门处。也正因为如此，这里的风俗与众不同，女孩子们"喜欢系条华丽的宽内带"（7 页），以至于"有些人见了就要闭上眼睛"；男孩子们"从小养成了的轻狂习气，年满十五岁就已经早熟得可怕"（9 页）。显然，中规中矩的信如便是一股清流，特别是在这纸醉金迷的吉原，他无疑是"出淤泥而不染"的，这也正是他的独特之处。对此，岩见照代、北田幸惠等（1996：130）也阐明："对俗气的父亲老和尚持有批判的态度，是最远离金钱法则的人物。在这一点上，信如是最无垢的纯正的少年，也最具有孩子本性。"

再者，长吉邀请信如加入"小胡同组"时曾直言："你什么也不用做，（中略），会有很多人喜欢我们这一组啦。"（19 页）显而易见，这便是长吉邀请信如的最关键因素，他是充分了解信如的个人魅力所在的——什么都不做就能招人喜欢。的确，信如与生俱来喜欢读书，学习成绩全校第一，且长相斯文。

2.2 长吉眼中的信如个人魅力

虽说《青梅竹马》中的信如是一种孤独的存在，但是，他并不是完全孤僻独行、与人格格不入的，反而受到长吉的青睐。比如说，庙会前两天，长吉找到信如苦苦哀求他加入“小胡同组”，即使打败也愿意。万般无奈下，信如答应了长吉的要求，同时承诺绝不失信。诚然，信如是一个受人信任且守信的孩子。但是，长吉为何如此执着于邀请不会打架的信如呢?

这里，首先介绍一下16岁的长吉，他是消防头的儿子，又是“小胡同组”的孩子头，外号叫“头子长吉”，每天任意妄为、惹是生非，堪称附近一霸。小说中也提到:“这个生来就不讨人喜欢的长吉，可怜从没有一个朋友诚心跟他要好。”（19页）虽然和信如同在育英学校里上学，但是二人却有着天壤之别。还有，诚如他自述“人人都说我太粗鲁，也许我是个粗鲁人”（16页）的那样，长吉是一个粗鲁的少年，并非细腻之人。

小说中，长吉甫一登场便是去寺院找信如。樋口一叶用了几个词语描绘出了一个小心翼翼的少年形象，先是“左思右想”，接着是“悄悄”来到信如的房间，然后“探进头”喊道:“信君，在家吗?”从这一连串的动作就可以看出长吉对待信如很谨慎，一改平日里的小霸王作风，与他平时的粗鲁性格也完全不同。究其原因，笔者认为主要有以下两点:

第一，长吉和信如的竹马之谊。《青梅竹马》中与信如关系密切的少年当属长吉。“长吉是从小在这龙华寺门前长大的孩子，方丈夫妻也宠爱他”（18页），可以说两人有着自幼的交情，再加上同学关系，对信如自然与别人不同。

第二，信如的个人魅力。东京大学教授小森阳一（1988:260、263）指出:“长吉需要的是信如‘会学问’的力量。（中略）以长吉为首，正太郎和美登利等都深受信如吸引。”长吉眼中的信如的个人魅力确实在于他是有学问之人。在小说中，长吉用了足有五百多字（中文译文）、声情并茂的一段话来游说信如，他邀请信如的决心之大不言而喻，也可看出他对信如的信服。其实，对于长吉来说，信如是有学问之人，可以用汉语回骂正太郎他们，尤其他又是育英学校的榜首，自然可以服众。

2.3 明治时代带有国家意识的教育

谈及学问，就必须再略微深入地探讨一下明治时代的教育。明治时代是重视人的学问与学历的，毕竟有学问、有学历的人也就意味着有机会出人头地。中村光夫（1979：23）就曾写道："对于我国知识阶级来说，从明治二十年代初期至日俄战争的这十几年间，是最安定最为安居的时代。（中略）教育制度及内容也与前代不同，基本稳定并形成了体系化，从学校出来的人其社会地位及发挥自己实力的机会也有了保证。"

《青梅竹马》中的孩子们也接受教育，他们或在公立或在私立学校求学。而且孩子们的世界是一分为二的，一方面是花街柳巷，另一方面是儿童社会的一个归属之地——学校，真可谓对照鲜明的两个地方。关于孩子们的教育，小森教授（1988：256）曾指出：

> 一方面引导孩子们幻想未来的自由与平等；另一方面又以"学历"这一抽象的、一般概念的价值尺度来约束孩子们，使他们成为按国家所需进行再分配的装备，发挥作用。而且《青梅竹马》中的孩子们生活的明治二十年代后半期也是基于《教育勅语》（明治二十三年）的发布而形成的国家教育机制的确立期。

说到《教育勅语》，明治天皇于1890年颁布了《教育勅语》（1948年6月19日废止），目的在于阐明大日本帝国的国民道德基本与教育的根本理念，其主要内容为基于家族国家观的忠君爱国主义和儒教道德，教育的根本在于历代天皇的遗训，强调以忠君爱国为国民道德，且在学校教育中将忠君爱国思想强加给国民。

总之，日本自确认近代教育制度以后，大力推进适合日本中央集权制统一国家及日本资本主义道路发展的教育制度，行之有效，使日本国民教育基本得以普及。与此同时，也确立了教育在日本近代化发展道路上的至关重要的作用及地位，肯定了学问、学历的价值所在。但是，教育也好，学问、学历也好，自然会带有国家主义倾向的，展现出一种国家意识，诚如王桂（1987：153）所指出的："明治中期（1885—1894），日本教育由改革实验阶段进入确立国家主义教育体制阶段。因为这个时期确立的教育制度、学校体系及教育内容的指导思想是国家至上主义，所以把它称为国家主义的教育体制。”

2.4 《青梅竹马》中明治时代学问·学历这一国家意识的再现

明治社会中，对于普通民众来说，学问·学历与衣食住行·出人头地是息息相关的，从中村光夫（1979：18）的论述“明治维新之后，‘学问’直接关系到衣食之路，获得学士称号就是得到了成功的保证”中便可了解，而学问·学历都与教育息息相关，因此，再一次证明这一社会共识中也内嵌着国家意识。换句话说，这是当时的社会风潮，亦为明治时代的近代价值观。

2.4.1 孩子们的“学问”世界

> 不言而喻，试图将孩子们内嵌于国家意识光环之下的这一姿态就是以钦定宪法和《教育敕语》的发布所象征的明治国家的确立为背景的。(272 页)
>
> 天真烂漫的童心流露受到抑制的孩子、被过度社会化的孩子，即便这是非现实性的，但毫无疑问这才是明治国家的大人们所期待的少年形象。(277 页)
>
> 除去信如，《青梅竹马》中的孩子们没有一人想要致力于学业，也没有一人具有跨越由吉原与大音寺前所形成的矮小生活圈从而开拓未知人生的干劲。(280 页)
>
> 这种男女角色的逆转可以说是摆在明治国家所期待的善良的孩子们——勤俭力行的立志少年眼前的阴郁的讽刺。(282—283 页)

以上是学者前田爱（1993）关于《青梅竹马》的解析。《青梅竹马》的舞台位于大音寺前的声色犬马世界，在这里，女孩子是个宝，男孩子却“仿佛是个无用的累赘”（61 页），男女之间天壤之别，与社会主流相悖。对于男孩子们来说，姑且不论“勤俭”，“力行”和“立志”都离他们甚为遥远，好似天方夜谭。因此好学的信如反而成为孤独的存在。

那么，是不是就可以说大音寺前的孩子们不受当时的社会风潮所束缚呢？答案显而易见是否定的。《青梅竹马》中，有“学问”的登场人物只有信如和正太郎，寥寥无几。其中，关于信如，长吉和美登利先后提到了他有学问、学问好这一点。而且如前文所述，信如的个人魅力也就在于他的学问。而说到正太郎，长吉的“小胡同组”的孩子暗中成了正太郎一组的，其中一点原因就是“怕他有学问”（15 页）。甚至就连长吉也是从学校、学问角度来游说信如的。可见，即使在孩子们的世界里，“学问”也是受人敬仰或敬畏的。当然，由于这些孩子们尚且年幼，并未意识到学历的重要性。

2.4.2 正太郎“学问”的实质

虽然说正太郎也被大音寺前的孩子们认为是有学问的，但是，正太郎的志向却不在学问上，因为他终究是要继承家业的，协助奶奶经营当铺。小说中，正太郎是惹人爱的有钱人家少爷，“他真不像个十三岁的孩子，处处都想得这么周到”（47 页）。为了照顾上年纪眼睛又不好使的奶奶，他 11 岁时就开始替奶奶四处收利钱，早早就接触了自家营生。小说第四章中曾描述过盛大庙会的场景，有一幕令人尤为印象深刻，正太郎身上穿了印有字号的外褂，这一打扮与众不同。按照当时惯例，这个字号多为商号、姓名之类的。显然，在此，应该是田中屋的商号了。可见，正太郎虽年仅 13 岁却不遗余力为自家营生做宣传。虽然知道奶奶的骂名，但是他也深知奶奶的不易，因此，即使再心软也照样收利钱。小说最后一章中，正太郎留给读者的还是替奶奶收利钱的身姿。所以，可以断言，学问之于正太郎而言，并不是将来谋生的手段。

其实，小说中第一次谈及正太郎时，曾如此描述：“正太郎由于在公立学校念书，所以连唱个同样的歌，正太郎的脸上也要现出自己是正统的神气。”（15 页）所谓正统，是针对私立学校的学生而言的。众所周知，正太郎与长吉互为死对头，长吉是私立学校的学生，因此，正太郎的“正统的神气”不自觉地会让人觉得学校甚至学问是被他拿来当作战胜他人的资本。这也恰恰映射出了学问这一明治时代近代价值观，即便正太郎将来无须凭借学问来谋生，但掌握学问也自然会高人一筹，会令其他孩子另眼相看。

2.4.3 “学问”的执行者、“学历”的践行者——信如

前面多次提及《教育勅语》，而《教育勅语》中则提出了“钻研学问，学习业务，培养知识才能，成为善良有为之人”这一要求。信如虽然就读于私立学校，但是接受的仍然是带有国家主义倾向、国家意识的明治时代教育。信如的个人魅力就在于他是有学问之人，也是《青梅竹马》中唯一一位致力于学业的孩子，颇有学识。后来，更是“为了钻研本派的教义”（130 页）而出门求学了。而且作为寺院出身的少年，信如谨守

佛教教规，较之父亲老和尚更像是佛门弟子，发誓一辈子不吃荤。因此，信如可以说是明治时代教育下的模范生，是《青梅竹马》中真正的学问执行者。

在《青梅竹马》中，信如是如此的与众不同，正如高良留美子（1994：208）曾论述：“他是对学历这个日本近代的又一价值观丝毫没有抵抗的少年。而且获取学历是获得‘货币’的最稳定的干净利落的方法，这一点，在明治这个时代较之现代一定是感觉更加强烈的。”诚然如此，信如要去某地的一所和尚学校求学。由于分寺院的住持是由前任住持推荐来任命的，所以，信如如果将所规定的学业修完顺利毕业的话，自然会由他父亲推荐接任龙华寺住持一职了。因此，和尚学校的学历对于信如来说是至关重要的，这是通向他住持之路的必备条件。同时，这点也完全符合当时的社会风潮，可以说，在信如身上再现了学历这一明治时代近代价值观的重要性。

特别是在小说的最后结尾处，关于信如的出路，樋口一叶明确交代给了读者，“信如为了求学穿上了法衣，离开寺院出门去了”。显然，信如最终也是继续走他的学问之路，为继承父亲的衣钵而储备学问，获取学历学成归来之际，也是他通过自己所学经营自己佛家人生的起点。当然，不能断言成年后的信如是否会成为一名善良有为之人，但是，从他正直、忠厚的性格上来看，想必不会有太大偏差。

总之，在信如的身上，读者们看到了一位按部就班、符合国家所期待的、顺应当时社会风潮的少年人物形象。

3. 樋口一叶在信如形象上的投影

《青梅竹马》的舞台设定在大音寺前，徐琼（2012：30）阐明：“人生经历是樋口一叶的创作之源。”的确如此，这与一叶自身的生活经历息息相关，一叶于明治二十六（1893）年七月二十日迁居下谷区龙泉寺町（通称为大音寺前）。关于这段经历，从一叶的日记中便可窥见一斑。关于这一时期的日记，高井有一、红野敏郎（1994：7）在对谈中也指出：“正是因为贴近一叶生活来撰写，所以能看到其背后的社会。”

在此，首先阐述一下樋口一叶的远大志向。在小岛政二郎（1941）编的《樋口一叶全集》中提到了明治二十六年八月十日的日记《尘埃中》（『塵の中』、23—26），刚刚8岁的一叶就日夜祈愿，想要成为一名比他人略为杰出的人物。关于这一点，小说家高井有一（1994：8）曾指出："一叶有着很强的复兴家业、自己成名的志向。"的确，作为一名小说家，在文学这一领域，一叶确实是功成名就的。然而，成为一名小说家果真是一叶所诉求的志向吗？以樋口一叶研究为其毕生事业的日本文学研究者和田芳惠（1970：486）就指出：从日记等中仔细研读樋口一叶的处世方法，会感觉到她祈愿出人头地的方式与成为小说家这条道路是不同的。换言之，一叶的志向并不在于小说家。其实，关于一叶的志向，在小岛政二郎（1941）编的、明治二十七（1894）年四月至五月二日的《尘中日记》（『塵中につ記』、98—108）中即可寻出，那就是：国家之根本。所谓"国家之根本"，可以说阐明了一叶的经国（治国）之志，松坂俊夫（1982：249—250）指出：与这个"国家之根本"相关联，一叶的本意就在于文章经国这一点。由此可知，一叶是通过文学创作来明志的。

众所周知，樋口一叶在生活上过得很窘迫。虽然如此，她却志存高远。细读一叶《尘埃日记》的原文，便不难发现，22 岁的一叶对社会不良风气深感痛心疾首，她发出一声叹息：道德颓丧、人情薄如纸，朝野人士重私利、不谋求正确的政治方针，这样的社会将会何去何从？一叶针砭时弊，字字切入要点。虽自知无能为力，但她言明自己绝不贪图一时之安逸，而是深思百世之忧虑。虽自知微乎其微，但她立志一生投身于社会，别无他求，不惧生死，遵循天地之法则行动，其心与天地融为一体。同为明治二十七年着手创作的《青梅竹马》说是她的明志之作也不足为奇。

其次，樋口一叶是一位执着于学问的女性。在日记《尘埃中》，一叶记述了自己的求学之路。有两点尤为令人钦佩，一是：在一叶 11 岁时，由于母亲认为女子多学无益，遂令其退学在家学习缝纫、帮忙做家务。纵然如此，她仍每晚坚持伏案苦学；二是：熟知一叶好学的父亲给她买了《和歌集》，在父亲的大力帮助下，一叶得以排除万难继续求学。简言之，迫于无奈而辍学的一叶执着于学问，通过自修继续自己的求学之路。

在《青梅竹马》中，信如是唯一一位"学问"的执行者和"学历"的践行者。对于学问，信如身上再现了樋口一叶的执着态度。当然，不同的是，信如由于自家生活富足而在求学道路上一帆风顺。试想，11 岁辍学在家的一叶在 14 岁时经由父亲友人介绍几经周折才得以进入中岛歌子的"荻之舍"学习和歌和书法，她的内心迫切希望自己能够顺顺利利求学。所以，信如一帆风顺的求学之路的设定不正是一叶自身所祈求的吗？特别是，徐琼（2012：30）指出了“一叶的作品是具有社会性的”这一点，笔者也颇为赞同，学问是当时的社会风潮，是明治时代的近代价值观之一，对于立志文章经国的一叶来说，这是她倍加认同的，她亦想通过信如来唤起民众对学问的关心。

最后，樋口一叶的侠义之心。在日记《尘埃中》，一叶自述 7 岁时喜欢草双纸（江户时代的通俗绘图小说），尤其是其中的英雄豪杰传记。她深深感动于侠义之士的行为，喜欢所有勇猛、辉煌的人物。特别是，一叶与当时的女孩子的喜好不同，她不玩拍球、打羽毛毽子这类女孩子的游戏。显然，彼时的一叶对于男性的、道义的世界充满了憧憬，也是一个有着侠义之心的少女。高原知子（1975：81）曾借用日本近代文学研究者关良一的观点，指出：《青梅竹马》是一部基于一叶所特有的道义的、关心社会的作品。其实，在《青梅竹马》中，即便在孩子世界里也存在长吉的“小胡同组”与正太郎的“大街组”之间的纷争。在这纷争之中，信如是一个关键人物，长吉对他很仰仗，他也向长吉展示了自己的那份义气，而正太郎又想与他一较高下。尤其是，他曾对长吉说过：“欺侮弱小的人是咱们的耻辱哩”（82 页）。如此看来，信如身上真给人一种孩子世界中的“英雄豪杰”之感。

同时，关于自己的性格，樋口一叶还有如下之叙述。一方面，在世人眼中，称赞她是一个温顺的孩子，也说她是一个记忆力强的孩子，父亲以她为傲，老师也因她出类拔萃而喜爱她。另一方面，在内心世界里，她却是一个刚强、不服输的人。一叶的这一内一外的性格特征与“外面软，里面硬”的信如形象重叠了。不仅如此，一叶轻视那些为利欲而奔波的世人，觉得他们的行为既卑鄙又令人厌恶，视金钱为尘芥。这一点，在信如身上也表现得淋漓尽致。通过信如，一叶再一次表达了自己对金钱至上主义的批判，这也正是她批判现实主义文学的意义所在。

综上所述，不难看出，在信如这一人物形象上，折射出了作者樋口一叶的身影。

4 结语

樋口一叶在《青梅竹马》中一反常态塑造了一个与众不同的少年主人公形象，这个外柔内刚的少年，对内，因他正直、敏感、重名誉、忠厚的性格而与家人产生隔阂，由此而滋生了孤独感；对外，与周围的同龄人格格不入，难以融为一体。如此特异的少年，却又凭借着个人独到的魅力征服了众人，在他身上尽显孩童的纯真。说到信如的个人魅力，首屈一指的便是学问，他也是《青梅竹马》中唯一的真正的学问执行者。为了求学，他毅然远走他乡，堪称明治时代教育下的模范生。学成归来之际，便是信如凭借自己的学问、学历立足于世的出发点，可以说，在他身上很好地显现出了明治时代学问、学历这一近代价值观。不仅如此，纵观作者一叶的人生经历，从她的远大志向、执着于学问，到她的侠义之心、视金钱为尘芥，都折射到了信如的人物形象身上，阅读信如的章节，就好似重温一叶的人生点点轨迹。

参考文献

岩見照代、北田幸恵等．樋口一葉事典［M］．東京：おうふう，1996.

本文中的日文引用部分皆为笔者译。

小島政二郎編．樋口一葉全集第四巻［M］．名古屋：新世社，1941.

小森陽一．「口惜しさと恥しさ——たけくらべにおけると言説（ディスクール）」文体としての物語［M］．東京：筑摩書房，1988.

高井有一、紅野敏郎．対談　樋口一葉と明治 20 年代［J］．國文學 解釈と教材の研究第 39 巻 11 号，1994.

高原知子．樋口一葉たけくらべについて［J］．駒沢短大国文 6 号，1975.

高良留美子．「無意識の加害者たち——たけくらべ論」新・フェミニズム批評の会樋口一葉を読みなおす［M］．東京：學藝書林，1994.

中村光夫．筑摩業書 9　明治文学史［M］．東京：筑摩書房，1979.

中村稔．樋口一葉考［M］．東京：青土社，2012.

前田愛．樋口一葉の世界［M］．東京：平凡社，1993.

松坂俊夫．鑑賞日本現代文学 2　樋口一葉［M］．東京：角川書店，1982.

和田芳恵．「樋口一葉」日本文学全集 3　幸田露伴　樋口一葉集［M］．東京：筑摩書房，1970.

曹顺庆主编：《比较文学概论》，高等教育出版社 2015 年版。

［日］樋口一叶：《青梅竹马》，萧萧译，中国和平出版社 2005 年版。

王桂：《日本教育史》，吉林教育出版社 1987 年版。

徐琼：《樋口一叶及其作品研究》，知识产权出版社 2012 年版。

“Xinru” in “Childhood Sweetheart” and Meiji National Consciousness

Han Chunhong

Abstract: Higuchi, a famous Japanese novelist, has successfully created the typical characters of young boys and girls such as Xinru, Maidenly and Zhengtaro in his masterpiece “ Childhood, sweetheart ” . Among them, the hero believes that he is an isolated being, but also he has a unique personal charm, that is, he is a learned person. Although Yiye is one of the pioneers of critical realism literature, she is also a woman who dedicated to learning, which exactly reflects her life experience. By means of text analysis, this paper aims to analyze the modern values represented by the character image Xinru in Meiji era— “knowledge” theory “and education background” theory, and at the same time it clarifies the national consciousness of Meiji era implied in the character image Xinru.

Key words: “ Knowledge ” theory; “ Education background ” theory; Meiji state consciousness; Character image Xinru

自然：自由与艺术的桥梁

闫军利*

摘　要：自然，作为相对于主体的客观存在，是主体赖以生存的物质条件，也是艺术家表现自我的不可或缺的重要因素。正如古语所说，文章多得江山助。艺术须借助自然使内在得以外化，集中的体现是人意志的自由。自由是人的基本属性，也是艺术所要追求和表现的重要方面。艺术展现美，美不能脱离感性，所以艺术不能脱离自然，人需要借助于自然并以艺术的方式来彰显人的自由本质。因此，在艺术活动中，自然在自由与艺术中间架起了桥梁。

关键词：自然；自由；艺术

1　引言

印度哲人泰戈尔在他富于哲理的格言诗集《飞鸟集》中，用清澈的文字描写了大自然的激情，意象奇崛美妙，在字里行间表达了对自然、宇宙和人生的哲理认识。在《飞鸟集》中，泰戈尔提到："艺术家是自然的情人，所以他是自然的奴隶，也是自然的主人。"（郑振铎，2015：15）这句话虽然看似简单，但蕴含着深刻的哲理，泰戈尔提到了艺术家、自然以及他们之间所存在的一种矛盾的身份关系。为了搞清楚这种关系，本文试图从以下方面进行分析。

2　自然与自由

2.1　人对自然的偏好

谈到自然，首先要说说什么是自然。"自然"一词在一般意义上来

---

* 作者简介：闫军利（1970—　），男，陕西师范大学外国语学院讲师，研究方向：典籍翻译。

讲，它指的是我们通常所说的大自然，如花草树木、山川河流、日月星辰。所以，“自然”一词包括自然界，但并非完全指的是自然界，它的概念要比自然界内涵深刻得多，所以不能将二者等同。对于“自然”，台湾学者卢建荣说：“魏晋时人喜欢用‘自然’一词，并从此引申出一连串的丰富思想。”“自然”一词根据他的解释：“由正面界定的意义是：物之本性自足。”由反面的界定意义是：“不使物自足之本性受到任何改变或破坏。”（郭廉夫，1996：82）

“知者乐水，仁者乐山。”（孔子，1998：74）这是为人们所熟知的一句圣哲之语，按照一般的理解，即儒家也是提倡以山水自然为乐的，但究其深层含义，绝不止于此。中国的儒家思想提倡以“仁”为核心的伦理道德观念，并在此基础上建立了“君臣父子”的伦理纲常和相应的社会秩序，主张“学而优则仕”以及“修身齐家治国平天下”的积极入世的思想。但在儒家创始人孔子的内心深处，还有更为令人向往的境界。这一点在《子路、曾皙、冉有、公西华侍坐》一篇中能够体现出来。其实，对于自由的向往，在儒家那里，也有所显示。儒家本来是主张入世的，但《论语》中也有这样的记载：孔子在倾听子路、冉求、公西赤、曾点各自的志向后，对于子路，“夫子哂之”，即微笑了一下，对冉求和公西赤则未置可否，当夫子问到正在鼓瑟的曾点时，曾点则停止了鼓瑟，然后毕恭毕敬站起来回答老师说：“异乎三子者之撰”，即不同于前三人的安邦务实之志，子曰：“何伤乎？亦各言其志也。”于是曾点说：“莫春者，春服既成，冠者五六人，童子六七人，浴乎沂，风乎舞雩，咏而归。”夫子喟然叹曰：“吾与点也。”即长长地感叹一声说：“我赞同曾点的观点。”（杨伯峻，2002：119）孔子为什么对前三人的治国理想未加评论，而对曾点顺时游乐的心态表示欣赏和赞同呢？宋代理学家朱熹对此有一个比较权威的解读，他说，曾点的理想看起来不过是“即其所居之位，乐其日用之常，初无舍已为人之意”（《四书集注》），好像他做的都是些日常小事，没有什么舍己为人的大理想。但曾点的内心是完美充盈的，他以自身人格完善为前提，以万物各得其所为理想，顺乎自然大道。将身心融入自然，充分享受自然给人的心灵所带来的自由欢娱，这和孔子“知者乐水，仁者乐山”的思想也是一致的。心灵的生命力就在于其能自由欢畅。由此我们也能体会到儒家和“独与天地精神共往来”的道家思想有某种契合点。追求心灵的自由，是人类从古代直至今天都在刻意希望达到的理想境界，儒家也是如此。

西方近代崇尚自然始于培根，王国维曾介绍说："培根对眩惑上古文学之徒，以现在三字警告之，大声疾呼曰：汝勿盲信传来之说，而躬就自然研究之。向来之科学，不使自然发言，待以任意构成之观念，加诸自然界，而由之以成虚伪之思想。"（蓝国桥，2016：113）于是培根就努力"使自然发言"，并使自己的言说以自然作为真正的起点。这样在教育上就可以做到："心常止于物之本身，而受纳其形象，如在其真。且也，不依赖教权，而尽舍得自传授之意见，一以无垢无邪之心，考察世界是已。"（蓝国桥，2016：114）

自然在康德那里，一方面是指经验的对象，美的现象可以在此表现出来，另一方面是指经验对象呈现的规律，因而是规定判断的对象，只有从规律中暂时摆脱出来，也就是说不再受人为（人为自然立法）概念的限定，自然才会向人舒展美的姿态。康德多是在自然的意义上谈美，原因可能是自然的丰富性，往往使概念的规范性失效，所以他常常提醒人们注意审美不涉及概念。康德由此表现出对自然新奇性的爱好，而对理性规范性则流露出厌倦的情绪，他这样表述自己的好恶："马尔斯顿在他关于苏门答腊的描绘指出，在那里大自然的自由的美处处包围着观者，而由此对他不再具有多少吸引力；与此相反，一个胡椒园，藤萝蔓绕的枝干在其中构成两条平行的林荫路，当他在森林中忽然碰到这胡椒园时，这对于他便具有很多的魅力。他由此得出结论：野生的、在现象上看是不规则的美，只对于看饱了和规则性的美的人因其变化而引起愉快感。但是只要他做一个实验，一整天停留在他的胡椒园里，使他内心感到，如果知性经由合规则性把自己置身于他处处所需要的秩序井然的情调里，那对象将不会长久地令他感到有趣，甚至对他的想象力加上了可厌的强制；与此相反，那富于多样性到了奢侈程度的大自然，他不服从于任何人的规则，却能对他的鉴赏不断地提供粮食。"（康德，2002：81—82）或许回到大自然，人才会从规范中解放出来，自然的魅力因此是无穷的，这或许也是康德从自然角度讨论审美的真正原因吧。

由于对自然偏好，这种趣味一直贯穿于康德对艺术的说明中，艺术若如自然，其价值会高些，相反如显露为人工的矫揉造作、人为的模仿就会使艺术价值打折扣，甚至有时会令人生厌。对自然的欣赏，而对人工对象的厌倦，自然的魅力显然胜过了人为的魅力，大自然之美达到了"豪奢程度”，毕竟它不服从于任何人为的规则，并可以向人的“鉴赏不断地提供粮食”，而人为的对象再美，也会有令人厌烦的时候。康德在涉及艺术讨论时这样写道：“诗人所赞美的莫过于夜莺在悄悄的夏夜，藏在孤寂的丛林里，发出它的动人的美丽的歌唱。但人们虽有这样的例子，即在这个场合并不是夜莺的歌唱，而是某一客店主人为了使那些在他客店里歇夏的旅客高兴，暗中叫一个顽皮的孩子藏在丛林里（用声管或竹管）模仿自然的歌唱。当人们一旦发觉这是欺骗时，他们就不再能长久忍耐下去听这先前那样认为多么美的歌声了”（蓝国桥，2016：118）。这样模仿自然的歌唱，就令康德变得无法忍耐了。也就是说，他对人工（人为）就显得很不满。

2.2　自然的呈美原理

自然是充满生命的有机整体。她的美也就在于生命的有机性。回归自然就是回归活的生命本身。摆脱了人为的缠绕之后，自然向人展现了它最本真的面貌，生命也因此变得晶莹而透明，也就是说自然呈美还在于它的直观性。培根与洛克等人都把自然当成与人距离最近的一种对象。也就是说，自然与人的接触采用了最短的距离。对自然的欣赏，一则必须是无功利的，二则需要排除概念，否则人与自然的距离就被推得无限远，康德在审美上要求“无功利”“无概念”，就是希望自然能无遮蔽地向人敞开。去除了人工束缚，自然以自由之名义为自己命名，自然在此意义上是自由的象征，排除了人为的因素后，自然界的充满生机性就被展露出来，那是一个流动着的活的整体，自然由此是生命的标志，人工、人为要素免除后，人与自然的距离也就变得最短，人以最直接的方式进入自然，在自然界中人展示了自己最本真的生命状态。自然展现的面貌，其实就是人自身要求到达的境界，自然之所以呈美主要是因为自然满足了人的要求，自然之美与人就发生了最为密切的联系，若还原为康德语言的话，自然之所以美，是由于自然合乎了人的目的，合乎了人的自由、生命、本真的目的，而这些目的只是在一种主观的意义被符合了，这样自然就具有了主观合目的性的意蕴。

对此，康德这样写道：“一个关于对象的概念在他同时包含着这个对象的现实性的基础时唤做目的，而一个物体和诸物的只是按照目的而可能的品质相一致时，唤做该物的形式的合目的性，所以判断力的原理，在涉及一般经验规律下的自然界诸物的形式时，唤做在自然界的多样性中的自然界的合目的性。”康德在此已经很明确地指出，自然呈美的基本原理就是“自然界的合目的性”，是自然“诸物的形式的合目的性”，而自然诸物的形式本身是人能动造型的结果，因此带有主观的色彩，自然在审美的意义上只是人主观愿望的一种延伸，自然的自由性、生命有机性、自然的本真状态，也只不过是人的自由、生命、本真状态要求在自然身上的主观折射而已。这样，自然之美也就由此转化为人之美。

康德在其《判断力批判》一书中，提出了无目的的合目的性理论。合目的性原理与审美和艺术又有何关系呢？某物具有自然的合目的性，就会使人愉快。为何自然的合目的性能与我们的愉快情绪相联结呢？康德认为，这是由于一种意图的达成就导致愉快，而意图的达成就是把单纯经验规律的多样性归结为原理的统一性。他说：“一切意图的达成都与快乐的情绪相联结；这意图的达成有一先验表象为其条件，象在这里对于所有反思着的判断力有一个原理一样，快乐的情绪也是被一个先验和对每个人都有效的根据所规定：并且也仅仅是由客体联系到认识机能。”（康德 2002：230）当一自然事物的形式，符合了我们头脑中先验的关于自然形式合目的性原理，因此，也符合了我们的认识机能的要求，从而使我们在知性力和想象力的和谐产生的表象中，产生愉快的情绪。而引起自然的合目的性的美学表象的对象就被称为美，而通过情感对美的对象的判断则被称为鉴赏。康德认为，艺术活动不同于自然活动，艺术活动是基于理性之上的自由创造。康德把合目的性原理作为始终不脱离感性形态去寻求审美的普遍有效性的根据，它不是为自然而设立的，而是为人自己设立的。基于合目的性原理，人们可寻求较为一致的有可能达成共识的共通感，从而为美学及各门艺术的发展奠定了坚实的基础。这正如鲍桑葵所指出的：“在鉴赏判断中所包含的关系方面，美是一个对象的合目性的形式，只要这个对象能在没有目的观念的情况下知觉到。”（戴茂堂，2005：162）

在艺术创作中，“无目的的合目的性”也具有很重要的指导意义。它可以简单地理解为：“主观上无目的但却在客观上合目的”，至于主观上无目的，延续英国的美学传统，认为审美判断的标志性特征是“无利害”（dis-interestedness），中文被翻译为“无所为而为”，很传神，于是审美活动是一种无利害的静观（contemplation）。

2.3 自由与自然：受制与超越

关于自由和自然，西方人谈得更多且更深刻。在西方，人们竭力用语言符号来穷尽一切真理。这也使科学有了迅速的发展。反过来，科学的发展也为思想的发展提供了依据，自然与自由的问题就是一个很好的体现。西方人用科学的方法论证了自然与自由的关系。

康德在其《纯粹理性批判》里就清楚地谈论了这一问题。他认为，自由是人的基本属性，人的自由是先验的，是可能的。他把世界划分为感性世界和理知世界。感性世界是指现象的世界、经验的世界、是我们的认识所及、知识形成的世界；理知世界是超验的世界，是我们不可认识但可以思维的世界。感性的、经验的世界是受因果律支配的世界。理智的世界是超验的，他用先验的范畴对在物自体的刺激下产生的感性杂多安排在时间与空间的秩序之中。人一方面是自然的产物，作为自然的一部分，他必然受到自然因果律的支配，因而是不自由的。另一方面，人又具有物自体的属性，并不服从于自然法则，因而是自由的。这里有必要对二者进行区分，以便说明其理论根据。康德认为科学知识是关于感性世界的知识，人是知识主体、感性主体，但又可以外在于知识、外在于自然因果链条，人为知识奠基并划定界限，这就为人的自由得到论证。康德有句著名的哲言："我不得不悬隔知识，以便给信仰腾出位置。"（康德，2002：209）

自由的概念是整个康德哲学的拱心石，是最关键的一环，他的《纯粹理性批判》和《实践理性批判》都是以自由作为他的立论基础而建立起来的。康德哲学的两个最主要的话题是自然和自由，自然涉及必然性，所以自然是有必然性的自然。自由涉及道德，它是《实践理性批判》的起点，是通过道德给自由立法。

康德认为人具有两重品格，一种是现象品格，也即经验性的品格，它使主体按照自然因果规律而处于现象序列之中，成为现象中的一环，即人处于现象世界并受因果律支配的特点；另一种是理知的品格，凭借这种品格，"主体虽然是那些作为现象的行动的原因，但这种品格本身并不从属于任何感性的条件，并且本身不是现象"（康德，2002：238），我们也可以把这种品格称为自在之物本身的品格。所以同一个主体，就其经验性的品格而言，是感性世界的一部分，这个主体自身及其行动作为现象将服从于自然因果规律，他的一切行动就必须按照自然律来解释；就其理知品格而言，主体不会从属于任何时间条件，他不会处于感性世界的现象序列当中，因而也根本不可能被认识。由于经验性品格和理知品格属于同一主体，这样一来，自由和自然，每一方在自己完全的意义中，就会在同一些行动上，按照我们把它们与自己的理知的原因还是感性的原因相比较，而没有任何冲突地被找到。

2.4 艺术家的能动作用

艺术家作为主体，在面对自然这一客体时，必须要充分发挥能动作用。艾默生在《论自然》一文的开篇诗中写道："……目光解读它触及的征兆，玫瑰诉说万语千言。……"（艾默生，2010：1）这两句诗中，玫瑰代表自然，向人类展现万千气象，作为主体的人用自己的感官来吸收、归纳和总结，从而形成知识。而艺术家，则会通过心与物的交融而产生艺术佳作。在文中，艾默生还提到："说实话，没有几个成年人能看得见自然。大部分人不认真看太阳。至少，他们那种看是非常肤浅的。太阳只照亮了成人的眼睛，但却不仅照亮孩子们的眼睛，而且透进他们的心灵。"（艾默生，2010：4）儿童世界与功利性的成人世界形成很大的不同。朱光潜提出："我们成人把人和物的界限分得很清楚，把想象的和实在的分得很清楚。在儿童心中这种分别是很模糊的。他把物视同自己一样，认为它们也有生命……人情化可以说是儿童所特有的体物的方法。人越老就越不能起移情作用，我和物的距离就日见其大，实在和想象的隔阂就日见其深，于是这个世界也就越没有趣味了。"（朱光潜，1988：35）

所以，艺术家作为审美主体，在面对自然客体时，不但要具有主观能动性，而且还要求达到儿童般的天真无邪的、透过心灵的专注。著名诗人柯勒律治的一段话也许更加清楚地说明了这一点："把儿童时代的情感注入成年人的理性中去，用儿童新颖和惊奇的感受去鉴定我们几十年来熟视无睹、习以为常的日常事物表象——这便是天才的独特个性和才能。"（刘绪源，2009：45）

3 艺术是对自由的表明，对自由的确认

自由是人类的重要属性，人是自由活动的存在。黑格尔（1996）说，精神的本性是自由……哲学告诉我们，精神只能依赖自由而存在；思辨哲学的结论认为，自由是精神的唯一真理……精神是以独立自足的形式存在。毫无疑问，这就是自由。因为如果我是有所依赖的，我即他物，而非我；我不可能凭借外物而自由自在。相反，我如果依靠自身，我则是自由的。黑格尔的"人不可能凭借外物而自由自在"这一思想和庄子的思想十分相似，如出一辙。这就是他在《逍遥游》的"无待"论中所确立的

"理想自由"。庄子在文中列举了那么多事物，不论是"水击三千里，抟扶摇而上者九万里"的鲲鹏，还是"御风而行，泠然善也"的列子，都是"犹有所待者也"，都是不自由的，而只有那"无己"之"至人"、"无功"之"神人"和"无名"之"圣人"才是自由的。

自由是艺术的反映对象的本质。按照马克思的观点，"艺术是自我的对象化，是人在他所创造的世界中直观自身，也即人在他所创造的世界中直观人的自由的感性现实的表现。如果我们从艺术中抽去了人对自由的追求，那么艺术就失去了它的生命和灵魂，再也不成其为艺术了。人类文化的进步，本质上就是人的自由的进步。而在一切文化中，艺术又处在自由的最高的位置上"（刘纲纪，1986：228）。

自由是人的本质之一，也是审美的主要条件，有了这个条件，审美活动才能开始。自美学学科创立以来，美的问题即被归结为人的问题，美的本质被规定为人的自由本质。美学的最高问题涉及人的自由和意义问题。在所有学科中，美学无疑是最接近人的本质的存在的。在艺术家和理论家心中，审美、艺术与自由和自然有不解之缘，艺术家和审美主体以及创造过程和审美活动都体现着自由精神。有了自由的人和人的自由，才能有审美和艺术。当代美国哲学家 H. M. 卡伦（1989：23）在其《艺术与自由》一书中提出，艺术家拥有其他人所没有的自由。

艺术的最高境界是一种有规矩的自由。朱光潜（1988）认为，从心所欲不逾矩，是道德家所追求的至境，也是艺术家的至境。通俗地讲，从心所欲就是自由，不逾矩就是不能超越规矩，因而是不自由的。用康德的话来讲，这种境界是合目的性与合规律性的统一。艺术家的创造活动看去既是随心所欲、高度自由的，同时又处处都是合规律的。这也就是中国古代艺术理论中所谓的"无法之法，乃为至法"。艺术美的合规律性，是一种自由中的合规律，或合规律中的自由。赵朴初先生称王羲之的书法为规矩方圆之至，规矩即法度，方圆即自由。

美本来是人的个性的自由的表现。美的本质从根本上决定了美的合规律性必然是一种自由中的合规律性。在这里，规律不是从外部来限定束缚人的自由的东西，而是已经和人的自由融为一体的东西，规律发生作用同时就是人的自由的实现。在艺术美的领域中，我们看到了目的的实现同时就是人的自由的实现，并且只有作为人的自由的实现来看，目的的实现才是美的。

4 人类自由的理性思考

康德把自然纳入了他所建立的目的论系统，在这个系统中，自然既有其内在合目的性，又有其相对合目的性。内在合目的性指的是自然作为一个有机的整体，其内部是自足的，无须依靠外部的力量来使其运行。相对合目的性指的是自然内部各组成部分之间是互为因果，互为目的和手段的。各个部分都处在链条当中，是整个自然链条的不可或缺的组成部分。在自然的链条当中，人也是其中的一部分，因为人是自然的产物。在天地万物自然运行中，各部分之间相互依赖，此物的存在成为彼物存在的条件或基础，彼物又是他物的条件和基础，这样循环往复，无始无终，呈现出一种有序但是无目的的状态。孔子说："天何言哉？四时行焉，百物生焉，天何言哉？"即是说万事万物的运行有其内在的运行机制，是一种自发的机制，但同时也是盲目的。自然的运行没有设定任何目标，不涉及从哪里来、到哪里去的问题，是纯任自然的。最基本的状态是，土地的存在成为植物生长的条件，植物成为动物的生存条件，依次类推，最终的推论是，人成为自然的最终目的，因为人是唯一一种能给自己设定目的的存在物。康德说："人是地球上唯一能够给自己造成一个目的的概念、并能从一大堆合乎目的的形成起来的东西中通过自己的理性造成一个目的系统的存在者。"（康德，2002：282）

人作为能够给自己设定目标的自然存在物之一，他最大的目标就是幸福。正如美国《独立宣言》中提到的，人生而平等，天赋人权。生存、自由、谋求幸福的权利不可剥夺。要想获得幸福，首先需要满足的是其感性需要，人类幸福的基础在很大程度上取决于感性需要的满足。所以幸福的获得取决于对满足感性需要的物质资料的占有程度。而且人类追求幸福的欲望是永远不能满足或达到的。欲壑难填一词深刻地揭示了这个问题。康德认为"人的本性具有不在任何地方停止并满足于占有和享受的性质"（康德，2002：286）。所以在人与人之间、团体与团体之间，国家与国家之间，就幸福的获得问题而进行不断的斗争。

既然人类为了满足欲望、追求个人的幸福而不惜损害他人利益，所以追求幸福不能也不足以成为自然的最终目的。因此，康德引入了道德，因为通过道德可以对人的私欲加以管束。这样一来，追求幸福成为一种有条件的人类活动，人作为一个道德存在物而成为自然的最终目的。另外，一方面人作为自然链条中的一环，受到必然性的制约，另一方面，由于人的理性而使其能够身处其中而又能超然物外。因为人类的理性以知性为对象，知性又以感性为对象，感性通过仰观、俯察、远瞻、近取，从感性杂多中获取信息，从而达到认识自然、改造自然的目的。同时，人还借助于理性而反观自身，对理性进行反思和批判来完善自身。所以，人是能够给自己创造目的的理性存在物。自然有机体中的各部分都是互为目的和手段的，唯有人能够超越自然，成为自然的终极目的。而这样的人兼备道德存在物和自由存在物的特性。“这是唯一这样的自然存在者，我们在它身上从其特有的性状方面却能认识到某种超感官的能力（即自由）。”（康德，2002：291）

按照康德的理论，人只有作为道德的存在物才能成为自然的终极目的，这种目的是不需要任何别的东西作为它的可能性的条件。

5 自然之中人类自由得以实现的条件

卢梭有句名言：“人是生而自由的，但却无往不在枷锁之中。自以为是其他一切的主人的人，反而比其他一切更是奴隶。”（卢梭，2003：4）由此可见，人类虽然具有理想自由的一面，又有现实生活中自由处处受阻的一面。所以，人类的自由是有条件的自由。康德作为一位数学家和天文学家，他通过使用数学般严密的逻辑思维对人类理性与自然的关系发表了自己的见解，认为人可以运用先验的知性范畴加之理性的整体思维对自然立法，从而达到认识自然，并在自然的有机体中脱颖而出，最终成为自然的终极目的，使自然最终向人生成。但正如泰戈尔所说“人既是自然的主人，又是自然的奴隶”。所以，这种人类的自由是有条件的，但也是有希望的。

首先，人必须是有道德的人，必须是克服了单单以幸福作为最终目标而不能把控欲望的人。在认识自然的过程中，人类为自然立法，而在社会实践领域中，人也必须为自身立法，这就是道德。由于近代科学技术的飞速发展，人类对自然的认识无论从广度和深度来讲，都达到了空前的高度，由此造成的后果也是不言而喻的，人类无情地攫取自然，为我所用。科学利己主义达到泛滥的程度。所以康德提出了要用人类理性建立一个能够给科学予以引导的科学，即哲学。在哲学的指引下，人才能够摆脱他物的束缚，而成为自己的主人，也即获得自由。因为人类虽然能够通过科学的方式最大限度的认识自然而获得利益，达成私欲，但最终的结果还是囿于物。丧失了人之所以为人的最本质的东西。

其次，人类是有理性的存在物，正是由于人类的理性才将自身从感性的束缚中解脱出来，正如前文所说，人类的幸福在很大程度上是由感性的满足程度来衡量的。所以，确切地说，人是有理性的感性存在物。康德认为自然界的一切“是为了人类的多种多样的利用，对所以那些被造物作这种利用是人的知性教给他的；人就是这个地球上的创造的最后目的，因为他是地球上唯一能够给自己造成一个目的概念，并能从一大堆合乎目的的形成起来的东西中通过自己的理性造成一个目的系统的存在者”（康德，2002：178）。

最后，人只有摆脱功利的束缚，才能获得审美体验中真正的自由。康德认为，在人类的演化当中，由于具有理性这一区别于自然中其他一切生物的特征，使人类能够在无目的的受机械律支配的自然之中脱离出来，成为自然的终极目的。当然，这种情况的造成也是有前提的，即人必须是具有道德自律的理性存在物。在物质层面，道德自律要求人类必须有能力克服为追求幸福而产生的无限膨胀的欲望，同时，在精神层面，能够超越自然律他律的束缚，从而达到真正的自由。

这种自由，在文艺作品的创作实践活动中能够得以充分的体现。众所周知，王羲之的《兰亭序》被称为天下第一行书，他是在天朗气清、惠风和畅、茂林修竹、清流急湍的自然风景的诱发之下，加之自己的人生体验而写成的，后世称之为文书双璧。因为是当时即兴而作，中间有涂抹之处，后来王羲之在重新整理时，也为自己的书作之妙大为惊叹。但当他想重造妙品时，发现怎么也达不到最初的效果，只能怅然作罢。这一典型事例说明了审美创造是超越功利的，有心于佳乃不佳，无心于佳乃佳。另有刘熙载《艺概》有言：“书非使人爱之为难，而不求人爱之为难。盖有欲无欲，此所以别人天也。”（彭庆阳，2019：135）

另外，文艺作品的外在形式所传达的是美，其核心却是创作者内心的自由，但是，必须首先克服自然律他律的束缚才能达到艺术的自由。这种自由也是在符合并熟练地运用机械律的前提下实现的。正如俗语所说：“艺术是戴着脚镣手铐的舞蹈。”这里所谓的脚镣手铐，指的就是艺术实践活动中的自然律他律。自然律他律要求艺术家在起初阶段必须亦步亦趋地按照自然规律行事，然后逐渐达到熟练的程度，所以艺术的低级阶段是技术，或者说技术是艺术的基础。技术要求不断地机械重复以达到娴熟，熟能生巧从而上升到艺术的境界。所以艺术佳作是在心和手都自由的情况下产生的。正如孙过庭《书谱》所提到的所谓心手双畅，翰墨神飞。

6 结论

自然，是人通过艺术实现人类自由的桥梁。自由是人的基本属性，艺术不能脱离开自由的人和人的自由。人是感性的理性存在物，人类可以通过给自然立法从而认识自然，自然人虽然身处自然有机体当中，属于自然链条中的一环，但由于人的理性，把自身同其他形态的生命区别开来，因而使自身成为目的而非他物的手段。最终结果是人使自身成为自然的终极目的。但人必须是在道德的指引和约束下，才能达此目的，从而使自然向人生成。尽管人类能够通过理性和道德而上升为自然的终极目的，但人的自由问题，和审美活动息息相关，并成为审美关键的一环。

审美活动使人从世俗生活以及道德的压力中解放出来。艺术展现美，美不能脱离感性，艺术不能脱离自然，人需要借助于自然并以艺术的方式来彰显人的自由本质。人是有理性的感性存在物，人生于自然，必然受到自然律的制约，但同时人能够通过理性认识自然，能够在道德律自律的基础上成为自然的终极目的，并且在对自然的审美中实现自身的自由的本质属性。

参考文献

[美] 艾默生：《论自然》，中国对外翻译出版公司 2010 年版。

戴茂堂：《超越自然主义》，武汉大学出版社 2005 年版。

高广文：《高等学校英语专业高年级阅读教材》，西安交通大学出版社 2000 年版。

郭廉夫：《王羲之评传》，南京大学出版社 1996 年版。

H. M. 卡伦：《艺术与自由》，工人出版社 1989 年版。

[德] 黑格尔：《美学》，商务印书馆 1996 年版。

[德] 康德：《判断力批判》，邓晓芒译，人民出版社 2002 年版。

孔子：《论语》，外语教学与研究出版社 1998 年版。

蓝国桥：《王国维与康德美学》，人民出版社 2016 年版。

刘纲纪：《艺术哲学》，湖北人民出版社 1986 年版。

刘绪源：《儿童文学的三大母题》，华东师范大学出版社 2009 年版。

[法] 卢梭：《社会契约论》，何兆武译，商务印书馆 2003 年版。

彭庆阳：《清·刘熙载〈艺概·书概〉》，中国书店 2019 年版。
申扶民：《自由的审美之路》，中国社会科学出版社 2009 年版。
孙过庭：《书谱》，赵宏注解，中州古籍出版社 2013 年版。
[印度] 泰戈尔：《泰格尔作品集 飞鸟与夏花》，郑振铎，冰心译，2015 年版。
杨伯峻：《论语译注》，中华书局 2002 年版。

Nature: the Bridge of Art and Freedom

Abstract: Nature, as an objective existence in relative to the subject, is the material condition on which the subject relies, and also an important factor for artists to show oneself. As the saying goes, articles are the fusion of man and nature. Art is a way to externalize something internal, the focus of it is man's freedom. Freedom is the basic nature of human being and is also an important aspect which art seeks. What art shows is beauty which can not be separated from sensation. And as a result, art is closely associated with nature, with the help of which man manifests his freedom via art. In this sense, nature serves as a bridge for freedom and art.

Key words: nature; freedom; art

重塑性别伦理：小说《奥兰多》的身体观和伦理愿景

巢 玥*

摘 要：《奥兰多》被公认为是伍尔夫双性同体书写的代表作，然而，当结合伍尔夫的艺术追求和20世纪初英国的社会背景，本文发现在重塑传统性别伦理的基础上，伍尔夫还诉说了自身的身体观和人类与世界融合的伦理愿景。文本通过文本细读，探讨小说中的性别“戏谑”描写、双性同体的身体在场和伍尔夫对人类与世界浑然一体之美的追求，揭示伍尔夫在一战后对人类身体和人类命运的思考。

关键词：性别伦理；身体；奥兰多；浑然一体之美

引言

20世纪初，一方面，处于爱德华时代的英国社会仍受维多利亚时期严苛的道德教条的影响，另一方面，世界大战给人类身体带来毁灭性的灾难，因此英国社会的性别伦理呈现出既受传统男女二元对立的影响，又涌动出新的性别意识的杂糅特点。尤其是女性长期受到维多利亚时期道德律令的压制，伍尔夫（1966：285）曾在《女性的职业》中写道：“她想到一些事情，一些关于身体、关于激情的事情，不消说，作为女人的她，说这些事情并不合适。理智告诉她，男人如果听见她说这些，会震惊的。”作为一名作家，伍尔夫深谙女性写作的困境，她迎难而上，一反异性恋的文学传统，在《一间自己的房间》中描述了女同性恋的可能性：“‘克洛依喜欢奥利维娅’，我读道。突然，我强烈地意识到，变化何等之大。在文学中，或许第一次有了克洛依喜欢奥利维娅。”（2003：71）小说《奥兰多》创作于第一次世界大战结束后和第二次世界大战开始之间，伍尔

---

* 作者简介：巢玥（1989— ），女，陕西师范大学外国语学院讲师，研究方向：英美文学。

夫不仅在其中书写了双性同体的情感，还通过描写主人公奥兰多运用变换装扮来扮演不同的性别，打破了传统性别伦理的严格界限，体现了她对战后人类身体宿命的深刻思考和两性融合的愿景。

一 性别“戏谑”

小说《奥兰多》的主人公以 16 岁的英国贵族少年形象出场，因忠诚、迷人的气质获得女王的青睐。年迈的女王恋上少年奥兰多，利用自己的权力将奥兰多封为皇家司库和总管，这份爱情萌芽于权力等级与男权思想的土壤之上。在奥兰多看来，“女王的手是一只让人难忘的手，瘦骨嶙峋，细长的手指佝曲着，好似王位上的宝球，又似象征王权的节杖。它是那么神经质、乖戾和病态，又是那么威严，稍稍一抬就会有人头落地”(10)。显然，在奥兰多眼中，女王所代表的权力是病态的。女王认为，作为下属的奥兰多理应在情感上也服从于她，当在镜中看到奥兰多亲吻她人，在盛怒之下她将金炳宝剑击向镜子。从这一条叙事线索来看，奥兰多与女王的关系由王权主导，暴力霸蛮的行为恰是女王受制于王权思想的体现。然而，对忠诚爱情的向往又体现出她少女般的心思。从性格互相矛盾、纠结的女王身上，不难看出，在王权与男权的双重裹挟之下，女王的自我认同产生了错位。

然而，从另一条叙事线索来看则能对伍尔夫有关性别伦理的重构有进一步的认识。伍尔夫借用人物视角，描述女王眼中的少年形象：“长长的深色鬈发”，“恭敬”，“天真无邪”，“两条笔直秀美的长腿”，“一双紫罗兰色的眼睛”(11)。女王用这些原属于女性的身体和性格特质来评价少年奥兰多，还将奥兰多秀气的外形与天真的性格解读为男子气概，与传统男权话语所描述的坚毅的外形和刚强性格恰好相反。这不同寻常的描述看似体现了王权对性别的曲解和上级对下级的权力，实则是伍尔夫有意将男性气概与女性特质颠倒，从而混淆性别话语的界限，通过讽刺现实生活中人们对男女特质的刻板印象，来颠覆传统性别伦理的禁锢。

一天，奥兰多一觉醒来发现自己变成女儿身。此后她再次邂逅曾经没有赴约与自己私奔的罗马尼亚女大公，而这一次，大公是以男性姿态出现在她面前的。原来，罗马尼亚女大公先前被作为男性的奥兰多深深吸引，为了能够接近他，故意男扮女装化身为女大公。如今，罗马尼亚大公发现奥兰多是女性，便展开对她的追求。奥兰多与罗马尼亚大公之间的误会不免让读者觉得啼笑皆非，可在感叹这戏谑般的情节背后，我们还能体验到一丝丝的熟悉和真实，那就是现实中受制于传统性别伦理所导致的性别偏见。所以，罗马尼亚大公的变装和奥兰多的变性看似超乎现实逻辑，实际则是伍尔夫借助对性别的戏谑来讽刺僵化的传统性别伦理观。这样对性别的处理看似颇有些玩笑成分，脱离了现实生活中人们对性别的普遍认知，然而，历经两种性别的奥兰多，分别以男性眼光和女性眼光看待世界，背后蕴藏着伍尔夫打破传统性别伦理界限，构建双性同体性别伦理的愿望。

虽然奥兰多体验过两种性别，事实上，男性身份和女性身份对奥兰多来说并不是单一的性别认同问题，因为当他穿上以往的男士装束，就可以继续以男性身份出现。在变性之后，奥兰多仍然经常穿上少年时期的装束，以男性身份示人，没有人发现男士装扮的奥兰多其实是女子。可见，在文本对性别的戏谑的表面之下，暗含着伍尔夫超越传统性别伦理的身体观念。根据法国身体现象学家梅洛-庞蒂（2008：325）提出的“触—被触”概念，事物是“我”的身体的延伸，“我”的身体是世界的延伸，通过这种延伸，世界就在“我”的周围——虽然“我”不能触及我的运动，然而这种运动完全是在和“我”的接触中构成的。这里的身体并非指狭义的躯体，而是融合躯体与心灵的身体。两种性别的装扮是奥兰多身体的延伸，“衣服能改变我们对世界的看法，也改变世界对我们的看法”（107），因为“性别虽有不同，男女两性却是混杂的，每个人身上，都发生从一性向另一性摇摆的情况，往往只是服装显示了男性或女性的外表，而内里的性别则恰恰与外表相反。对由此产生的复杂和混乱，人人都有亲身体验”（108）。与其说她能够通过变换装束和变性驾驭两种性别，不如说，双性同体便是她的身体在场和世界在她身上的体现，通过换装，既作为男性，也作为女性，她/他可以与世界进行双重对话，同时也用自己的身体的延伸来颠覆传统性别的限制。

二　双性同体的身体观

身体既是活生生的体验结构，同时也是认知的物理机制；身体既是内在的，又是外在的，是包括全部知觉在内的现象学的身体（梅洛-庞蒂，2005：303）。伍尔夫在重塑性别伦理的基础上，用小说人物的身体知觉表达其理想的身体观，用双性同体的身体冲破维多利亚时代对身体施加的道德律令，体现了伍尔夫将身体视为世界的第一见证者在文学中的应用。

奥兰多想成为文学家，一直混迹于伦敦的文学圈。然而，鉴于诗人蒲柏对女性才智上的偏见，她无法就文学与诗人侃侃而谈，为他斟茶倒水倒成为自然而然的事情。“女人很清楚，才子虽请她过目诗作，称赞她的判断力，征求她的意见，喝她的茶，但这绝不表示他尊重她的意见，欣赏她的理解，也绝不表示虽不能用剑，他就会拒绝用笔刺穿她的身体。”（123）在蒲柏看来，女性喜怒无常、难以捉摸，因此，他主张得体、节制、明智。奥兰多因给他端茶时打了个喷嚏，糖块扑通一声掉进茶杯，蒲柏便用男权的眼光审视她，讥讽她不得体。奥兰多带着滚烫的双颊走到花园中才如释重负，与男权主义者蒲柏的相处让她发现，“才智尽管很神圣，却栖身在肮脏的躯壳之内，头脑太大，心胸就给挤得透不过气来”（123）。这是伍尔夫借奥兰多之口影射现实中的英国诗人蒲柏对待女性的态度，因为他曾在《道德论》的第二篇信札《给一位女士》中谈论女性性格特征与道德的关系：“大多数女人根本就谈不上有什么性格”（Pope，1966：599）。

当奥兰多开始审视自己，发现虽在男权对女性进行道德归罪的高压之下做了女人多年，却并没有因为道德专制而束缚住自己的身体，“她站在镜前左顾右盼，发现自己虽穿衬裙多年，腿脚依然活动自如，这才放了心”（124）。她脱去女性装束，拿出多年前的黑色天鹅绒衣裤穿上，俨然一位翩翩少年的样子出了门，是对蒲柏所宣扬的“得体、节制、明智”的女性特质的一种反叛。

以男性装束出门的奥兰多碰到一位站在街头的妓女，并跟随她回到她的住处。她为了讨好这位“客人”，开始涂脂抹粉。然而奥兰多却能看出她的心不在焉。直到奥兰多承认自己其实是女人，这位姑娘自在地大笑起来，完全放下了恳求和感伤地讨好男人的作态。在奥兰多眼里，“这姑娘的谈吐虽然粗俗，但比起她习惯了的文雅辞令，却像美酒一样醉人”（126）。从文本表面看，这是奥兰多被她自在的美而吸引，然而在情节叙述的背后，伍尔夫用双性同体的奥兰多解构了妓女讨好男性的社会现象，又用奥兰多赞赏妓女的视角解构了社会话语对妓女的诟病，她用这些看似荒诞的情节颠覆了传统的性别伦理。

奥兰多通过变装在男性和女性之间穿梭：

> 上午，穿一件分不清男女的中国袍子，在书中徜徉……此后，到

花园里给坚果树剪枝，这时穿齐膝的短裤很方便；然后换一件塔夫绸花衣，这最适合乘车去里齐蒙德，听取某位尊贵的贵族的求婚；然后回到城里，穿一件律师的黄褐色袍子，到法院去听她的案子有何进展……最后，夜幕降临，她多半会从头到脚变成一个彻头彻尾的贵族，到街上去冒险。(127)

不断换装的奥兰多发现自己可以游刃有余地游走于男人和女人之间，轻而易举地拿捏两种性别，从而找到了身体与世界接触的独特方式。“她的性别变化之频繁，是那些只穿一类服装的人所无法想象的。她用这种办法获得了双重收获，生活的乐趣和阅历都因此增加，可以轮番享受两性的爱。”（127）作为男性时，他敏感、善良；作为女性时，她又独立刚毅，融合了两种性别优势的奥兰多成为男女两性互补的完美存在。当奥兰多能够让脑中的男性因素和女性因素达到平衡，她最终完成了耗费毕生心血的诗集《大橡树》，对文学的追求让奥兰多看到世界，并被世界看见。她问道：“难道写诗不是一种秘密的交流，即一个声音对另一个声音的回应？”（192）变换性别并不是目的，诗歌才是奥兰多与世界的对话的载体，是她给予世界的回应。

两种性别的身体经验让奥兰多从对性别持有偏见走到两性融合。一开始“她说不清自己到底是男是女，因为她洞悉个中奥秘，兼有两性的弱点。她招惹两性对立，轮番发现两性都有可悲的缺陷，因此不能确定自己此身谁属，也就不足为奇”（146）。分别体验了两种性别的偏见，奥兰多才最终明白双性同体观的重要性。其实，奥兰多究竟是以男性形象还是以女性形象示人并不重要，形象与性别的转换让她从性别的刻板印象抽离出来，以不断变化的姿态建构多元的主体性。伍尔夫的双性同体观描绘了一个和谐的理想社会，这里没有传统意义的“第一性”“第二性”男女性属的二元对立，没有强加在女性身上的男权社会的价值秩序、社会规范及文化意识（郑茗元，2018：76）。可见，双性同体是伍尔夫发掘小说人物身体感觉，探索真实自我的手段，她将“男女性属的二元论”对性别的遮蔽揭开，体现了对建构更为包容的性别伦理的期望。

三 浑然一体之美的愿景

有评论认为伍尔夫对双性同体的文学形象塑造主要源于其女性主义的

政治立场，因为伍尔夫早在20世纪初就提出了20世纪80年代女性主义思潮提出的摒弃男女二元对立的双性同体观（蔡芳、谢葆辉，2005：33）。的确，伍尔夫的双性同体思想比女性主义理论超前，但并不意味着伍尔夫对双性同体的文学呈现仅仅止步于女性主义所涉及的两性融合。实际上，她在文学中建构双性同体的性别伦理来源于她对身体的重视。伍尔夫曾批判道："文学尽其最大努力强调它关注的是心灵，而躯体则是一片白玻璃，通过它能直接而清楚地看到心灵，除了诸如愿望和贪心等一两个欲求外，它是毫无价值、微不足道和不存在的。恰恰相反，这种说法的对立面才是真实的。"（2016：113）因此，伍尔夫的文学理想不仅包含两性融合，还有对身心融合以及人类身体与世界融合的深远追求，正如梅洛-庞蒂所说，对于作家来说，可感的身体就像生命一样是有许多东西可说的宝库（2008：322）。伍尔夫力求在文学中描写两种性别身体的感性体验，建构积极主动的伦理身体，不仅超越了性别的界限，也超越了人的界限，将自然纳入其中。

当奥兰多感到与怀有性别偏见的蒲柏之间存在交流困难，她将目光投向自然，发现"谷仓与大树，谷垛与马车的某些随意搭配，会给我们一个完美的象征，象征那些可望而不可即的东西，于是我们又开始了追求"（124）。消弭性别壁垒，进行真实的交流看似可望而不可即，但她体察到在人之外的自然中，即便是谷仓与大树，谷垛与马车也能构成和谐的画面，受此触动，奥兰多开始继续对文学的追求。在自我与自然的融合中，奥兰多感到愉悦，从乡间的居所中获得慰藉：

> 她眺望花园，遐想酣睡的番红花、休眠的大丽菊，看到仙女们袅娜的白色身影在雪地和大片的紫杉丛中闪现，那些紫杉丛在漆黑夜幕的衬托下，浓密如房屋。她看到柑橘园和参天的欧楂树。她从这一切以及我们粗粗记下的每一景象、每一声响中得到慰藉，心中充满渴望和欢乐。（159）

城市生活充满追名逐利，乡村生活让奥兰多获得久违的快乐，酣睡的花和郁郁葱葱的植物展现出一片祥和又具有生命力的和谐美景。不仅如此，她发觉自己的身体与自然紧密相连，当她走进一片沼泽地，被植物的根绊倒在地，耳边是秃鼻鸭的笑声，鼻尖是绣线菊的香气，她说："我找

到了自己的伴侣，那就是沼泽。我是大自然的新娘。”（144）

> 所有这些年，对树林古老的低吟，对农庄和门边的枣红马，对铁匠铺、厨房、辛辛苦苦孕育出的麦子、芜菁和青草的田野，对鸢尾和贝母花怒放的花园，她作出了踟蹰的回应，还有什么能比这些回应更神秘、更舒缓、更似恋人之间的交媾呢？（193）

听古树的低吟，感受农田里的庄稼，给大自然以踟蹰的回应，奥兰多与自然达成了人伦最高级别的融合，构成一股抵抗现实中工业化社会弊病的力量。做自然的新娘，聆听自然的声音，与动植物对话，奥兰多与自然的互动还描绘出一幅人与自然和谐共生的图景，在经历战争洗劫后的时代，这幅生机盎然的画面尤显得珍贵。以沼泽为伴，视天地为自我归宿的生态观念也映射出“一战”后遭受苦难的人类对自然家园的向往。由此可见伍尔夫希望构建和谐的天人合一的自然生态观，宣扬应摒弃人类中心主义的观念，要“与大自然同呼吸共悲喜”（Woolf，1992：170）。有研究分析伍尔夫的伦理观属于女性伦理观，即从女性视角出发来构建男女关系以及人与社会的关系等（郑茗元，2018：175）。然而，通过伍尔夫想要建构男女和谐，人与自然和谐的伦理愿景已经可以看出，其伦理观超越了性别界限，且源于一种更广阔的世界观和身体认知。

根据梅洛-庞蒂的身体现象学，人类最终要通过世界的肉身来理解身体——世界的肉身，就是被看—存在，就是一个显著地被知觉的存在，正是通过世界的肉身，我们能够理解知觉（2008：319）。奥兰多通过大自然的肉身感悟到自身，与自然界的对话让她体验大自然的拥抱，体会到个体身体的存在。虽然在伍尔夫所处的时代，梅洛-庞蒂的身体现象学还未出现，但伍尔夫的文学创作已经有意无意地表达了她对身体的认知以及对个体身体与世界融合的认识。这种意识并非偶然，童年时，伍尔夫在圣艾夫斯的花园里发现了花朵与世界的关系，当她看到花坛中的植物“舒展着嫩绿的叶子，突然感觉一切都豁然开朗，花朵本身就是世界的一部分；黄土围住的才是花，是真正的花：既是花朵，又是世界”（伍尔夫，2016：83）。这是伍尔夫最早关于审美的认识，她发现“整个世界就是一件艺术品；我们都是这艺术品的组成部分。我们就是语言，我们就是艺术，我们就是事物本身”（伍尔夫，2016：85）。她将其称为“浑然一体的美”（Wholeness）[①]（伍尔夫，2016：83）。

浑然一体的美不仅涉及双性同体的文学视域，如德里克·莱恩（Derek Ryan）所说，伍尔夫的作品呈现了对物质世界新的理解，其中人类和非人类之间普遍存在的以及亲密的缠绕处于重要的地位（2013：4）。她打破了西方科学主义将人类身体感知降格的秩序和用理性把握外部世界的传统，在她的小说中，人物之外的物质和世界，包括动植物，常与小说人物的身体之间有着极为紧密的联系，这也是为什么奥兰多要做自然的新娘，并且虽在现实生活中遭遇文学交流的挫折，却能从外部世界中找到继续追求的动力的原因。性别本是自然的馈赠，人类给性别施加了原本不属于它们的话语，造成两种性别进行交流的障碍，奥兰多反观自然界，全身心地感受自然，给予自然回应，其亲密程度完全不亚于情侣之间的亲昵，达成自我与自然界的融合。这浑然一体之美不但跨越了性别界限，也超越了人与自然的边界。让人类在自然界中感受自己的身体存在，是伍尔夫用艺术的形式给战后荒原般的世界开出的一剂良方。

结语

弗吉尼亚·伍尔夫在伦敦的住所于“一战”期间被炸毁，与丈夫伦纳德都被列入希特勒的黑名单。1927 年，在“一战”过去十年后，45 岁的伍尔夫开始创作《奥兰多》，这部作品不乏伍尔夫对战后人类命运的体察和思考。她从超越男女性别的伦理界限出发，构建人类与自然共生的和谐图景，双性同体不是她的创作目的，只是手段。她在文学生涯中一以贯之地追求浑然一体之美，《奥兰多》中的少年奥兰多与女性奥兰多“合而为一”，体现了她对男性与女性和谐共存的希冀。“合而为一”是伍尔夫对浑然一体之美追求的文学表征，在战争和工业革命的背景下，人与自然，男性与女性，个体与他人之间的距离越来越远，而她则在文学中力求各方面的融合共生，试图从文学审美的角度为遭遇现代性重重危机的人类提供出路。

① 本文参照刘春芳、倪爱霞的译本，将《存在的瞬间》中伍尔夫提到的“wholeness”译为“浑然一体的美”。

参考文献

Pope, A. Epistle to A Lady. *The Poems of Alexander Pope*. Newhaven: Yale University Press, 1966: 599.

Ryan, D. *Virginia Woolf and the Materiality of Theory: Sex, Aninmal, life*. Edingburh: Edingburh Univeristy Press, 2013: 4.

Woolf, V. *Virginia Woolf*. A Woman's Essays. Ed. Rachel Bowlby. Hwrmondsworth: Penguin, 1992: 170.

Woolf, V. "Professions for Women." *Collected Essays*. London: Hogarth Press, 1966: 285.

蔡芳、谢葆辉：《从〈奥兰多〉感悟伍尔夫小说创作的文脉：双性同体观》，《外语与外语教学》2005 年第 12 期。

[英] 弗吉尼亚·伍尔夫：《奥兰多》，林燕译，人民文学出版社 2003 年版。

[英] 弗吉尼亚·伍尔夫：《存在的瞬间》，刘春芳，倪爱霞译，花城出版社 2016 年版。

[英] 弗吉尼亚·伍尔夫：《太阳和鱼》，孔小炯，黄梅译，上海文艺出版社 2016 年版。

[英] 弗吉尼亚·伍尔夫：《一间自己的房间》，贾辉丰译，人民文学出版社 2003 年版。

[法] 莫里斯·梅洛-庞蒂：《行为的结构》，杨大春译，商务印书馆 2005 年版。

[法] 莫里斯·梅洛-庞蒂：《可见的与不可见的》，罗国祥译，商务印书馆 2008 年版。

郑茗元：《弗吉尼亚·伍尔夫当代文论思想研究》，中国水利水电出版社 2018 年版。

Reconstruction of Gender Ethics—Body Ideal and Ethics Vision of *Orlando*

Chao Yue

Abstract: Though *Orlando* is widely recognized as a representative of

Virginia Woolf's androgyny narrative, combined with Woolf's art pursuit and British social background in the early 20th century, this essay puts that Woolf was trying to tell her concept of body and integration of human being and the nature based on her endeavors on constructing gender ethics of androgyny. Thus, this essay discusses the bantering narratives of genders, androgynous body presence and Woolf's ideal of "Wholeness" in an effort to reveal Woolf's reflections on human body and destiny after the First World War.

Key words: gender ethics; body; Orlando; "Wholeness"

语言与文化

从翻译忠实性看网络热词英译的语用意义

——以2019年度热门网络用语英译为例

吕敏宏　杨　澜*

摘　要：在翻译过程中，源语文本与目标文本之间的信息不对称情况时有发生，其原因之一在于二者语用预设不对称。语用预设的差异，根本上而言，是由双方文化环境不对称的现状造成的。从翻译的忠实性角度分析时下网络热词的英译，有助于我们把握翻译的基本原则和方向，探究具体翻译现象。本文尝试结合翻译的忠实观及语用预设理论，对受众群体较广的网络热词译例进行客观分析，将原文与译文进行多层对比，深入描述文化现象，并对这些译例作出尝试性解释。

关键词：忠实性；语用预设；网络热词；翻译

引言

新词语指形式、结构和内容在以往词汇系统中不存在，或者虽存在却与之前使用有很大差异的全新的词语。新词语能够比较客观地反映当前社会和时代的发展。从词汇系统的历时层面分析，在社会发展的高峰期，产生新词语的概率和频率都更高。自1978年改革开放以来的四十几年间，整个国家各行各业处于高速发展的黄金时代，语言以凸显个性的方式来记录社会发展中“人”的个性的彰显。（赵艳梅，2018）反映在语言系统中的便是新词汇的产生及自身意义的延伸。

新词语的生成主要有三种类型：迎合当下交际趋势所生成的词语，原

---

* 作者简介：吕敏宏（1968—　），女，陕西师范大学外国语学院教授，研究方向：翻译理论与实践。杨澜（1993—　），女，广东省中山市中山一中铁城中学教师，研究方向：翻译理论与实践，英语教学。

有词语语义变迁和延伸形成的词语，以及借自他国他民族语言所形成的词语。一般而言，网络热词作为词汇现象，与前两类新词语生成的联系密切，通常凝结着当前社会新事物、新现象和新趋势，是当代社会的一面隐形镜子，能直观真实地反映各社群、组织以及大众间发生或出现的客观事物和现象。所谓网络热词，简言之，即借助“全能”的数字化多媒体平台和网络技术所带来的内容公开性、多向互动性、速度实时性等优势手段，在规模巨大、分散的、流动的社会上一般大众的范围内，流行一时的热门词汇或表达。

顾名思义，语用指语言应用，旨在研究一定交际情境（语境）中，人们使用语言的学问。语用研究立足于交际情境这一广阔视角，重点探究语言交际者在特定场景和情境条件下，如何对符号本体的意义产生影响，使交际意义得到准确传达。探索网络热词的丰富含义，首先应从概念意义出发，概念意义作为其字面意义，具有相对稳定性，属于意义的核心部分。然而其文化语义作为人与社会存在及社会实践互动的衍生物，属于意义的外围部分，比较容易随时代和使用群体的差异而产生不同的理解。在研究当下网络热词的含义之际，应将词语与宏观的社会结构和环境联系起来，进行共时的比较和讨论，从这个视角出发，对词语的使用语境和本质特征起决定作用的应是其文化语义，即意义的衍生部分。从翻译的忠实性视角来分析新词语中网络热词的翻译研究，对解读新词语的文化语义，深化对新词语翻译规律的认识有重要意义。

当前，新词语翻译研究主要基于语用对等研究模式及原则，研究问题往往大多限于对新词语的界定、特点分析、地域考察、语域划分、认知解释以及新词语分类及流行动因的探讨（汤志祥，2002；吕世生，2014）。关于新词语翻译研究所涉及的文化问题，这类研究未从语用预设与文化语义和新词语语义的本质联系上作出完整解读，在意义、内容及文化表征等的忠实性层面还需进一步纵深挖掘。

有鉴于此，本文尝试从翻译的忠实性视角分析新词语中网络热词英译的语用预设及所涉及的文化语义的内在机制。

1 翻译的忠实性

忠实性是翻译最重要的准则之一。大部分理论家都主张翻译应当对原文忠实，大多数翻译工作者也都认为自己的翻译作品能够对原文忠实。纵观中国翻译史和西方翻译史，在讨论翻译原则时，忠实观一直占据主流地位。学界对翻译忠实性的讨论主要从以下几个方面进行阐述。(1) 翻译的层次性。即“忠实于什么”的问题，是原文内容、原文形式、原文作者，抑或是译文读者及译文文化特征等的因素。发挥译语优势，将译文与原文及其他译文之间进行比较竞争，试看哪种文字能更好地表达原作的内容（许渊冲，2000）。(2) 忠实的伦理属性。翻译活动的忠实性既涉及人际关系，更涉及文际关系（王东风，2004）。(3) 在翻译的文化层面，如源语文化与目的语文化的地位、文化模式、审美观、伦理道德等方面，对翻译的忠实性进行讨论（刘亚猛，2006；马会娟，2008）。(4) 忠实的适用范围问题。如翻译的方向、翻译的体裁、翻译的题材、翻译的标准等（何瑞清、马会娟，2015）。

1.1 忠实性：“描绘”原文本的意义与精神

本文所提之“忠实”主要是从上文阐述的第二点出发，强调翻译的忠实，主要是立足于其文际关系。当前大多翻译理论者提出翻译忠实的对象包括源文本、源文本创作者、源语文化、目标语读者、目标语文化、或者跨文化交流及翻译自身的发展等。本文认为对于翻译所忠实的对象应尽量避免扩大化，从原文出发，不拘泥于原文结构，而是“描绘”出源文本的意义和精神。下面以“盘”字为例进行说明。

“盘”是今年较为流行的新词语。说到这个字，一般人都会想到“盘核桃”，“盘保健球”这个动作，在英文里面，具有对应概念意义的词语是“rotate”。但借助新媒体及网络传播的手段，这个字已经暂时形成其自身词义的变迁。最初“盘”来源于孟鹤堂、周九良的相声《文玩》，其中有句台词是这样说的：“干巴巴的，麻麻赖赖的，一点都不圆润，盘他！”。德云社是中国最知名的演出团体之一，在社会上享有极高关注度和人气，台上风趣幽默、同时蕴含多样文化内涵的相声表演，深受大众喜爱，成为炙手可热的偶像团体。受众群体庞大，年龄范围广，使相声这种中国传统文化艺术逐渐走入新媒体和大众的目光，是当下最为喜闻乐见的表演方式之一。由于其社会影响力和网友对某种意义使用的频率，使“盘”字产生更多的文化意义。一种是在面对一些令人不爽的人或事物时，它的意义多了“反抗、反对、找茬”等，在英语里便是“picky on”。它还涉及言语上的攻击，与之对应的是“slam”，“lash out”，或者“bash”。另一种意思是，当看到喜欢的事物，盘也可理解为把他/她/它捧在手心，反复揉捏，表现出“喜爱”的心情。此时，“盘”对应的英文表达便是“stroke”，或者“be fascinated by...”。基于至少两种意义方面的考虑，从翻译的忠实性角度来看，“rotate”不是理想的对应语言选择。

1.2 忠实性的限度

网络热词的翻译是一种跨文化交流行为，真正优秀的翻译必须保留文化本质，这就要求汉语的词语进入英语文化和语境的过程中，不是完全迎合外语文本的语言和文化差异，而应保留自己的本土文化特征，把握忠实原则的“度”。“扎轮胎”是词义变迁形成的新词语，其新词语的文化语义是故意作出一些破坏、捣乱或恶搞动作，对他人施以报复的一种行为。在英语中，“扎轮胎”对应的概念意义的词语是“slash tires”，意为用利器将车用的橡胶轮胎割破。在概念层面，二者的意义相似。然而，基于这一网络词汇的使用情景、目的和意图的分析研究发现，使用中的“扎轮胎”并非实施破坏车辆轮胎这一实际行为。这一词汇因中央电视台著名主持人康辉在刊播《国际锐评》时，针对近期美国对中国施加的种种打压政策和措施，表示“这些怀着怨妇心态的美方人士，看人发展就心态失衡，使出各种损招阴招扎轮胎”，央视的金句热词内容在网络上爆红，一度将这个词送上热搜。如果按照最基本的概念意义，显然美国并没有向中国实施扎破轮胎这一实际行为。故而得体地翻译成英文时，应考虑其语境意义和文化含义，即实施故意报复、捣乱行为，我们应从这个文化语义出发，寻找恰当且对应的词语或词组。“Revenge”一词的字典意义，即概念意义是“hurting or punishing someone”。“Revenge”的概念意义和“扎轮胎”的文化语义处于类似“对等”地位。这也表明文化差异的存在不足为奇，不同的文化、生活经验，交谈群体等，使不同事物的属性在人们的认知过程中凸显程度有所差异。

从以上关于网络热词英译的论述中，我们不难得出这样的结论，我们应忠实于词语的内容和风格，在摸清概念意义的前提下，将二者的文化环境考虑在内，选取较为接近源文本意义的目标词语。我们应当重视的是，即使做不到完全的忠实，翻译时，也应将译成相关词语的可行性和可能性考虑在内（Gao，2017），做到尽可能地忠实。

2 语用预设

预设分为两类，分别是语义预设和语用预设。在语义学中，预设被视为两个语义命题之间的关系，这种关系是不变的，不受语境支配的意义（Yule，1996）。后来学者发现预设对语境这一因素非常敏感，预设的信息与说话人及言外知识关系密切。Stalnaker（2002：701）将语用预设定义为交际双方共享的背景信念。“某一命题P是某个语境中说话人的语用预设，必须满足以下条件：说话人对命题P作出假设或相信命题P；说话人设想或相信听话人对命题P作出假设或相信命题P；说话人设想或相信听话人意识到自己在作出这些假设或具有这些信念。”

2.1 语用预设：文化特征

语用预设与文本的连贯性和一致性有着一定的紧密联系。贝克（1992）曾将语用预设定义为语用推断，语用预设与语言和言外知识有关，是发言者假设听众应具备或有必要具备的知识，以获得发言者的信息。不论是语言知识抑或是言外知识，理解话语的过程涉及多种因素，在这些因素中，文化因素属于最基本的因素（吕世生，2003）。它包括说话者和说话对象的情况，言语的环境因素以及对话的目的、意向等。

当下流行的汉语新词语中文化语义特征突出的这类词数量比较多，语用预设理论对这类词的翻译解释也比较充分，以“柠檬精”一词为例，“柠檬精”一词想要表达的是心里酸酸的、羡慕嫉妒恨的感觉，现多用于自嘲似的表达对他人从外貌到内在、从物质生活到感情生活的多重羡慕。汉语中柠檬的定义是“果实椭圆形，淡黄色，味酸”。中国文化中，有“拈酸吃醋”的说法。柠檬和醋都具有“酸”的特征，是中文语言文化中共享的概念，酸又有痛苦之意，人们才把拈酸吃醋与嫉妒联系起来喻指心酸，有时也称为“酸意”，“酸劲儿”。总之这个成语的汉语解释是因嫉妒而产生不快情绪。柠檬本指味酸的果实，在当下的中国文化模式下，在新媒体、网络及八亿网民的创造力影响下，这一过程生成的文化语义便是羡慕和嫉妒的一种心态和状态。从这个文化语义开始，寻找英语中与之相对应的词语，然后分析其概念和文化语义演变过程及其要素特征，以确立其是否与汉语中“柠檬”对应的人际关系。汉语中“柠檬”一词，英语中的对应词是“lemon”，其概念意义与汉语中“柠檬”一词几无差别。但是“lemon”一词在英语中的文化语义不包含“嫉妒、羡慕”之义，故而二者之间缺乏文化经验的关联，因此“lemon”一词的属性映射不到“羡慕、嫉妒”这一目标文化含义。如要寻找另一与之对应的英语词语，便需要尝试转换视角，以“柠檬”的映射特征为起点，在英语中寻找对应其文化语义特征的词语。

与汉语“柠檬精”文化语义对应的英语词语是“green with envy”或者“green-eyed”。green在英语中除了指绿色，还有妒忌之意。基于green的这一延伸意义，“green-eyed”除了有绿眼睛的意思外，还有眼红、妒忌之意。试举例示之：

例句：在他们纯洁的友谊面前，我变成了柠檬精。

译例（1）I become a lemon monster in the face of their pure friend-ship.

译例（2）I become a green-eyed person in the face of their pure friends-hip.

译例（3）I become green with envy in the face of their pure friendship.

从以上三种译文分析发现，（1）中lemon monster是字对字，词对词得出的英语翻译，在英语文化里面，是“柠檬怪物”，暂时没有眼红的含义。反之（2）和（3）中的“green-eyed”和“green with envy”，在英语文化中具有“羡慕、嫉妒、眼红”之意，故而这两个词语汉语中的“柠檬精”在文化含义上对应更为恰当工整。

从上述对网络空间流传甚广的热词英译案例研究中，我们发现，语言符号所携带的意义本身具有多义性与暧昧性，在特定的传播情境与文化环境下，会受到外部事物、条件、因素的直接或间接影响，产生区别性的情境意义，即文化语义。文化语义属于词语意义的引申部分，较容易发生变化，其自身携带较为明显的文化特征和时代印记。在许多情况下，传播情境是生成文化语义的重要机制。这一认识有助于我们以新的视角理解新词语英译，并将其运用到跨文化交流中，完善翻译实践的理论逻辑建构。

2.2 语用预设：群体性使用特征

在网络热词的翻译过程中，我们发现语义变迁形成的新词语所占比重也很大。比如：ETC一词。在当前社会文化语境中，词语意思的演变呈现出明显的非常规、非主流的特征。ETC是electronic toll collection的缩略词，意为电子不停车收费系统。ETC原是为缓和道路收费口的交通拥挤问题，加快车辆通行速度而建设的。它的一个重要特点是能够给装了ETC车载器的车辆通过收费站时，自动抬起拦路杠杆。当下在数字网络中有一句时兴语：“做人不要太ETC”。分析其使用情境和特征，“ETC”在网络上的语用含义是“抬杠”，尤指一类管不住自己的嘴巴，遇事忍不住自动抬杠的人，容易随随便便因一两句微不足道的话而辩驳，对人不对事，爱挑毛病，忽略曲解事件本身的逻辑，选取没有客观依据的观点胡说八道，也就是我们常说的“杠精”。由此看来，“抬杠”的人或“杠精”的做事风格和行为与ETC的系统工作原理比较相似。读者很快可从字面含义上推导出所指事物的引申属性，将其与现实世界的事物联系起来进行思考，从而得出背后的文化语义，生动形象，通顺流畅，忠于原意。

许多热词都关乎娱乐产业，这一现象可以从两个维度进行理解和解释。一方面，网络与娱乐产业相互补给，相互借势，相互代言，以期共同增进影响力；另一方面，当下娱乐产业声势浩大，在大众群体中喜闻乐见，娱乐新闻老少皆宜，是大多数群体熟悉亲近的领域，在日常生活中的能见度高，故而网络热词的“娱乐味”很重，同时也有着很浓郁的“生活味”，其本身便代表着大众的某种选择，是反映人们生活的一面镜子，进而影响着大众的生活。不一样的网络热词，显示出有所差异的社会和文化大环境，背后也蕴含着丰富的价值观念和人们不尽相同的对待事物的心态和立场。

值得注意的是，词语的文化语义既有多数成员共同使用的，也有个人或少数成员基于自身联想在小范围内使用的。因此，对于同一类事物，包括新词语，不同群体之间的理解未必一致。社会大众并不是同质的孤立个人的集合，他们分属于不同的社会群体和组织，具备丰富的社会多样性，在词语理解上，会得出各异的反应和解释。用具体事物来表示某种抽象概念或思想感情的行为，属于人类的象征性活动。这种行为的特点是使所表达事物的字面意义向引申意义发生转化，群体特征在转化过程中扮演着重要角色。群体特征主要包含性别、年龄、文化程度、人格特点、群体规范、个人经验经历等。这些方面作为人们理解词语意义的既有背景和倾向，潜移默化间规定着人们的态度和看法，同时对意义理解产生深刻的影响。

3 结束语

文化差异是翻译行为存在的内在驱动力，这些在社交平台上流传广、使用频率高的网络热词更是文化差异存在的显性表现。以翻译的忠实性角度分析时下流行词，有助于我们把握翻译的基本原则和方向。我们否认忠实的绝对性，在合理的范围内，可允许译者发挥个性特征，对译文进行灵活变通处理。同时，也尽量避免忠实对象与目标的扩大化，紧随原文本的意义和精神，进行靠近和复刻。对于语用预设而言，文化层面必然是最根本的因素，受到文化因素的制约和影响。语用预设的差异，根本上而言是源语和目标语的文化环境不对称造成的。再者，文化信息具有群体性。由于翻译行为是跨越时间和空间的，译文读者和原文读者的世界观，认知方式，社会环境和文化环境等都有所不同，故而会对翻译文本提出一定的群体性要求，译者应对其认知环境作出较为准确的评估，最终选出恰当贴切的意义体进行表述。

参考文献

Gao, F. Domestication? Over-Domestication?: Feasibility of Applying Chinese Internet Buzzwords in Subtitle Translation. 3rd International Conference on Education and Social Development, 2017.

Munday, J. *Introducing Translation Studies*. Routledge, British Library, 2001.

Stalnaker, R. Common Ground. *Linguistics & Philosophy*, 2002, 25 (5): 701-721.

Yule & George, *Pramatics*. Oxford: Oxford University Press, 1996.

段红鹰：《忠实与现实的矛盾——论翻译的忠实性限度》，《中国外语》2008年第4期。

冯全功：《翻译忠实观：争议与反思》，《解放军外国语学院学报》2019年第3期。

何瑞清、马会娟：《忠实始终是第一标准——评目的法则和〈翻译质量保证标准指南〉》，《天津外国语大学学报》2015年第3期。

吕世生：《语用前提对称与文化信息等值——〈红楼梦〉英译本译例分析》，《外语学刊》2003年第1期。

吕世生：《汉语新词语英译的隐喻认知模式分析》，《中国社会科学院研究生院学报》2014年第6期。

刘亚猛：《从“忠实于源文本”到“对源语文化负责”：也谈翻译规范的重构》，《中国翻译》2006年第6期。

马会娟：《论汉译英的标准：有条件的忠实》，《解放军外国语学院学报》2008年第2期。

汤志祥：《汉语新词语和对外汉语教学》，《语言教学与研究》2002年第2期。

王东风：《解构“忠实”——翻译神话的终结》，《中国翻译》2004年第6期。

赵艳梅、杨文全：《当代汉语新词语表人词语模主观性解析》，《新疆大学学报》（哲学·人文社会科学版）2018年第1期。

机构话语中的沉默言语行为与身份建构

段李敏*

摘　要：言语交际中的沉默是一种有意义的空缺言语行为，是说话人在一定交际时刻发出的一种意向性行为。沉默的含义丰富，可以表示肯定意义、否定意义及各种主观评价意义。沉默具有标记身份和调节人际关系的功能，在一定程度上体现了交际者之间的权势关系。机构话语中的沉默体现了身份的不对称和权势的不对等。强势方的沉默是其建构权势机构身份、实现机构目标的交际策略，弱势方的沉默则是无声的人格标记，是其反对权和质疑权的体现，也是一种自我保护的方式。

关键词：沉默；空缺言语行为；机构话语；身份

一　引言

作为言语交际中一种普遍存在且不可忽视的现象，“沉默”（молчание）在俄罗斯学界的研究已有 200 多年历史。20 世纪 80 年代，随着俄罗斯语言学中“人类中心主义研究范式”的兴起，“沉默”也成为俄罗斯语言学特别是语用学关注的对象。1986 年，在 Н. Д. Арутюнова 的组织和领导下，苏联科学院语言研究所成立了一个“语言的逻辑分析”（Логический анализ языка）课题组。该课题组至今已经出版 20 多部论文集，为俄罗斯语言学的发展作出了重大贡献。其中的《语言的逻辑分析——言语行动语言》（*Логический анализ языка. Язык речевых действий*）论文集中［特别是第三部分《言语行动语用学》（*Прагматика речевых действий*）］有数篇论文都以“沉默”为主题，从独特视角详细分析了沉默作

---

* 作者简介：段李敏（1981—　），女，陕西师范大学外国语学院讲师，研究方向：语用学、话语分析。

为一种言语行为在交际中发挥的重要作用。在 Арутюнова1999 年出版的《语言与人的世界》（*Язык и мир человека*）一书以及 2000 年由其主编出版的论文集《关于语言的语言》（*Язык о языке*）中收入的《沉默现象》（*Феномен молчания*）一文，更进一步深化和完善了沉默作为语用现象的理据。

二　沉默——一种有意义的空缺言语行为

（一）“沉默”的含义

1. “沉默”（молчать）与“不说话”（не говорить）

Арутюнова 之所以将沉默作为语用学的重要话题之一，是因为她认识到，“沉默是交际活动的最高形式（высшая форма коммуникативной деятельности），是表达和传递心理感受和感觉的纯粹方式”（Арутюнова 1994：178）。Арутюнова 认为，对“沉默”可以有两种理解，一是作为零言语行为（空缺言语行为）（нулевой речевой акт），二是通过语言手段（如动词“молчать”及其派生词）来描写这种零言语行为（Арутюнова 1994：106）。如果仅研究词汇意义，俄语动词 молчать（沉默）的内涵为无标记的否定特征 не говорить（不说话）。但如果从言语行为角度看，молчать 和 не говорить 的外延有很大区别。“沉默”这一概念是在“说话”这一概念的背景上形成的，也就是说，“沉默”是以“说话”为前提的。M. H. Эпштейн（2006）也明确指出：“不可说出的东西也不可沉默，因为沉默只能针对那些可以说出的东西。”但不说话并不都是沉默，沉默并不都意味着没有言语活动。只有在言语交际（现实的或虚拟的言语交际）的条件下，即有可能完成言语行为的条件下，才有沉默可言。也就是说，молчать 预设着“实施某个言语行为的可能性”，但 не говорить 并没有这个预设，可能仅仅表示没有言语活动的能力（не способность человека к речевой деятельности）。例如，婴儿不会说话可以说 Он не говорит，但不能说 Он молчит。не говорить 还表示没有掌握某种语言（невладение каким-либо конкретным языком）。例如：Он не говорит по-русски.（他不会说俄语），但是 молчать 就没有这种意义。此外，二者的区别还在于，молчать 一般表示的是自觉的、由人所控制的行为，而 не говорить 同“自我控制”则没有严格的关系（Арутюнова 1994：107-108，2000：418—419）。

2. “沉默”（молчание）与“寂静”（тишина）

许多学者在研究“沉默”时，都将其与“寂静”进行了区分。Арутюнова（2000：433）形象地将二者进行了易位：“寂静是一种转移到人类世界的自然现象，沉默是一种转移到自然世界的人为现象。”寂静对于所有人都是一样的，但沉默却因人而异。寂静没有主观性和人称，而沉默既有主观性，也有人称。Эпштейн（2006）也指出，寂静没有主题，没有发出者，例如，不能说 тишина о чём-то *，或者 быть тихим о чём-то *。寂静只是一种自然的现实的状态，而沉默则是由主体发出的针对客体的行为。М. М. Бахтин 也明确区分了“沉默”与“寂静”，他（1979：338）指出：“用声音打破寂静是机械性的、生理性的（作为一种感知条件），而用话语打破沉默则是有意义的……在寂静中，什么都不发出声音（或某些东西不发出声音），而在沉默中，没有人说话（或某个人不说话）。”尽管“沉默”和“寂静”在形式上都是“没有声音”，但是沉默在结构上更接近于说话，与说话一样有着意识中的针对性，正如 Гуссерль 所说，沉默也是一种意识形式，是意识的发声方式，在下列各种形式中占有合理的地位：думать о……，говорить о……，спрашивать о……，писать о……，молчать о……（Эпштейн 2006）。将“沉默”与“寂静”区别开来，能够进一步明确沉默的主观性、人称性和意向性，也是研究沉默言语行为及其交际功能的语用基础。

（二）沉默的类型及其语用含义

沉默言语行为有其原因（Почему/отчего ты молчишь?）和动机。例如：Я предпочел молчать, так как боялся обидеть мальчика（我选择沉默，因为害怕伤害男孩）。作为一种有意义的“空缺言语行为”，对沉默的理解必然离不开语境。也就是说，只有在实际的言语交际中，沉默才能获得具体的语用含义。沉默行为的特征不仅决定了动词 молчать 的外延，还决定了其使用的语境。沉默用于规约程度不同的交际语境。其中最规范的就是对话。在对话中，作为空缺言语行为的“沉默”体现得最为明显。“沉默既是会话内容的组成部分，也是话语建构的一种方式。”（彭艳虹 2007：26）对话沉默是言语反应的缺失，可能由不同的原因引起。对话中的沉默是一种有意的行为，沉默背后往往隐藏着某种对立、拒绝、怀疑和反对。受话人也可能通过沉默来表示其不会阻碍说话人的行为，但也不想承担责任。沉默还可以表示不回答、对召唤不回应、不提供信息、由于害怕或规避不良后果而不表态、不反对、不干预等，还可以表达不置可否、故作深沉、犹豫不定等丰富多样的含义（Арутюнова 1994：110）。对话中的沉默既是对上一话轮反应的缺失，同时也是对继续谈话的刺激的缺失。交际中言语的空缺不等于说话人意向的空缺，相反，是其有意识或潜意识运用“沉默”这一方式来传递更为丰富的语用意义，所谓“此时无声胜有声”，沉默本身就成为一种有力的武器。沉默指的是没有言语活动，但不是所有的对话空白都能用 молчать 来描述。由于 молчать 同 говорить 一样，不属于施为动词，不能明示语力（иллокутивная сила），因此不能描述施为性言语行为的空缺、礼节性言语行为及礼貌的空缺（лакуны вежливости）。也就是说，并不是所有的空缺言语都属于对话沉默（диалогическое молчание）的范畴（Арутюнова 1994：110）。

除了对话沉默外，还有一种“社交沉默”（светское молчание），表现为在社交场合中的沉默，不参与对话、不交换意见、不参加活动等。社交沉默是在社团中以及人际和家庭关系中表现得不爱说话、默默无闻。例如：Все пели，а он молчал（大家在唱歌，而他默不作声）；В обществе он больше молчал（在社交场合他多半默不作声）。这里的沉默具有量化意义，即参与言语活动的相对比例。此时沉默呈现了人的心情和一般的行为或性格特点（Арутюнова 1994：111），体现了个体层面的身份特征。

Арутюнова 区分出的第三种类型的沉默为“社会沉默”（молчание в социальном контексте）。这类沉默指的是对侵犯他人尊严和人权的行为不作回应和反抗，也就是不履行道德义务。如：Его задевают，а он молчит（他被人羞辱，而他却默不作声）。这种沉默意味着软弱和恭顺。认为沉默不违反禁忌的观点是一种“弱道德”立场。而在“强道德”的框架下，沉默无异于撒谎、背叛等负面行为。如：Сбили самолёт с детьми，а телевидение молчит：как лгали，так и лгут（一辆载着儿童的飞机被击落，而电视台却保持沉默：一如既往地撒着慌）。要完成“强道德”的要求，不能用反义词 молчать – говорить，而要对沉默加以否定，如：Писатели не молчат（作家不会沉默）（Арутюнова 1994：112）。尽管 молчать 与受话人没有配价关系，但是 не молчать 隐含了“被听到”之意，而 говорить 尽管与受话人有配价关系，但却仅限于说话人的范围。试比较 Я не молчал（我没有沉默）和 Я говорил（我说了），前者指具有效果的行动，而后者仅仅是悬而未决的言语。

除了 Арутюнова 之外，还有许多学者也将沉默视为一种有意义的言语行为或交际行为。Корнилова（2002：215）认为，沉默是一种多功能的交际单位，在一定的社会作用条件下充当交际策略。她（2001）将交际看作沉默言语行为和其他言语行为在不同比例之下不断互动的过程。Формановская 认为，不能将沉默看作是一个单独的言语行为（единый речевой акт），因为这一行为背后隐藏着各种不同的意向和情感意义。沉默可以表示拒绝，也可以表示同意，可以表示不知道，也可以表示委屈、责备、不满等。有意义的沉默往往伴随着一些非言语交际手段，如表情、神态、动作等。因此，她认为，将具有交际意义的沉默看作是表达意向意义的非言语交际手段较为合理（Формановская，2002：119）。沉默是听话人的角色责任和礼貌合作行为（不打断对方的话、认真聆听、听对方说完等），听话人在交际中发出自己参与其中的言语和非言语信号，如点头，注视，发出 угу 一类的感叹词等，从而确认自己对于交流的关注与理解。这种听话人的"规范的"沉默符合说话人的期待。与此不同，另一种类型的沉默是说话人的沉默，当对方期待其发出言语时，他却一言不发。这种情况下，就要根据上下文、交际场景和环境以及交际双方的相互关系等，将沉默解释成一种具有意向性、情感性和评价性的独特言语行为。沉默可能表示同意（例如"默认"）、不愿回答、很难找的合适的词、拘谨、犹豫不决、责备、指责、委屈等。因此沉默可以被解释为一种特殊的言语行为，一种非言语交际要素（Формановская，2002：207）。Я. В. Шабанова 认为，作为一种言语行为，沉默的命题内容就是零位叙事行为（нулевая локутивная сила），真诚条件是说话人和听话人都应该理解该言语行为的恰当性。发话人（即沉默一方）刻意使用沉默来达到一定的目的，即影响交际对象（即受话人）。与其他言语行为不同的是，沉默言语行为没有严格规定的预定条件和本质条件，需要密切结合语境和话语参数对其作出解释（Шабанова，2007：185—186）。

总之，沉默这一现象本身是复杂的，甚至是"自相矛盾的。一方面，沉默是言语形式、信息和互动的缺失，是空白，是封闭；另一方面，沉默又代表着感受的深刻、立场的严肃和能量的积蓄"（Шабанова 2007：183）。作为空缺言语行为的沉默与其他任何言语行为一样，是说话人在一定交际时刻发出的一种意向性表述，只是这种表述所使用的言语形式为零，而"形式上的缺失使其更具想象空间和隐含意义"（李凤琴，2010：

57)。言语交际中的沉默具有多重意义，既可以表示否定意义，也可以表示肯定意义，还能表示各种主观评价意义，能够传达丰富的信息，反映交际者的心理活动，可以作为建构身份的有力手段。

三 机构话语中的沉默与身份

（一）机构话语与身份

机构话语（институциональный дискурс）是机构语境中的言语事件，是在特定组织和机构中生产和传播的话语，是“社会群体或机构代表在业已形成的社会机构框架内进行的言语互动”（Карасик，2002）。在机构话语研究中，身份研究是重点之一。一方面是因为，近年来，不同学科都在广泛关注“身份”这一议题，身份的话语建构观逐步确立；另一方面则是因为“身份”是机构话语的核心，机构话语的机构属性取决于话语行为和内容与交际者的机构身份之间的相关性（Drew & Heritage，1992）。“身份”这一概念含义丰富，其本质是关于“我是谁?”“我属于哪一群体?”“‘自我’”与“‘他者’的关系如何?”的问题。本文从语用学角度，将“身份”界定为“交际者在言语互动中为满足交际需要对自我和他人的定位”。该定义强调了身份的话语建构性，既包括对自我和他人个人层面的身份定位，又包括人际层面和社会群体层面的身份定位。机构身份通常是成对出现的，学界习惯上称之为机构代表（агент）和客户（клиент）。如教师和学生、神甫和教民、医生和病人、记者和读者（听众、观众）等（Карасик，2002）。这种基本的“角色关系对”，或者说是“默认身份”（Richards，2006）之间的互动就构成了机构话语的内核。机构话语是一种“特点鲜明的不对称交际”（王晋军，2007：24），这种不对称体现在话题的不对称和交际任务的不对称，但本质上还是机构身份的不对称。机构语境下的交际者处于身份不对称和权势不对等的状态，但这种状态并非固定不变，有时，机构交际者也会通过各种方式展开权力的动态争夺和身份的动态抗衡。身份是在话语实践中建构起来的，反过来也在某种程度上决定着话语方式的选择。

（二）沉默与身份

Карасик（1991：56）也认为，沉默具有交际意义。他借鉴 В. В. Богданов（1990）的观点，将沉默分为“为了说话的沉默”（молчание для говорения）和“代替说话的沉默”（молчание вместо говорения）。前者

与对话中的话轮交替有关。通常情况下，对话过程中，话轮主导者会力图控制话轮，即保持其说话人的角色，而沉默就是对话中地位相对较低者的标记。“代替说话的沉默”含义十分丰富。按照 Богданов 的观点，这种沉默可以表示对上一话轮的赞同，也可以表示不愿说话，犹豫不决，遵守礼貌原则等。沉默在一定程度上体现了交际者之间的权势关系。不愿说话可能是说话人不愿意与身份地位较低的群体交往的标志。这种情况下沉默就成为身份地位较高者的标记。沉默也可能是被支配者的语言，是“无权者的语言”（Moreau，1984：47）。“在不同地位的交际者之间，位尊者的沉默显示出权威和霸气，而位卑者的沉默则暗示着顺应和服从”（Sifianou，1997：68）。Крестинский 曾划分出了沉默的十八种交际功能，其中的“角色标记功能”（ролемаркирующая функция）和“社会角色功能”（социально-ролевая функция）都与身份密切相关。前者是指沉默能够标记行为主体在对话中的交际角色，后者是指沉默能够标记交际者在社会等级结构中的社会角色（Крестинский，2010：213）。沉默除了能够标记身份之外，还具有调节人际关系的功能。Jenson（1973）曾总结出沉默的 5 种功能，每一种均有其正反两面，其中的合分功能就是表示联结或分离说听双方的关系（彭艳虹，2007：27）。

（三）机构话语中的沉默与身份

日常话语中，沉默随处可见，如夫妻吵架时一方的沉默。机构话语中，沉默也普遍存在，如法庭话语中被告的沉默、警察询问中犯罪嫌疑人的沉默、企业管理话语中下属的沉默、课堂话语中学生的沉默等。受机构规则的制约，机构代表拥有机构赋予的权力，同时也应当履行机构的职责，按照机构约定的话语规则展开其话语，通过机构互动最终达到机构的既定目标。鉴于此，机构代表的话语中一般很少出现沉默现象，因为如果沉默则代表其不履行机构职责，言语行为上“不作为”。例如，政府新闻发布会中，无论记者提出什么样的问题，发言人都没有沉默的权利，必须作出回应。而非机构代表的机构权势相对较低，其身份不代表机构，因此受机构制约相对较小，有时可以通过沉默来表达某种语用意图，从而建构某种身份，巩固其在机构话语中的地位。正如费尔克拉夫所说，“保持沉默是 N-P（即 non-powerful，不强大的参与者，即权势较低者）在不平等会谈中的典型防范手段”（费尔克拉夫，2003：147）。但从另一方面来看，机构话语中权势较高者如果一旦沉默，则沉默就成了其权力的标记，

“P（powerful，强大的参与者，即权势较高者）而非 N-P 可以实际上不必说话便拥有‘操纵发言权’的权利，例如，保持沉默以作为一种重申某人控制的方式，或是作为含蓄批评他人的方式”（费尔克拉夫，2003：143）。可见，机构语境下，沉默是特定身份的体现，既可以被用作一种权力来源，也可也被当成一种反抗形式。下面通过几种不同类型的机构话语实例，分析沉默言语行为如何体现身份的不对称和权势的不对等，如何参与身份建构过程。

1. *法庭话语*

在当代刑事诉讼发展史上，众所周知“米兰达警告”。美国联邦最高法院在 1966 年米兰达诉亚利桑那州一案的判例中，最终确立了米兰达规则。按照该规则，警方强制讯问之前，必须告知“米兰达警告”，即“你有权保持沉默，但如果放弃沉默权，你所说的一切均有可能成为法庭上不利于你的证据……”（卡罗尔，2012：146）。许多国家的法律中都明确规定，犯罪嫌疑人、被告人被赋予沉默权。沉默权是犯罪嫌疑人、被告人面对官方讯问时的诉讼权利，是刑事诉讼的基本权利，反映了警察与犯罪嫌疑人之间怀疑与辩解、公诉人与被告之间指控与辩护的关系（王戬，2013：29）。但目前我国现行的刑事诉讼和宪法规范中还没有赋予被告人沉默权，因此，我国庭审中被告人无权用沉默的方式拒绝回答公诉人或其他机构代表的提问。机构交际中，沉默有时能达到某种施为用意，但有时却适得其反。在法庭上，原被告或者证人的沉默可能会被理解为对某证据没有异议而被法官采信，也可能会被法官看作是藐视法庭，从而影响其形象和信誉，甚至对审判结果产生影响。但一般情况下，当非机构代表由于某种原因沉默时，机构代表会通过重新问话或者直接要求等方式迫使非机构代表对问题作出回答。因此，权势地位较低的非机构代表的沉默与否在一定程度上受到权势地位较高的机构代表的控制。

例（1）

辩护人：在此之前，你是否受到过刑事或者行政处分？
被害人：有过行政处罚。
辩护人：被行政处罚过几次？
被害人：前后一共有三次。
辩护人：为什么被行政处罚呢？

被害人：**（沉默）**

辩护人：邱××，请你回答，你为什么被行政处罚呢？

被害人：因为盗窃。

（2015年6月18日福州市××区人民法院刑事审判庭依法公开审理××区检察院起诉的刘××、王××抢劫、绑架案庭审笔录）

该例中，辩护人试图证明被告人没有抢劫与绑架，而只是在帮助那些被被害人邱××盗窃的受害人要回财物。辩护人在询问被害人时，一步一步让被害人陷入自己的设定，即让被害人自己说出自己是盗窃惯犯的事实。在被害人沉默时，辩护人并未就此止步，而是要求被害人回答，最终说出了自己因为盗窃被行政处罚三次的事实。可见，法庭上对非机构代表的沉默的干涉是机构代表建构其权势身份的方式之一。

2. 医患话语

在医患话语中，医患双方都会使用沉默作为一种交际手段或交际策略。医患关系的不对称决定了医患话语中医生掌握着更多的话语权，其沉默是自由随意的，是其权力的一种反映。

例（2）

（背景：60多岁男性眼病患者就医）

1 患者家属：大夫您好，我们是神经内科过来的，需要在这儿进行一下眼科会诊。（将会诊申请单递给医生）

2 医生：（**沉默**，在电脑上开检查单，打印，递给患者）去10号诊室检查。

3 患者：10号诊室？好的，谢谢！

（检查结束后，患者将检查报告递给医生）

4 医生：（看了一眼检查报告，**沉默**，写病历和开处方）

5 患者：大夫，我这干眼症严重，有啥办法？

6 医生：（**沉默**，写病历和处方）

7 患者：看了好几家医院了，没缓解。

8 医生：（**沉默**，写病历和处方，将打印好的病历和处方递给患者）回去滴眼药吧！

9 患者家属：他还有其他症状，眼皮眨得很厉害，也是干眼症引起的?

10 医生:(**沉默**)

11 患者:眼药滴了没用,滴了大半年了,看了好几家医院,还有白内障,你看还有啥治疗的办法?

12 医生:干眼症本来就不能根治!

13 患者家属:那您看还要做啥检查?

14 医生:(**沉默**)

15 患者:要不要查一下眼底?

16 医生:你要查就查吧!

(2019 年 12 月 26 日西安某医院眼科门诊)

该例中,医患会话一开始,医生既没有询问病情,也没有给患者陈述病情的机会,而是直接让患者去检查。拿到检查单之后,也未对患者的疾病进行诊断,而是直接开始写病历和开处方,这意味着此次医患会话即将进入结束阶段。到此时为止,医生只说了一句话。但患者(及家属)求助心切,主动向医生陈述既往症状和就医历史,以寻求治疗方案,而医生对患者的问话进行回应的主要方式就是沉默。在患者对医生给出的治疗方案(滴眼药)提出质疑之后,医生才说了一句"干眼症本来就不能根治",以维护自己的专业权威。患者显然觉得问题没有得到解决,便向医生询问还要做什么检查,医生依旧沉默,不给出建议。直到患者自己提出要查眼底,医生才说"你要查就查吧",也并未给出明确解释(是否需要检查眼底及其原因)。该例共 16 个话轮,其中在医生的 8 个话论中,有 4 个话轮完全以沉默代替(第 4、6、10、14 行),2 个话轮(第 2、8 行)中先是用沉默应对患者的诉求,之后则是发出强指令言语行为(强势一方常用的言语行为)。医患双方在医学信息和机构权力方面的不对称导致了医生的权力强势和病人的权力弱势。医生对患者的诉求和疑问不作回答,只是按照自己的方式开出检查和药物,而不做详细解释说明,患者的诉求和疑问没有得到回应,心中的不满可想而知。医生的沉默是其权势的符号,也是其个性的体现。该例中的沉默言语行为刻画了一个对患者麻木冷淡、不愿与患者交流的医生形象。这一形象在医生群体中并不少见,而患者对这类医生一般满意度较低。可以说,医生的沉默不利于构建和谐的医患关系。

医生需要为患者诊断病情，因此会有一系列提问言语行为来了解患者情况。当医生提问时，患者有时也会沉默。这种沉默有时是对医生话语的不理解，体现了医患双方在医学信息方面的不对称；有时是对医生诊断的默认；有时也会用沉默的方式对医生的建议进行回应，此时沉默多是一种委婉性的拒绝或者不满。由于医患权势的不对称，患者很少会直接拒绝医生的诊断，而沉默则凸显了患者这一身份在机构话语中所拥有的反对权和质疑权，尽管这种反对和质疑是无声的，但仍在内心发出了反对和质疑的声音。正如 Крестинский（1998：77）所说，“沉默是一种内在的言语，人们由于某种原因没有发出有声言语，但并未停止思考”。沉默同时也是一种自我保护，“用沉默反抗权力，实际上是弱势者在挑战强势者的话语权。虽然不能颠覆强势者的绝对权力，但至少可以保护边缘个体的某种尊严”（杨石乔，2008：80—81）。

3. 管理话语

除了法庭话语和医患话语，其他机构话语中弱势者的沉默也随处可见，请看下例：

例（3）

（На производственном собрании начальник УГИБДД отчитывает подчиненного за плохое и недобросовестное исполнение служебных обязанностей:）

Начальник: То, что вы сделали за семь месяцев, вы должны были сделать за месяц.

Подчинённый: По нскоторым позициям мы занимаем первые места.

Начальник: Я считаю, что каждый командир роты должен каждый день брать распечаткуи видеть результаты работы, и по какому направлению он движется: или ты отстаешь, или ты забегаешь. Если ты забегаешь, то притормози и возьми ту позицию, по которой ты отстаешь. Вы сегодня в мелких нарушениях пытаетесь показать себя, а основное вы не делаете.

Подчинённый: **(Молчание)**

Начальник: Ты сколько лет уже командир роты? Поставьте

мне молодого пацана, с которого можно было бы спросить. У тебя спроси – ты лоб морщишь, отчитаться ты не можешь, заверить коллектив ты не можешь, что у тебя будет порядок в роте. Как такого человека можно держать на такой должности?

Подчинённый: **(Молчание)**

Начальник: Садитесь, Алексеев.

(语料出自 Евтушенко 2011: 13–14)

该例是机构语境下的上司和下属之间的对话，属于机构话语中的管理话语（административный дискурс）。对话的内容为上司在会议上公开批评下属未能尽职尽责完成任务。可以看出，这段对话的独白性很强，上司大部分时间都在说，而下属大部分时间则保持沉默。在上司一开始指出下属的失职行为时，下属试图为自己辩解，但辩解无果，上司仍然继续指责，下属则在接下来的几个话轮中都保持沉默。上司的第三个话轮中有两个问句，但此处的目的不是提问，而是用提问言语行为来间接实施指责言语行为。此时下属的沉默不仅是弱势者迫不得已的闭口不言，也不仅是下属对上司的服从，还是下属自我保护的一种体现。“弱势者的被动沉默是一种相当积极的意志表现。当受到权威话语的威胁或压迫，而言说又只能带来损失或痛苦时，弱势者采取沉默掩盖自己的轻蔑或异议，是意志的体现和对话语的控制，也是对内在自我的保护。”（杨石乔，2008：81）尽管是一种言语行为上的空缺，但很多时候，沉默远比争论更有力，恰当地运用沉默，能产生“无声胜有声”的效果。该例中由于下属一直用沉默应对上司，上司最终停止了指责，让下属坐下。

4. 课堂话语

课堂话语中，沉默也具有重要作用。课堂上，教师和学生都可以成为沉默言语行为的主体。对于教师来说，沉默可以作为管理课堂、启发学生思考、鼓励学生积极参与课堂互动的一种手段。例如当课堂秩序变得混乱时，教师会突然停止讲话，用刻意的沉默来引起学生注意，从而快速恢复课堂秩序，此时的沉默建构的是教师课堂秩序管理者的角色。当学生在课堂上发言时，教师可以采用认真倾听、不打断、保持沉默，同时伴随着注视和微笑的方式，鼓励学生继续畅所欲言，此时的沉默建构的是学生的主体角色和教师的倾听者角色。教师还可以通过适当的沉默来转换话题，建构其课堂话题引导者的角色。与课堂中教师沉默的积极作用不同，学生的沉默往往是消极被动的。学生过多的沉默在建构其弱势者身份的同时，也从反面凸显了教师的专制身份。当学生对教师的提问沉默不语时，有可能是对问题的答案没有把握，但在心理层面可能是害怕回答错误而被教师批评或者丢了面子。因此，学生的沉默往往是课堂话语中身份不对称、权力与资源不平衡的一种体现。难怪有人将学生的课堂沉默称为一种“被规训的沉默”（庞妮，2011）。从沉默的视角来看，也证明了课堂话语中交际参与者的身份是师生共同建构的。因为“身份具有交互性（Tracy，2002；Van De Mieroop，2008），为自己建构某种身份的同时也为交际对象建构了与之相对的身份，反之亦然”（任育新，2013：139）。

四 结语

综上，言语交际中的沉默是一种有意义的空缺言语行为（零言语行为），与其他任何言语行为一样，是说话人在一定交际时刻发出的一种意向性行为，只是这种言语行为所使用的言语形式为零。沉默含义复杂，可以表示肯定意义、否定意义以及各种评价意义。沉默具有标记身份和调节人际关系的功能，在一定程度上体现了交际者之间的权势关系。机构话语中的沉默体现了身份的不对称和权势的不对等。对于权势较高的机构代表一方来说，沉默是其机构身份的权力标记，是为实现其目的而采取的一种交际策略，而对于权势较低的非机构代表一方来说，沉默则是无声的人格标记，是其反对权和质疑权的体现，也是一种自我保护的方式。将沉默看作是一种言语行为，拓宽了言语行为理论的研究范围，为我们分析会话中交际者如何利用言语行为手段建构包括性格特点、行为特点等属性在内的自我身份以及他人身份提供了思路和方法，对会话中沉默的研究有助于更全面地了解会话各方的身份博弈和权力抗衡。

参考文献

Арутюнова Н. Д. Молчание и чувство. *Логический анализ языка. Язык речевых действий.* М.：Наука，1994：178-183.

Арутюнова Н. Д. Молчание：контексты употребления. *Логический анализ языка. Язык речевых действий.* М.：Наука，1994：106-117.

Арутюнова Н. Д. *Язык и мир человека*（2 изд. Исправл.）. М.：Языки русской культуры, 1999.

Арутюнова Н. Д. Феномен молчания. *Язык о языке. Под редакцией Н. Д. Арутюновой.* М.: Языки русской культуры, 2000.

Бахтин М. М. *Эстетика словесного творчества.* М.: Искусство, 1979.

Богданов В. В. *Речевое общение: прагматические и семантические аспекты.* Л.: ЛГУ, 1990.

Евтушенко О. А. Административный дискурс: институциональные характеристики. *Известия ВГПУ.* 2011 (5): 11-14.

Карасик В. И. *Язык социального статуса.* М.: Институт языкознания АН СССР, Волгоградский педагогический институт, 1991.

Карасик В. И. *Языковой круг: личность, концепты, дискурс.* Перемена, 2002.

Корнилова Н. Б. Молчание в культурной коммуникации: гендерный аспект. *Гендер: язык, культура, коммуникация.* М.: Рудомино, 2002.

Корнилова Н. Б. Слово и молчание: аспекты взаимодействия. *Ярославский педагогический вестник.* 2001 (1).

Крестинский С. В. Молчание в системе невербальных средств коммуникации. *Тверской лингвистический меридиан: Теоретический сборник.* - Вып. 1. Тверь: Тверской гос. ун-т, 1998.

Крестинский С. Молчание как средство коммуникации и его функции в языковом дискурсе. *Коммуникативное пространство: измерения, пределы, возможности.* М.: Изд-во Моск. ун-та, 2010.

Формановская Н. И. *Речевое общение: коммуникативно - прагматический подход.* М.: Русский язык, 2002.

Шабанова Я. В. Речевой акт《Молчание》в структуре вербальной и невербальной коммуникации. *Язык, коммуникация и социальная среда*, 2007 (7): 183-192.

Эпштейн М. Н. *Слово и молчание. Метафизика русской литературы.* М.: Высшая школа, 2006.

Drew, P. & J. Heritage (eds.). *Talk at Work: Interaction in Institutional Setting.* Cambridge: Cambridge University Press, 1992.

Moreau, N. B. Education, ideology and class/sex identity. In Ch. Kramarae, M. Schulz and W. O'Barr (eds.). *Language and Power.* Sage Publications, Inc, 1984: 43-61.

Richards, K. "Being the teacher": Identity and classroom conversation. *Applied Linguistics*, 2006, 27 (1): 51-77.

Sifianou M. Silence and politeness. In: A. Jaworski (ed.), *Silence: Interdisciplinary*

Perspectives. Berlin: Mouton de Gruyter, 1997: 63-84.

［美］卡罗尔·S. 斯泰克:《刑事程序故事》, 吴宏耀等译, 中国人民大学出版社 2012 年版。

李凤琴:《“沉默”的话语意义与交际功能》,《外语学刊》2010 年第 6 期。

［英］诺曼·费尔克拉夫:《话语与社会变迁》, 殷晓蓉译, 华夏出版社 2003 年版。

庞妮:《课堂沉默: 一种被规训的“自由”》,《现代中小学教育》2011 年第 1 期。

彭艳虹:《意义沉默的语用解读》,《外语与外语教学》2007 年第 9 期。

任育新:《学术口语互动中专家建议者的身份建构策略》,《语用学视角下的身份与交际研究》, 高等教育出版社 2013 年版。

王戬:《刑事程序改革续留问题研究》, 上海人民出版社 2013 年版。

王晋军:《国外机构语篇研究回顾》,《山东外语教学》2007 年第 4 期。

杨石乔:《交流的无奈——试析〈掷铁饼者〉中的医患“沉默”》,《医学与哲学》(人文社会医学版) 2008 年第 5 期。

Silence Speech Act and Identity Construction in Institutional Discourse

Duan Limin

Abstract: Silence in verbal communication is a meaningful vacant speech act, which is a kind of intentional behavior of the speaker at a certain communication moment. The meaning of silence is rich, which can express positive meaning, negative meaning and various subjective evaluations. Silence has the function of marking identity and regulating interpersonal relationship, which reflects the power relationship between communicators to some extent. The silence in the institutional discourse reflects the asymmetry of identity and the unequal power. The silence of the strong party is the communicative strategy to construct the powerful institutional identity and achieve the goal of the institution, while the silence of the weak party is the silent personality marker, the embodiment of its right to oppose and question, and a way of self-protection.

Key words: silence; vacant speech act; institutional discourse; identity

20世纪以前西方镜像中的中国形象解析

潘　婧*

摘　要： 国家形象研究是中西文化交流史上的重要话题，它影响本国民族精神的独立与自信，影响其他国家之于本国的政策与关系。本文通过梳理史料，对西方中国形象特征进行概括整理，认为20世纪前期，中国的国家形象经历了赞美颂扬的巅峰期，理性与情感交织的调整期，以及贬斥鄙视的没落期。这些形象建构源于西方国家所处的特定历史阶段，早期西方宗教势力强大，在其他方面发展缓慢，因此他们倾慕东方文明的繁华与富足；其后西方地理大发现与启蒙运动使西方在制度与认知上获得了极大的自信，对东方文明开始产生疑惑动摇；最后随着在鸦片战争以及后续的一系列对华战争中取得胜利，西方国家开始全面按照其价值体系建构东方文明的劣者形象。

关键词： 颂扬；贬斥；他者；殖民话语权；文化形象

国家形象是一个国家对自己的认知以及国际体系中其他行为体对它的认知的结合，它作为国家的软实力，不仅影响国家间的关系、政策走向，更影响社会公众的认知。纵观20世纪以前的中西文明交流史，中华文明的形象在西方的话语体系下经历了几次重要转变，从光辉灿烂的巅峰，一路跌至谷底，沦为某些国家眼中的“黄祸”。这一转换包括过度渲染、客观理性以及主观偏见三个阶段。正视它们有助于我国客观分析自身所面临的问题与挑战，提升国家软实力。近年来，国家形象建构成为诸多学者热议的话题。有的以西方游历文本为中心进行考察（李朝军，2015），有的对中西作者的书籍进行对比（李想，2011），有的从

* 作者简介：潘婧（1981—　），河南郑州人，陕西师范大学外国语学院讲师，研究方向：西方翻译史，中国传统文化与传播。

来华传教士的视角进行跨文化分析（李霄鹍，2015）。这些研究虽然勾勒出西人对中国的形象概括，却不够深入具体，本文试图从20世纪以前中华文明的三个重要历史阶段，概括分析西方镜像下中国形象的主要特征及成因。

一 18世纪前被颂扬的中华文化：富饶理性的帝国

早在公元前4世纪，希腊文献中就出现了将中国人称为赛里斯人（Seres）的记录。公元2世纪，罗马帝国历史学家阿里安（Arrian）就在其著作中，将中国称为“秦人”（the Sinæ or Thinæ）。在蒙元统治时期，旅行者与商人则用自己的旅行游记使西方对东方产生了梦幻般的联想。1254年，柏朗嘉宾在自己的著作中描述了一个遥远、辽阔、富饶而神秘的东方王国“契丹”（Cathay），此后整整200年间，西方不同类型的文本中，包括游记、通信、诗歌等都有关于契丹的记叙。名噪一时的《马可波罗游记》，极尽所能描述中国无穷无尽的财富，巨大的商业城市，极好的交通设施，以及华丽的宫殿建筑。对于仍处在黑暗的中世纪的西方来说，这些文本无疑是文明的灯塔，照亮了他们的心灵，开阔了他们的视野。

自15世纪至17世纪的两百年中，宗教革命席卷了欧洲，天主教传教士为了传播天主的福音开始陆续前往东方传播天主教。他们学习中国语言文字、社会风俗，与儒家官员交往，了解仕族的精神追求与平民的市井生活。在向东方传播西方宗教、科学的同时，又将东方的文化输入西方。其中较有代表性的包括：1585年门多萨所著的《大中华帝国志》，该书自出版至1600年，印刷19版，英、法、德、荷等7种欧洲语言的版本共印出46版，其畅销程度可见一斑（李想，2011：188）；1615年意大利耶稣会士利玛窦（Matteo Ricci）所著《基督教远征中国史》（*De Christian Expeditione apud Sinas*），又名为《中国传教史》，该书在欧洲引起了巨大反响，被誉为“欧洲人叙述中国比较完备无讹之第一部书”（费赖之，1995）。除此之外，还有卫匡国（Martia Martini）的《中国上古史》（*Sinicae Historiae Decas Prima*，1658）（张西平，2009：387）记叙了从盘古开天地至西汉哀帝元寿二年（公元前1年）的历史，是第一次向欧洲展示中国悠久历史的书籍。这一系列书籍摆脱了最初的商旅游记的特征，是传教士向西方描述中国镜像所作出的初步尝试，向西方展现了一个地大物博、统治有序、贸易兴旺的帝国形象。

1700年的“礼仪之争”[①]，使西方对中国的认识开始由曾经的物质丰富转变为制度先进的“孔夫子的中国”，以孔子为代表的重伦理制度的文化中国形象由此应运而生。在介绍东方先进文化制度的著作中，比利时耶稣会士柏应理（Philippe Couplet）所主编的《中国哲学家孔夫子，或中国知识的拉丁文译本》（*Confucius, Sinarum Philosophus sive Scientia Sinensis*）可以算是欧洲最早介绍中国思想，且最有影响力的作品，它虽然未能完全准确地解读中国儒家思想，有时为了理解与接受，甚至附会西方文化中对圣人的认知，但不可否认它确实是第一次全面系统地向西方展示了中国文化形象。到18世纪后期已经有许多欧洲人借用中国的文化历史，批判《圣经》、教会，歌颂理性与科学。（毕诺，2000）著名启蒙思想家伏尔泰（Voltaire）曾客观地比较了中西两种信仰。“中国的读书人，除了崇拜信仰，他们尊崇正义公道。他们无法了解上帝赋予亚伯拉罕和摩西的一系列律法，以及长期以来西欧和北欧民族闻所未闻的弥赛亚的完善的法典。”（伏尔泰，1996：593）对于中国的孔子，他评论道“孔子是传授过古代法律的贤明官吏……中国儒生的宗教从来没有受无稽神话的糟蹋，也没有为政教之争和内战所玷污。”（伏尔泰，2003：88，225）除此以外，莱布尼茨（Leibniz）也对中国文化表现出极大的热情，他说：“如果说我们在手工艺技能上与他们不分上下、在理论科学方面还超过他们的话，那么，在实践哲学方面，即在人类生活的伦理道德和政治学说方面，我们不得不汗颜地承认他们是远胜于我们的。”（伏尔泰，2005）又说：“相对于其他民族，中国律法促成了大众的安宁和社会的和谐，以至众人所受的干扰可以降至最低；其律法之完美，简直无法形容。”（Lach，1977：46）1716年，他完成了最后一本关于中国的著作《中国人的自然神学》，其中驳斥了一些对中国加以谴责的声音，认为西方文化由于过于年轻，因此才无法认同古老帝国的规范的。

① 17世纪至18世纪西方天主教传教士就中国传统礼仪是否违背天主教教义的争议。罗马教廷对中国教区传教产生分歧，耶稣会认为天主教需要利用中国本土的文化，利用两者的相似性，减少教众的心里抵触。而多明我会等则认为应该彻底摒弃异教思想，将中国文化中的“天”“帝”的概念与天主教的“上帝”严格区分，避免混淆，同时反对中国教众尊孔、祭祖的传统。教皇克雷芒十一世支持多明我会，打压耶稣会，结果引发清朝廷与罗马教廷的冲突，并直接导致清朝雍正时期全面禁止天主教传教活动，驱逐传教士。

西方对中国这些美好的印象主要源于其自身的需要。16 世纪天主教在欧洲受到宗教改革的巨大冲击，耶稣会传教士来华传教，既可以缓和基督教内部由于教义之争而产生的矛盾，满足将基督教传播到世界的每一个角落的使命感，又可以通过化解中华文明对基督教的普世价值的冲击，把中华文明收编到基督教世界中，巩固基督教的教义。正如利玛窦所说："我处心积虑地借用儒教先师孔子来证实我们的见解，因为我把某些含义模糊的文字解释得对我们有利。"（裴化行，1995）随后的 17—18 世纪，启蒙思想家需要一个基督教以外的异族文明形象，来证明宗教自由对国家繁荣稳定的影响。这一时期，中国形象是欧洲人审视"自我"的一面镜子，中国的道德观被启蒙思想家看作反对宗教权威的自然理性与道德哲学，中国就是在世俗的理性上建立起的思想自由、经济繁荣、社会安定的理想国。启蒙思想家利用中国为参照物，反思自己的政治制度与宗教文化，为了推翻封建教权，他们讴歌中国道德哲学的宽容，为了批判暴政，他们以中国的开明君主为典范，意图证明依靠自然理性也能道德地生活。不难看出，这一时期的中华帝国在西方眼中，是一片祥和、安定的正面形象，这种单一化的趋势，完全是由于启蒙思想家片面地理解颂扬中国思想及道德观，忽略了对中国文化理性的分析所造成的，其出发点完全是为了服务自身政治利益的需要。

二　18 世纪下半叶中华文明的衰落：腐朽专制停滞的帝国

18 世纪后期，随着西方启蒙运动的深入，西方对中华帝国的态度从最初普遍颂扬逐渐转变为贬斥，批评者主要来自新兴资产阶级作家、启蒙思想家，以及政府官员。英国作家笛福可谓开启了这一风潮。笛福对中国的描写和评论主要见于三部文学创作——《凝结录：月球记事》（*The Consolidator*: *Memoirs of Sundry Transactions from the World in the Moon*, 1705），《鲁滨逊漂流续记》（*The Farther Adventure of Robinson Crusoe*, 1719），以及《鲁滨逊感想录》（*Serious Reflections during the Life and Surprising Adventures of Robinson Crusoe*, 1721）。在这三部文学作品中，从最初含蓄地讽刺中国统治者的昌明，到后期露骨地批判，他描述了一个粗鄙的充满异教徒的野蛮邦国，经济落后、人民生活困苦、政治腐败、君主专制、野蛮愚昧，是许多野蛮国家中一个还算开化，但却是许多开化国家中最愚昧的国家（张影，2015：156）。研究者们认为：笛福像一道分水岭，他一改西方对中国繁荣、富强的认识，虽然该论调与当时社会趋势背道而驰，偏离了主流借用亚洲的优点批判西方社会的弊病，但其对其后来的乔治·安生（George Anson）、孟德斯鸠（Montesquieu）等对中国持批判态度的作家来说，无疑是具有开拓性的。（史景迁，2013：72—75）此后的1748年，孟德斯鸠在其巨著《论法的精神》中，针对中国落后的政治制度与传统道德进行了大量批判。在第八卷的最后一章（第二十一章）“论三种政府原则之沦丧——论中华帝国”（On the Corruption of Principles of the three Governments—On the Chinese Empire），他认为中国由于人口众多经常出现饥荒盗匪，专制政治使人民缺少自主性，他自豪地宣称“自由的尺度一直无法在亚洲扩大，而欧洲的尺度则视环境不同有所增减”。（史景迁，2013，121）至此，西方对中国的赞颂开始受到更为广阔的怀疑与批判，成为否定中国文化之滥觞。然而，对这个古老帝国的更为清晰、全面的了解则是在马戛尔尼（George Macartney）与阿美士德（William Pitt Amherst）先后两次代表团访华后，方得以最终呈现。

1793年，以向乾隆皇帝祝贺八十大寿为名，具有丰富外交经验的马戛尔尼英国代表团来到中国，意图建立平等的外交关系。这是自西方传教士被驱逐以后第一次东西方的正式会面，虽然由于礼仪问题，该使团未能完成其既定的使命，然而使团成员撰写的与中国相关的著作使西方对中国有了较为真实的认识。主计员巴罗把他对中华民族的性格总结为自大和自卑，假正经和真浅薄，彬彬有礼和粗鄙下流的奇异组合（马戛尔尼，2013：220），并把这一切归结为政治制度的腐败与无能。不得不说巴罗的观察并没有过多偏颇。此外，英国代表团的正使马戛尔尼勋爵在日记中将中华帝国看作是“一艘陈旧不堪而处在风雨飘摇中的巨舰，幸而她靠了一些能干的头脑清醒的军人掌舵，才在过去的150年中免遭沉没，并以其庞大的身躯和外表镇住了邻国。但只要遇上在甲板上执行指挥的是一位无能的人，那么这条船就会失去秩序与安全。她可能不致马上沉没；她或者会像一艘失事的船在海上漂浮一阵子，然后在岸边撞得粉碎，但将永远不会在旧甲板上再度建造起来”（Byne，1963：222）。20年后的1815年，阿美士德使团在中国同样因为礼仪问题与中国产生分歧，最终被嘉庆皇帝下令离开。然而使团副使小乔治·斯汤东（George Staunton）（曾随父亲一起出使中国）日后在《大清律例》英译本所写的“译者序”中，描述了中华帝国的衰落以及英帝国的崛起："中国人惯于认定他们在知识和美德方面优于其他民族，而这趟行程（指马戛尔尼使团）已足以表明，这种盲目自信的心理及其欧洲史学家对此的默认大都是错误的。近年来，欧洲在某些知识领域取得了巨大的进步，并特别热衷于此，但中国人在这些方面的知识水平并不尽如人意。他们的美德更多地表现在礼节仪式而非道德义务中，而且往往言过其实，言行不一。他们不合时宜的恶习也理应遭到强烈谴责。"（斯汤东，2015：202）

由此可见，从启蒙运动后期至鸦片战争这段时间，西方对中国的认识更为全面深刻。全面性体现在超越对上层文化的关注，如中国传统儒家经典，开始关注中国底层人民真实的生活状态，以及人民生活的方方面面；深刻性则体现在用科学的论证方式呈现中国形象。如孟德斯鸠在批判中国专制政体时，运用地理环境等因素作为论证手段，试图用较为客观科学的分析说服西方读者。这种深入的认识与启蒙运动所建立起的新型社会文化模式有着紧密的关系。随着启蒙运动的深入，民众思想的解放，西方民族国家要求建立一个全新的由市民阶层普遍参与的新型国家，它崇尚以理性主义为基础的自由、平等、民主的价值观，即西方自我认同下现代文明社会的基本要素。另外，18 世纪 60 年代西方工业革命使西方在社会科学和自然科学获得巨大发展，西方各国经济繁荣，人民生活富足，开始全面超越古老的中华帝国。再加上与中国的交流日益深入，西方开始以自己客观冷静的"理性"的态度，重新审视那个自己曾经学习的楷模。因此，西方社会文化自身的巨大变革促使它改变了对中国的看法，从一味崇拜，到多方争论，再到最终走向反面。"停滞"的，"东方专制主义的""落后腐朽"的中华帝国形象使西方在建立现代自由主义精神中，确立了民族自信，民族优越感，从而彻底摆脱了曾经的"精神挫折感"。（布费、利特尔，2004：281）

三 19 世纪遭遇贬斥期的中华文明：劣等未开化的民族

如果说 18 世纪的西方对中国的评价还算较为客观、冷静的话，那么 19 世纪特别是下半叶，西方则对中国充满了鄙夷与偏见。哈罗德·伊萨克斯（Isaacs Harold Robert）把 1840—1905 年这段时间定义为美国对中华文明的"蔑视的时代"（The Age of Contempt）。（Isaac，1973：71）德国

社会则认为应将中国文明和历史排斥在一般性的文化学科研究领域之外。(张西平，2011：161)

自1840年中国在鸦片战争中失利后，中国在西方的形象一泻千里，日益增多的来华传教士与外交官构成了这些中国形象的主要建构者。西方传教士多以“征服者”自居，对中国文化不但鄙视，还企图以西方文化取而代之。他们视中国人为“半开化的异教徒”“劣等民族”，而把自己扮作“救世主”和要当“中国人的先生”。不少传教士有“白种人的负担”，处处表现出对中国人的种族歧视。(顾长声，2004：432) 美国传教士明恩溥（Arthur Smith）在1894年《中国人的性格》一书中总结了“丑陋”的中国人的21个性格特征，如“好面子”“辛勤劳作”“漠视时间”“天性误解”“因循守旧”“遇事忍耐”“麻木不仁”“缺乏公众精神”等，他认为“如今的中国人对己对人都无真诚可言，对他人缺少利他主义，他们的宗教信仰是多神论、泛神论和不可知论……他们真正缺少的是品格和良心”(Smith，1890：316)。这些言论虽然有合理的成分，但更多的是对中国人不全面的负面的解读。在书的结尾，作者认为要解决中国的问题，不仅需要发展科学技术，而且需要外力以及建构物质文明的发展条件——基督教：“我们发现，中国的各种需要只是一种需要，这种需要，只有基督教文明才能永恒而又完整地给以满足。”(Smith，1890：330) 由此可见，西方传教士将中国内部存在的问题与异教信仰联系在一起，其绝对的宗教自信促使他们为在中国传播基督教寻找可能的现实依据。事实证明，基督教的确在19世纪后期在中国发展迅速。鸦片战争前近一个世纪天主教徒有30万，1900年全国已经有了70万天主教徒和8万新教徒，1901—1910年十年间，天主教徒更是从70万激增至130万，至1918年增至190万。传教士也从1901年的800名增加到1400名(顾长声，2004：233、428)。自耶稣会传教士入华以来数百年间，也未曾见过天主教徒如此迅速的增长，这大概和西人对中国人的态度，以及我们对自己的认知有关。

此外，西方的外交官、军官与探险家大量涌入中国，对中国的研究更深入、广泛，他们不再关注中国经典艺术等方面的内容，而是主要围绕社会整体、政治教育、道德宗教等主题，建构了病态可笑的中国人身体、颓败丑陋的社会整体、腐朽专制的政治和教育、异端罪恶的道德和宗教。例如：英国驻中国领事麦华佗（Sir Walter Henry Medhurst）写道：“有关中国人的突出观点是：他们是非同寻常但却愚蠢昏聩的人类，他们无休止地吸食鸦片，生出女婴就把她们溺死；他们日常食物中有小狗、小猫和老鼠，以及诸如此类的东西；他们在荣誉、诚实和勇气方面水平是最低的；对他们来说，残忍的行为是一种消遣娱乐。”（罗伯茨，1999：201）又如英国海军上尉艾略特·宾汉（Eliot Bingham）在《远征中国纪实》中写道：“禁止鸦片走私是绝对不可能的，除非整个中华民族彻底改变自己的性格。他们是不会放弃鸦片的。而且过去的经验已经证明，禁令愈严，吸食的人愈多。”（宾汉，2004：302）这些牵强武断的论断误导了那些不了解中国实际情况的西人，构建了“劣等他者”的中国形象，为西方殖民者进一步侵略中国提供了理由与借口。

当然，在充斥着唱衰中国的大背景中，仍有少数“亲华”者较为客观公正地看待这一古老的文明，并认识到西方看待中国的局限性。比如，赫德（Robert Hart）作为中国海关的总税务司在日记中写道：“在绝大多数情况下，关于中国和中国人的著作都陷入”毫无根据的以偏概全的错误中。从局部看整体在许多事情上是适用的，但是对于一个具体的中国人，中国领土的某一具体地点，人们却无法确定有关他们的什么应该是这个帝国另一地区的习俗特点，或者应是另一省里某些个人的习惯。（布鲁纳等，2003：143）毋庸置疑，赫德的描述更为全面和客观，他看到了中国文化的地区多样性，以及上层文化与下层文化的隔离，出于道德良知为中华文明辩解，发出异类的声音。但西方对中国的主流印象仍然是一个“劣者”的形象，就连对中国文化颇有好感的理雅各爵士（Sir James Legge），也是在其回国后担任了牛津大学首席汉学教授时，才开始重新审视中国道教文化的。总之，这一时期西方被政治、经济、宗教利益羁绊，企图确立自身在全球至高无上的霸权，于是将中国置于其自身的权利话语框架下，构建了一个二元对立的他者与自我的关系。也就是说，中国的落后与衰败对应着西方的文明与现代，中国需要向西方学习，西方需要通过扩张来传播自身先进的文化，及普世价值。毫无疑问，这些观念为西方列强在华进行政治、经济与文化侵略包裹了一层漂亮、得体的外衣，为那些标榜自身是民主自由的国家提供了侵略他国的“合理的、科学的”借口，为残忍的战争提供了道德避难所。

四 结语

1750 年以前，西方构建出三种形象类型“大汗的大陆”“大中华帝国”“孔夫子的中国”。然而随着西方现代性的确立，这个被美化了的乌托邦则转变为“停滞衰败的帝国”“东方专制的帝国”“野蛮或半野蛮的帝国”（周宁，2006：9）。这些形象无论是正确还是错误，出于友谊抑或敌意，都是基于西方自身价值观所建构起来的。他们虽然有客观合理的成分，但仍主要是以西方的认识框架及需求作为建构的基础，也就不可避免带有某些歪曲甚至是丑化的成分。从辩证法否定之否定的原则，它是一种对中国形象二次批判的螺旋式上升进程。了解西方对中国形象建构的过程，是在现代世界秩序语境中，获得“正义”支持的合法性所在，它避免我们再一次陷入西方设定的意识形态的论述框架，也避免我们以民族虚无主义的自卑态度接受西方的批判，为我们在世界话语权中建构更为公正平等的中国形象提供了可以借鉴的依据。

参考文献

Arthur，S. *Chinese Characteristics*. Singapore：Graham Brash Ltd. 1890.

Byng，J. *An Embassy to China*，*being the Journal kept by Lord Macartney During his Embassy to the Emperor Ch'ien-lung*，1793-1794. Hamden，Connecticut：Anchor Books. 1963.

Lach，D. *The Preface to Leibniz's Novissima Sinica*. Honolulu，1977.

Harold，I. *Scratches on Our Minds*. Westport：Greenwood，1973.

毕诺：《中国对法国哲学思想形成的影响》，耿昇译，商务印书馆 2000 年版。

布费·巴里、利特尔·理查德：《世界历史中的国际体系：国际关系研究的在构建》，刘德斌主译，高等教育出版社 2004 年版。

［美］宾汉·艾略特：《远征中国纪实》，见周宁著/编注：《鸦片帝国》（《中国形象：西方的学说与传说》之四），学苑出版社 2004 年版。

［美］布鲁纳，费正清，司马富编：《进入中国机构：赫德日记 1854—1863》，中国海关出版社 2003 年版。

［法］伏尔泰：《路易十四时代》，商务印书馆 1996 年版。

［法］伏尔泰：《风俗论》上册，梁守锵译，商务出版社 2003 年版。

［法］伏尔泰：《中国近事》，大象出版社 2005 年版。

顾长声：《传教士与近代中国》，上海人民出版社 2004 年版。

李想：《丑陋—温良—智慧——19世纪末20世纪初西方中国形象的变迁及原因探析》，《牡丹江教育学报》2011年第5期。

李霄鹍：《美国传教士的中国形象》，《武汉大学党报》2015年。

李勇：《西欧的中国形象》，人民出版社2010年版。

[美] 罗伯茨·约：《十九世纪西方人眼中的中国》，蒋重跃、刘林海译，时事出版社1999年版。

费赖之：《在华耶稣会士列传及书目》上册，中华书局1995年版。

[美] 裴化行：《利玛窦神父传》（上），管震湖译，商务印书馆1995年版。

[美] 马戛尔尼·乔治，巴罗·约翰：《马戛尔尼使团使华观感》，何高济、何毓宁译，商务印书馆2013年版。

史景迁：《大汗之国——西方人眼中的中国》，广西师范大学出版社2013年版。

[美] 托马斯·乔治，斯当东：《小斯当东回忆录》，屈文生译，上海人民出版社2015年版。

张西平：《欧洲早期汉学史——中西文化交流与西方汉学的兴起》，中华书局2009年版。

张西平：《西方汉学十六讲》，外语教学与研究出版社2011年版。

周宁：《西方的中国形象研究》，北京大学出版社2006年版。

张影：《笛福与18世纪欧洲中国观的转变》，《理论月刊》2015年第12期。

Chinese Cultural Image in the eyes of Western World before 20th century

Pan Jing

Abstract: National image is a crucial topic in intercultural studies, since it influences the independent identity, national confidence and even diplomatic policy-making. This paper uses the method of literature study to categorize and analyze the characteristics of national images. It has found that there are three phases in western conception. The earliest phase was mostly of positive and admiration because the western world was under the powerful reign of religion, which left itself developed at a slow rate. The second could be considered skeptical phase since the western exploration of the Enlightenment movement has enable the west a high level of confidence. The third phase of denouncement has set up an inferior image of China since the a series of victories had been achieved by the western world and the new world system had started to reshape people's notion of China.

Key words: praise; denounce; the other; colonist power of discourse; cultural image

俄罗斯汉学家克罗里和他的《史记》学研究

路　博　余　香*

摘　要：俄罗斯著名汉学家克罗里长期致力于汉代史学家以及史料学研究。出版发表大量汉学研究专著和学术论文，在俄罗斯乃至世界汉学界产生了很大影响。而其对《史记》的研究更是贯穿其学术生涯。笔者认为其《史记》学研究思路和观点对中国学术界有一定的借鉴意义。通过对其学术论著及以往研究成果等相关资料的整理和分析，本文从汉代文献写作手法，司马迁的文化理论与文化实践，以及《史记》文本相关问题的研究三个方面对其汉学研究，尤其是其《史记》学研究的观点进行梳理总结。

关键词：克罗里；汉学家；史记；研究

《史记》是中国的第一部纪传体通史，也是一部优秀的文学著作，在文学史上有着重要地位，具有极高的文学价值，被鲁迅誉为“史家之绝唱，无韵之离骚”。

在俄罗斯汉学家尤里·利沃维奇·克罗里看来，《史记》不仅值得尊重，同时也是值得研究的对象，通过《史记》不仅可以研究中华文明的起源和各种政治学说的本质，还可以了解中国古代国家体制的形成以及中国古代的对外政策。

1931年8月9日，尤里·利沃维奇·克罗里出生于列宁格勒（今圣彼得堡）。1954年毕业于圣彼得堡国立大学东方学院，主修中国历史。后于圣彼得堡国立大学东方学院继续攻读副博士学位，主要研究方向为中国

---

* 作者简介：路博（1984年），男，陕西师范大学外国语学院，讲师，研究方向：俄罗斯语言文学，15802956818，陕西省西安市雁塔区长安南路199号，nicsnow520@163.com。

余香（1997年），女，陕西师范大学外国语学院，研究生，研究方向：俄罗斯语言学，17791990756，陕西省西安市雁塔区长安南路199号，1065459749@qq.com。

古代史。1957年克罗里就职于苏联科学院东方研究所的列宁格勒分院。1963年他通过了副博士学位答辩，论文题目为“秦朝覆灭后的历史学家——司马迁”。1991年发表题为“汉代中国文化的丰碑——盐铁论”的论文，并通过了博士答辩。曾先后就职于苏联科学院东方研究所的列宁格勒分院和俄罗斯东方文献研究所，并担任高级研究员（1980年至今）以及首席研究员（1986—2014）。克罗里曾是苏联科学院东方研究所历史部分局的成员（1960—1970），并担任过中国及中亚汉代时期史学家研究以及史料学研究办公室主任（1984—1991）。目前，他是苏联地理学会东部委员会主席团成员（1987年至今）。

克罗里用俄语及英语发表和出版了超过150篇论文和学术专著。他的研究涉及秦汉时期的政治、经济、思想文化和法律制度。在他所出版的论文中，对汉代史料中所记载的地理经济、传统文化、计量学、哲学和文学等相关领域进行了尤为深入的论述。

他还参与了东方文献研究院中国木板书藏品的整理工作，根据中国古代不同的文体将藏品进行归类；他的研究还涉及了北京话中的歇后语以及20世纪俄罗斯东方学研究发展史。

司马迁的《史记》是中国历史文献的一座丰碑，并作为中国文化的独特范式对诗歌的文学形式产生了巨大的影响。克罗里对《史记》的研究贯穿其学术研究生涯，并留下了大量的关于《史记》研究的文章和著作。本文在对其相关资料和文章全面了解的情况下，对克罗里的汉学研究，特别是他对《史记》的研究观点进行梳理和总结。

一 汉代文献的两种写作手法

（一）杜撰式写作手法

在研究中国古代历史文献的过程中，克罗里总会遇到虚构的对话和人物。他认为这些对话和人物不仅是以真实的历史事件为背景虚构出来的，同时也是神话的产物。因此对于这些虚构的对话和人物，只有通过批评分析才能体会到其隐藏的意义。有时他会产生疑问：如果文献中出现这种虚构的对话和人物，那么这算是一种文学写作手法吗？如果是的话，那么是否存在这样一种体现杜撰方式的写作规则呢？

他猜想：如果确实存在着这样一种写作规则，且它在汉语中被称为寓言。古代著作《庄子》（公元前4世纪—前3世纪）一书中就有大量的寓言故事。此书中寓言一词共出现了 2 次：27 章《寓言》开篇 和 33 章《天下》。27 章中写道："寓言十九，藉外论之。亲父不为亲子媒。亲父誉之，不若非其父者也。"郭象对这一段做了以下注解："寄之他人，则十言而九见信。言出于己，俗多不受，故借外尔。肩吾、连叔之类，皆所借者。"肩吾和连叔是第一章中两个杜撰出来的人物。

克罗里在研究中指出，关于寓言一词更加详细的解释出自刘向所著的《别录》。书中写道："作人姓名，使相与语，是寄辞于其人，故《庄子》有《寓言篇》。"这样一来，就可以解释何为寓言：言是言语、对话，而寓却很难用现代文字来解释。《说文解字》一书中用寄来解释它，意为：予以、转移。于是结合上述解释，克罗里就得出了寓的含义：借他人之口的。并且他认为，根据刘向的说法，寓言中多为杜撰的人物。《庄子》一书中利用杜撰的人和话所记述的故事都带有深刻的寓意，所以《庄子》中的寓言具有讽寓、寓意的意思。《庄子》中提到的人名都带有抽象含义。孙绰记述了《庄子》两则故事中的人名：混沌（《庄子》第七章）和罔象（《庄子》十九章）。在克罗里看来，作者正是借助这样的名字古怪离奇且话语中充斥着神话色彩的人物来表达自己内心的想法。

克罗里认为，《庄子》和《列子》书中虚构对话和人物的创作传统对中国的文学艺术产生了巨大的影响，这种影响主要体现在汉朝的艺术形式——乐府中。大部分乐府诗歌作品的主人公都是虚构的人物，且这些人物的对话也洋溢着诗意的幻想。在《史记》和班固的《汉书》中都提及了公元前 2 世纪乐府代表辞赋家司马相如："相如以'子虚'，虚言也，为楚称。"（《史记》117 章 、《汉书》57 章）班固在《汉书》100 章中写道：子虚乌有，寓言淫丽。

（二）历史写实手法

克罗里认为，与杜撰式写作手法相对的是真实记录史实的手法，而这种写作手法的代表人物是西汉时期的历史学家司马迁。

首先，在克罗里看来，司马迁系统性地将过往文献中假借他人之口所述的片段分为虚与实，实就是真实的史实，虚则是杜撰之言。且司马迁曾数次赞美司马相如作品中的意境："相如虽多虚辞滥说，然其要归引之节俭，此与诗之讽谏何异。"（《史记·司马相如列传》）从中可以看出司马迁对司马相如的虚辞有着深刻的领悟。

同时，克罗里认为，司马迁是汉朝著名思想家之一。司马迁站在朴素唯物论角度来分析以虚实手法著称的作品。借助唯物论思想，司马迁在历史学评论领域也取得了非常大的成就。这种唯物论文学思想在王充的作品中也有所体现，他认为很多艺术现象都是对“实”（真实）的“增”（夸大），缺少真实描写。他同时反对以“虚”写“实”，并以激烈的言辞批评其他作品中的虚（虚伪）和华（浮华），王充的这种思想是司马迁创作思想的延续和升华。

根据克罗里的观点，理解和把握历史学家的文学观点和写作特点有助于正确认识其写作目的，及其对史实的态度。所以令他感兴趣的是，司马迁是如何看待史实的呢？他指出，司马迁在《史记·太史公自序》中写道“故述往事，思来者”。经过研究，克罗里发现在叙述中国历史时，司马迁主要对以下两种史实进行了描写：一是在文献或民间口述中记录的前人的事迹和传说，即并非他亲眼目睹的史实；二则是他亲身经历的史实。在《史记》中司马迁对历史各个时期的人物及传说进行了系统的梳理和记述。并且克罗里认为，司马迁是一个有着崇高理想的历史学家。在司马迁看来，记录历史应当力求真实、尊重史实。同时也将这一崇高理想付诸实践。在对所记录史实不确定的情况下，比如司马迁在撰写《孔子世家》时，根据对史实的调查向读者提出了自己的质疑，或是针对之前有争议的史实向读者作出了解释。克罗里认为，司马迁批判性地对文献、口头传说的史料及自己对民众道德和习俗的观察进行了深入的调查研究，然后从中选择写作素材。这种写作手法在巧妙地叙述史实的同时又描写出历史事件背后所反映的深层次的思想内涵。由此可以看出，司马迁在写作过程中力求史料的真实性，拒绝利用艺术创作篡改历史。这也就是为何司马迁在《史记》中运用了汉代虚与实的手法而摒弃了空与华。遵循着这一写作原则，《史记》中所运用的人物语言都源于史料记载或口头传说，并非根据历史人物和事件进行的主观编造。因此在克罗里看来，司马迁既是一位伟大的历史学家又是一位出色的作家，他的创作体现了他对待史料真实性严格要求的一贯态度。也正是这种对待史料的态度，解决了《史记》写作中所遇到的各种文学创作材料选取和艺术加工的问题。

其次，克罗里发现，司马迁在作品中运用了独特的叙述方式，他通过选取相对应的历史事件，以两种完全不同的叙事方式生动直观地阐述历史。一种方式是司马迁作为叙述者，以第三人称客观的叙述历史事件；另一种则是司马迁作为作者在篇末的主观叙述，即“论赞”部分。《史记》

通书贯穿着这两种叙述方式，第三人称客观的叙述与第一人称的论赞形成了鲜明的对比。

一方面，作为第三者的客观叙述，司马迁的语言平淡、温和，语句简练，极少表达个人的看法及个人情感。而且克罗里经过研究发现，司马迁在《史记》编撰过程中引用了大量的史料，其中既有传闻逸事亦有历史文献，他将这些史料串联起来，并统一叙事风格。比如在《高祖本纪》中司马迁将有关高祖的一些传说编于本篇末尾，将高祖塑造为顺应天命的英明君主。另一方面，他行文上使用篇前作序、篇后作赞、篇中夹议的方式，以“太史公曰”引出自己的见解。通过第一人称的叙述来阐发自己对人物、事件的主观看法和意见，并用极具感情色彩的文字对每一篇的内容进行评议和褒贬。

克罗里如是说：司马迁犹如历史事件的亲历者一般，将文献以及口头传说中的历史娓娓道来。伯顿·沃森也指出司马迁将这种叙述方式运用得恰到好处，使读者感觉《史记》乃是司马迁亲笔写出的而不是编撰而成；由此可以看出司马迁选择这样的叙述方式是有意而为之。司马迁在作品中着重突出了自己的见解，而书中客观叙述的史实则如同他的影子。这种写作方式使读者感觉到书中史料的陈述者仿佛不是作者本人，又好像是作者。两种叙述方式各得其所，使《史记》中的文字具有了独特的感情色彩和修辞特征。综上，司马迁的两种叙述方式在《史记》中得到了统一。

总而言之，克罗里对司马迁有着极高的评价。他认为，司马迁作为中国第一部编年体通史的作者，为中国文学的发展作出了巨大的贡献，并且其历史写实的写作手法对后世的叙事性文学产生了深远的影响。

二　司马迁的文化理论与文化实践

（一）关于“志”的见解

克罗里在研究中发现，在司马迁时代广泛地传播着公羊学的观点，即对于《春秋》的注释。和哈拉（T. Хихар）总结到：公羊学在研究春秋时，对于行为的道德评价具有绝对的客观性，不过其中也包含了对人意志的关注。这种对人意志的理解和对人的评价方式，在现实面前提供了更理想的偏向。在文学理论方面，克罗里认为司马迁的观点可以很明显看出这种文学思想的影响。

克罗里在文章中指出，司马迁在公元前190年前后的两个典籍中概述了其文学理论。这种文学理论，确切地说，指的是文学动机和文学目标。司马迁也列举了哲学、政治、军事思想、历史和诗歌等方面的经典之作，并且认为这些作者之所以能创作出这些作品，是因为其内心难以抒发的痛苦阻碍了其现实生活中思想的实现。尤其是一些遭受刑法而致残、无法实现自己仕途的作家（比如司马迁本人），转而专注于笔端来表达自己的愤懑之情。这些人有着共同的创作动机——不满于现状以及共同的创作目标——自显。关于这点克罗里指出：在司马迁来看，志指的是在创作时，作者的良好志向受到阻碍、无法实现的情况。由此，根据司马迁的观点，文学作品传递了作者意志的信息及其对后代的期许。也正是由于文学作品的存在，后世的人们得以获得作者的意志并完善对作者的道德评价，最终实现作者获得名望的期许。

克罗里认为，司马迁的文学理论表达了“志”对于个人评价的重要性，而这吸收了公羊学派的观点。并且有直接的记载表明，司马迁是在公羊学思想的指导下完成《史记》的。据司马迁本人所说，他听取了大量公羊学派的理论。由此克罗里得出结论：司马迁在创作《史记》时应用了公羊学对《春秋》的注释。

（二）“志”对于司马迁写作的影响

克罗里在著作中指出，公羊学用“志”对个人进行评价，不仅对司马迁的文学理论产生了巨大的影响，也对司马迁的文学传记写作产生了影响，即他对历史重要人物的评价。

首先，在克罗里看来，这种认识影响到了司马迁对历史人物传记的选择上面（《列传》）。司马迁认为，《列传》中所记载的是“扶义俶傥，不令己失时，立功名于天下”。关于这一点司马迁也指出，“每一个人都应遵循自己的‘志’”。因此在《列传》中他主要给那些努力建立自己声誉的人作传。而要被记载、建立声誉首先要经过道德评判，而评判标准是由历史学家所决定的。克罗里指出，司马迁的评价标准和现存的文化标准并不一致。在文章中他举了这样一个例子：从现代欧洲历史学家的观点来看：宦官赵高在《史记》中所占比例高于其他人，因为他在历史中扮演着重要的角色；但是司马迁本人并不认为赵高需要单独列传，这就体现了司马迁的个人意志。

在克罗里看来，司马迁编写《列传》原因在于一个人虽然在历史中并未发挥丝毫的作用，但是在某个事件中他却表现出了好的意志，并因此获得了好的评价。关于这一点他举例道：现代历史学家会一笔带过荆轲险些成功刺杀秦始皇的事实。因为荆轲的刺杀没有成功，并没有对历史产生任何影响。但在司马迁在《刺客列传》的结尾写道：“自曹沫至荆轲五人，此其义或成或不成，然其立意较然，不欺其志，名垂后世，岂妄也哉！”用沃森的一句话来说，司马迁专门写一章《刺客列传》是受董仲舒和公羊《春秋》的影响。

其次，根据克罗里的观点，司马迁对《列传》中人物的评价，很大程度上受到了公羊学说的影响。在他看来，司马迁试图创造“正义维护者”的形象，并运用较大篇幅去介绍这些人物的志。并且《列传》中所记载的人物之所以被司马迁列入《史记》，是因为他们虽然名望很高，但却都未实现自己的“志”。而事实上，在司马迁看来，根据一个人的文学作品来评价他的“志”和“意”，完全符合他的文学理论。历史学家所写记的两种“其他人的话语”都是他们“志”和“意”的重要表达。

克罗里指出，由于在许多情况下，《史记》中引用的“别人的话”是对一个人物形象的认识来源，那么就出现了这样的问题：在众多的关于一个人不同的人物传记中，历史学家应该如何挑选并运用被描写人物的评价？

对这个问题克罗里给出了回答，他认为，司马迁的《史记》可以称之为一部独白作品，其中以引文开篇的模式是文章写作的出发点。因此，司马迁引用历史学家们的补充观点是基于不改变其意思和语气的前提下，从而使他人的观点服务于自己的创作。

在研究中克罗里发现，如果司马迁认可主人公的自传，那么就会引用这种自我评价的话语来表达他的观点。在这种情况下，司马迁通常会把“别人的话”放在文章或传记的结尾，通过文章结构来强调其特殊作用，例如鲁仲连和屈原的文章节选。同样，司马迁也使用第三方的评价，其中包含传记中对主人公与历史学家观点不一致的评价。例如，儒家学者对叔孙通的低评价是为了通过比较他的言行与普通人的标准观点来反映这个人的非凡之处；事实上，这些“别人的话”代表了普通人的庸俗观点，同时也突出了非凡之人的追求和意志。

克罗里总结道：公羊学派关于为评价个人而突出其意志的做法不仅影响了司马迁的文学理论，也影响了他作为传记作家的文学实践。而司马迁文学理论和文学实践的棱镜反映了评价一个人的意志价值的概念。这一事实可以表明，每个人都被认为有一定的自由来追随他的自然愿望，而“正义拥护者”则表达了对“光荣名称”的渴望，而这种渴望只能通过他人对其意志的高度赞赏而获得。尽管如此，正如 Я. Прушек 指出的那样，传统的中国传记并不具有人生活中个性化的、特定的和独特的兴趣特征。原因之一就是历史学家只能看到个体与其他“同类人”（氏族或阶级）的共同点，而看不到个体独有的特征。另一个原因则正如 Д. Тунчет 所指出的，传记取决于个人的地位。这种状态决定了传记必然是一个杰出人物的单方面形象，并作为社会的、特别是国家关系的一个要素。回想一下，大部分《英雄》《传记》《史记》描述的都是官员。然而，在那些官僚之外的人的传记中，例如“周游列国的正义之士”，个人的意志更为明显。所以，在克罗里看来，司马迁文学理论中的“英雄”，其实是“失败者”，他们未能履行其作为官员的职责，并因此而从事写作。按照 В. М. Алексеева 的说法，“这是儒家个体的悲剧”。

三　对《史记》文本问题的研究

克罗里经过长时间的研究发现：两千多年来，人们对《史记》进行了大量的补充。但遗憾的是，这些补充过于久远，并不确切，甚至很难与续补《史记》的人联系起来。因此，《史记》增补的研究者面临不少文本问题。

克罗里在研究中指出，人们最感兴趣的问题之一是《史记》卷六和卷四十八结语中的“赞”。在这些结语中解释了秦朝（公元前 221—前 207）灭亡的原因。而汉代学者贾谊（公元前 201—前 169）的《过秦论》对司马迁（公元前 145？—前 87？）评价秦朝及其灭亡产生了至关重要的影响。这部作品现在被列为贾谊《新书》的章节之一。它也被完全编入《秦始皇本纪》（《史记》卷六），部分被编入《陈涉世家》（《史记》卷四十八）。《史记》第六章的注释者指出，在本章中所引用的《过秦论》与《新书》中引用的同一段有着明显的差异。《新书》中贾谊的《过秦论》共分为三篇：上篇关于秦始皇，中篇关于秦二世，下篇关于秦三世。《史记》卷四十八篇末的选段是贾谊的《过秦论》中的上篇（根据如今对《新书》的文本划分）。而参见《陈涉世家》“褚先生曰：地形险阻，所以为固也；兵革刑法，所以为治也。犹未足恃也。夫先王以仁义为本，而以固塞文法为枝叶，岂不然哉！吾闻贾生之称曰：……”《史记》卷四十八似乎证明了在这种情况下贾谊作品的选段是褚少孙的增补部分。同时在卷四十八中缺少“太史公”应有的“赞”。在《史记》卷六结尾处，贾谊的《过秦论》被全部引用，但是顺序却与《新书》中不尽相同：首先是下篇，其次是上篇，最后是中篇。

克罗里总结到主要存在以下问题：（1）为什么贾谊的《过秦论》两次出现在《史记》中？（2）为什么《史记》卷四十八没有“太史公”的“赞”？（3）为什么《过秦论》在《史记》卷六中的顺序混乱？

克罗里在自己的研究中指出，早在唐朝就已经出现这些问题的解释了：

1. 邹诞生认为，司马迁将《过秦论》以缩略的形式放于《史记》卷六结尾处，后来褚少孙续作了本章的“赞”，并且司马迁的原作和褚少孙的续作之间的界限是不清楚的，因为抄写者将两人的文本混在一起抄写了。

2. 裴骃认为，司马迁将《过秦论》的上篇、下篇分别作为《史记》卷六和卷四十八的“赞”，并且在卷四十八错误地插入“褚先生曰”。

3. 司马贞认为，卷四十八处应是“太史公曰”，而不是“褚先生曰”。

克罗里同时还指出上述问题也引起了清朝学者的关注：王鸣盛（1722—1797）认为在《新书》中《过秦论》按照一定顺序被分为三篇，这一顺序在《史记》卷六末尾处被破坏。他根据徐广、裴骃和司马贞的证据提出这一观点，即司马迁将《过秦论》的上篇作为《史记》卷四十八的“赞”，而《过秦论》的中篇和下篇作为卷六的“赞”。他指出，班固看了司马迁的书，因此贾谊作品的部分以上述的方式被放于其中。在魏晋时期，某个“鲁莽的人”将贾谊《过秦论》的上篇添加到了《史记》卷六的结语中。随后，另一个人注意到了，并怀疑这是褚少孙的作品，便将卷四十八“太史公曰”改为“褚先生曰”。然而王鸣盛的理论存在一处错误，日本学者泷川龟太郎认为王鸣盛有关班固似乎看过《史记》中的引文的根据是不充分的。但王的观点得到了爱德华·沙畹教授和嵇辽拉的支持。

为了厘清上述问题，克罗里引述了多个学者的观点：

著名史学家赵翼（1727—1814）认为，司马迁在《史记》卷六结尾处援引了《过秦论》，而褚少孙在卷四十八结尾处再一次援引了《过秦论》中有关陈涉的语句。这一猜想有很多薄弱之处。因为并没有证据证明有人看过《史记》的古本。在其他学者看来，赵翼的猜想是非常不合理的。赵翼提出的观点虽然没有根据，却由于满足《史记选注》的编写而被采纳。

泷川龟太郎曾提出关于《史记》卷四十八的问题。他认为，根据班固的引述，卷四十八中的“褚先生”应该写为“太史公”。为了证明自己的观点，他提出，《史记》每一卷都有“赞”，《陈涉世家》不可能是其中唯一的例外。

梁玉绳（1745—1819）曾试图阐明这个问题。他认为贾谊将其作品分为上下两篇。“太史公”根据《过秦论》的上篇作了《史记》卷四十八的结语，根据下篇作了卷六的结语。后来在卷六中插入了作品的上篇。在卷六中两篇作品的顺序在誊写过程中被打乱。然而，梁玉绳的理论需要证明，即证明在班固的时代贾谊的作品是分为两篇的。

朱东润教授也提出了相似的观点。他以班固的援引为基础，从《过秦论》上篇被引用在《史记》卷四十八这一观点出发，作出了结论：首先在卷六的结语中只有下篇可以被引用。因为朱东润认为《过秦论》分为三篇，由此他得出结论，在司马迁的原稿中，卷六的结尾处只有贾谊作品的下篇，而作品的上篇和中篇，就是在《史记》卷六中按现代顺序位于下篇之后的，只是后来被插入了其中。

在通过上述学者的观点分析后，克罗里得出以下的结论：除了赵翼和《史记选注》的编者，其他所有学者的观点是一致的，那就是司马迁将《过秦论》的上篇放于《史记》卷四十八的结尾，并用“褚先生曰”代替“太史公曰”。

至于是谁对《史记》卷四十八中“赞”的标题做了修改，以及谁补写了贾谊作品之前的一些文字，主要有以下几种观点：(1) 这些文字是褚少孙写的，他还擅自将“太史公”改为“褚先生”（司马贞）；(2) 这些文字是“太史公”写的，至于是谁修改了标题，我们无从得知（泷川龟太郎）；(3) 将“太史公”改为“褚先生”是后来插入进去的，他们试图通过这种方式解决贾谊作品的上篇在《史记》中重复出现这一问题（王鸣盛）。王鸣盛的观点成功地对泷川龟太郎的解释作了补充。褚少孙不可能在《史记》卷四十八“赞”的标题处做修改，因为据班固的观点，“太史公”根据贾谊作品的选段作成了《陈涉世家》的结语。自然也就可以得出结论，在由班固执手的《史记》副本中，在卷四十八结尾处，记载有“太史公曰”，而不是“褚先生曰”。因此在《史记》卷四十八结语的标题的修改，不是褚少孙干的，最可能是在2世纪末至5世纪司马迁作品编者中的某位干的。很有可能是为了解决贾谊作品在《史记》中重复出现的问题。

关于贾谊作品的哪些篇被引用到《史记》卷六的结语中，就只需要研究两个观点。中井和朱东润断言，在本卷的原文中也只引入了《过秦论》的下篇，而梁玉绳和王鸣盛认为，其中引用了《过秦论》的中篇和下篇。班固认为贾谊作品的上篇和中篇被司马迁使用，朱东润在此基础上建立了自己的理论。并且他的理论完美回答了这一问题，那就是在为何《史记》卷六结语处贾谊作品的顺序是混乱的。他认为徐广读过《史记》副本，其中卷六结语处引入了贾谊作品的中篇和下篇。班固执笔的《过秦论》副本按照现在作品的分法被分为三篇，在这一条件下朱东润的观点是不可反驳的。但是克罗里有严谨的根据来怀疑它。应劭在《汉书》卷三十一的注解提供了以下证据：“贾生书有《过秦》二篇，言秦之过。”由此可见，在应劭那个时代，贾谊的作品只分为两篇，后来下篇被分为现在的中篇和下篇。应劭生活在班固的时代。因此，如果说“太史公”根据《过秦论》的上篇和中篇作了《史记》的卷六和卷四十八的“赞”，班固完全能说司马迁将《过秦论》的上篇引入卷四十八的结语，并将中篇和下篇引入卷六，中篇和下篇在那一时期是合为一篇的。

由此看来，朱东润的主要观点是完全可以反驳的。所以克罗里不得不同意梁玉绳的看法。在克罗里看来，《史记》卷六的结语首先引于贾谊作品的中篇和下篇（当时属于合为一篇的《过秦论》下篇），这两篇按原本的顺序排列（先是中篇，后是下篇）。同时对于在《史记》卷六结尾处的贾谊的《过秦论》两篇混乱，这个猜想目前并没给出令人信服的解释，因此，问题仍需进一步明确。

参考文献

Кроль Ю. Л. , О двух традициях отношения к материалу в ханьской литературе [A],《История, культура, языки народов Востока》, 1970, 124–131.

Кроль Ю. Л. , Одна из текстологических проблем, связанных с главами 6 и 48《Записей историка》,《Письменные памятники Востока. Ежегодник. 1968》, 1970,

208-216.

Кроль Ю. Л. , Литературная теория и литературная практика Сыма Цяня, 《История и культура Китая (Сборник статей памяти академика В. П. Васильева)》, 1974, 200-216.

Russian Sinologist Krol and his study of *The Historical Records*

Lu Bo, Yu Xiang

Abstract: the famous Russian Sinologist Krol has been devoted to the study of historians and historical materials in the Han Dynasty. He has published a large number of monographs and academic papers on Sinology, which has a great influence on Sinology in Russia and even in the world. Much of his academic career has been devoted to the study of the Han Dynasty's literature writing methods and the textual research of *The Historical Records*. The writer thinks that his research philosophy and research approach have great reference significance to Chinese scholars. Based on the research of his academic works, this paper summarizes his Sinology research from three aspects: the literature writing technique of Han Dynasty, Sima Qian's cultural theory and practice, and the research on the related issues of the text of *The Historical Records*, especially his views on the study of *The Historical Records*.

Key words: Krol; sinologist; the research of *The Historical Records*

文化与教学

高校英语教学融入“课程思政”研究综述*

戴　琨　王　琳　景婷婷**

摘　要：自“课程思政”这一概念提出以来，许多学者对高校英语教学中融入“课程思政”开展了一系列相关研究，取得了丰硕的成果。学者们从不同的角度探讨了高校英语“课程思政”的内涵、高校英语教学融入“课程思政”的可行性和必要性、实施路径以及具体英语课程的改革实践。本文通过对相关文献进行梳理总结，发现目前高校英语教学融入“课程思政”的实证类研究相对较少，且相关研究比较宏观，可操作性不强；实施效果的评价研究比较匮乏。笔者也展望了该领域未来的研究趋势，以期为推进高校英语“课程思政”改革提供参考和借鉴。

关键词：课程思政；高校英语教学；综述

引言

习近平总书记在全国高校思想政治工作会议上指出：“要坚持把立德树人作为中心环节，把思想政治工作贯穿教育教学全过程，使各类课程与思想政治理论课同向同行，形成协同效应。”（习近平，2016）。自“课程思政”理念提出以来，国内许多高校英语教育学者对此进行了大量研究，也发表了一系列相关学术成果。截至 2020 年 4 月，在 CNKI（中国知网）上以“课程思政”“英语”为主题进行搜索，共检索到文献 301 篇，

---

* 本研究成果为陕西师范大学 2020 年度校级“课程思政”示范课建设项目资助项目成果［课程名称：大学外语（二）］。

** 作者简介：戴琨（1980—　），女，陕西师范大学外国语学院副教授，研究方向：英语教育、跨文化交际。

王琳（1995—　），女，陕西师范大学外国语学院硕士研究生，研究方向：英语教育。

景婷婷（1987—　），女，陕西师范大学国际交流与合作处科员，研究方向：英语教育。

经过文献梳理，发现该领域的研究成果呈逐年增加趋势，英语教育融入“课程思政”已经成了高等教育英语研究领域的热点。

一　高校英语教学背景下“课程思政”的内涵

2017年12月，教育部颁发的《高校思想政治工作质量提升工程实施纲要》中明确指出要大力推动以“课程思政”为目标的课题教学改革，自此有关“课程思政”的研究也开始如火如荼地展开。英语作为高校非英语专业学生的公共基础课程和英语专业学生的必修课程，其教学对象广，时间跨度长，且在该门学科中融入思政元素也有许多切入点。因此，国内许多高校英语教育工作者在中央精神的指导下，探讨了高校英语教学背景下“课程思政”的内涵。

夏元芬（2020）论证了大学英语“课程思政”的内涵，认为大学英语课程思政是一种综合的教育理念和实践模式。它指的是将思政元素有机融入大学英语教学过程中，充分挖掘出课程中的思政价值，进而使思政教育与大学英语课程实现协同育人的效果。也有学者指出提升人文素养、增强跨文化意识、培养批判性思维、引领文化自信是英语学科课程思政的内涵指向（胡恒，2020）。高校英语课程思政是以立德树人为导向，以明确的思政元素为主题，以英语知识技能和人文素养的提升为目标，以此来实现全方位育人。陈丽霞（2019）以一门具体英语课程为例，论证了专业课程的思政价值内涵。认为高校英语教学“课程思政”的内涵就是将显性语言知识传授与隐性价值引领相结合，以此达到全课程育人的格局。

综上，高校英语“课程思政”是一种新的教育理念和课程观，它是将显性语言知识的教学与隐性思想道德培育有机融合，将思想政治教育内容全方位地渗透到听、说、读、写、译等英语教学当中。它不是思想政治教育与英语教学的简单叠加，也不是为了思政而思政，将英语教学思政化，而是坚持英语教学本位，充分挖掘高校英语课程的社会主义核心价值观培育功能，实现英语课程融思政、思政寓于英语课程的局面，使知识传授与价值引领有效协同，在潜移默化中完成立德树人的目标。

二　高校英语教学融入“课程思政”的可行性和必要性

许多学者对大学英语、高职英语以及商务英语教学融入“课程思政”

的可行性和必要性进行了探讨和论证，如朱芮的《“课程思政”视域下的高职英语教学研究》、卢军坪的《大学英语课程推进“课程思政”的可行性探索》、韦金凤的《高校商务英语专业推行“课程思政”探析》等。总体看来，这些研究从课程性质、课程内容、课程功能等方面对实施“课程思政”的可行性和意义进行了深度探讨。

（一）课程性质与“课程思政”本质相吻合

从课程性质来看，不论是大学英语、商务英语还是高职英语，这些英语课程都兼具工具性和人文性的双重性质。就其人文性而言，其核心就是以人为本，注重人的综合素质培养和全面发展。英语课程教学承担着全面育人和培养优秀英语复合型人才的任务，所以在传授英语语言知识的同时，也兼顾学生综合素养的提高，把社会主义核心价值观融入高校英语教学当中，也是大学英语课程人文性的体现。高校英语课程的性质与“课程思政”的本质相吻合（卢军坪，2019：130；王小玲，2019：79）。

（二）课程内容既适合又需要“课程思政”教学

一方面，高校英语课程的内容比较广泛，涉及政治、经济、社会、历史、文化等诸多方面，可以深入挖掘教材当中的思政元素。另一方面，这些英语课程的教材内容都与西方思想文化内容紧密结合，基本上是直接从西方国家的报纸杂志或书籍上选取的英文原文，学生很容易在西方思潮的影响下摈弃本国优秀的文化，对西方国家的价值观取向产生盲目崇拜（张莹，2019：34；张巨武，2020：95）。因此必须要开展思想政治教育，一方面深入挖掘教材中的思政元素，以讲授西方语言文化为契机，因势利导，引导学生批判性地学习西方文化，学习中国优秀的文化；另一方面，要添加一些带有中国特色的思政元素作为教学素材，使学生在学习外国文化的同时也要坚定社会主义核心价值观，明晰中西文化差异，在通过语言学习了解外国文化的过程中，增强民族文化自信，传播好中国声音，阐释好中国的价值理念和思想文化。

（三）课程功能与“课程思政”功能有一致性

从课程功能来看，这些英语课程都具备隐性课程的功能，与“课程思政”的功能存在一致性。语言是文化的载体，也是意识形态的载体，任何语言都蕴含着丰富的文化内涵和思想道德因素（夏文红、何芳，2019：108；周帆，2019：52）。一直以来，英语教学只注重学生语言技能的传授，而忽略了意识形态方面的教育。学生在学习语言时，也会无意识地接触语言中蕴含的文化和价值理念，会在知识学习中潜移默化地发生理想信念层面的转变（蒋婷婷，2019：122）。在英语课堂中渗透思想政治内容，不仅会使英语课堂变得更加丰富多彩，也会使思政元素在英语课堂中得到有效的表达（杨琼，2020：50）。与传统的思想政治课程相比，英语课程中隐性地进行思政教育更能吸引、感染学生，使思政教学达到意想不到的效果。

这些英语课程的教学目标都与“立德树人”这一根本任务有非常高的契合点，在学生综合素质的培养上有着其他学科不能媲美的优势。教师通过隐性教育将思政元素融入课堂，赋予了传统的思想政治教育鲜活的生命力，又增添了英语课程本身的内涵，充分发挥了其协同作用和功能，是实现全过程、全方位育人的有效途径。

三　高校英语教学融入“课程思政”的实施路径

一些学者从宏观层面探索了“课程思政”在高职英语、商务英语、大学英语中的实施路径，也有一些学者从微观层面探索了“课程思政”在英语听、说、读、写、译教学中的融入和具体实施方案。就宏观层面来看，主要从课程教材建设、师资队伍建设、教学方法创新、课程考评机制等方面进行研究。

（一）加强课程和教材建设

从课程教材建设角度看，有学者认为要以修订英语课程标准作为实施“课程思政”的切入点（张莹，2019：35）。丁水芳（2020：69）认为，大学英语教材是实施“课程思政”的重要内容之一，在选取或编写教材过程中，要融入中国文化特色素材，提高学生用英语表达中国文化的能力。大学英语“课程思政”的课程设置应该从基础课程和文化素养培养课程两方面入手，通过挖掘课本中的思政元素和引领学生学习英文版中国文化等著作，来提高学生的英语水平，培养学生的文化自信和民族自豪感（孔标，2020：181）。夏元芬（2020：157）提出从大学英语必修课、中国文化概况等选修课和“第二课堂”来加强课程建设，提高学生的综合素质和跨文化交际能力。此外，还有学者认为加强教材建设，丰富高校英语教材的思政内容，在教材内容上融入更多的思政元素，也是实施“课程思政”的有效策略（杜刚跃、孙瑞娟，2019：125；夏元芬，2020：157）。为了从源头上推进“课程思政”建设，将思政元素潜移默化地融入高校英语教学，必须要加强课程建设和教材建设。

（二）加强师资队伍建设

从师资队伍建设方面来看，学者们也进行了细致的探索，强调了教师在实施英语“课程思政”方面的重要性。教师是“思政”元素融入的关键，加强教师专业化建设是课程思政教学改革的前提（刘瑛，2019：122；卢军坪，2019：131）。夏元芬（2020：156）指出，教师应该首先革新教育教学理念，树立协同育人的观念，在此基础上，再通过课程思政专题培训、专业化技术培训等提升自己的思政能力和育人水平。由此可以看出，教师育人观念和人文素养的提升是实施“课程思政”的先决条件。一些学者还从示范课、集体备课、组织教师集体学习、申报“课程思政”相关课题等方面探讨了英语“课程思政”教学团队的建设（孔标，2020：180；张巨武，2020：97）。大学英语课程思政建设，需要教师个人和教学团队的共同努力，只有坚持团队先行、引领示范、全员参与、同向同行的原则才能发挥出思政育人的最大功效。

（三）创新教育教学方法

从教学方法创新来看，许多学者都主张创新教学方法，利用互联网技术，采用“线上+线下”“课内+课外”相结合的混合教学模式，利用图片、音频、视频等多模态呈现方式，借助慕课、微课、网易公开课等优质网络资源，探索实践翻转课堂、混合式教学等新型教学模式、拓展“第二课堂”，完善多元化教学模式，精心筛选出有意义的、学生感兴趣的、含有思政元素的英文版内容作为教学资源，增强思政教育的吸引力，在潜移默化中实现知识传授和价值引领的有机统一（王小玲，2019：79；陈雪贞，2019：47；靳秀莹，2019：63；蒋婷婷，2019：123；夏元芬，2020：157；渠天花，2020：109）。英语教学“课程思政”应创新教学方法，利用多种教学资源辅助教学，充分利用课堂和课外、融通线上线下，实现英语教学思政育人时间与空间上的双向拓展，在引人入胜、潜移默化中提升教学和育人效果。

（四）优化课程考评体系

有学者也主张优化课程评价体系，推进“课程思政”有效落实。在评价中注重课程思政导向，做到评价主体、评价体系和评价内容的多元化（蒋婷婷，2019：124）。对学生进行评价的时候，要把过程性评价和终结性评价结合起来，避免由单一的专业知识维度来决定，要从学生的人文素养、思政素养等多维度进行评价，注重思政元素育人的导向作用（陈雪贞，2019：47；张巨武，2020：98）。对老师进行评价也要坚持多维度的评价体系，不能只注重教师的业绩，也要将教师的思想政治水平、职业道德等指标纳入考核体系。夏元芬（2020：156）提倡将文化素养作为对教师业务能力的衡量指标之一。对教师要加强动态监管，规范科学考核，对教学质量和教学纪律进行监控，以保证高校英语“课程思政”的顺利实施（张莹，2019：37）。通过优化对学生和教师的评价体系，可以达到以评促学、以评促思的效果，将思政教育真正落实在高校英语教学当中，实现高校英语“课程思政”的预期目标。

（五）听、说、读、写、译教学中思政元素的融入

学者们也对“课程思政”在英语听、说、读、写、译教学过程中的具体实施路径进行了探讨。在听力教学中，借助 BBC，China Radio International，Ted Talk，China Daily 等优质网络资源和一些反映中西方文化差异和政治理念的影视材料，挑选含有“课程思政”元素的内容应用于听力教学，有意识地引领学生学习和掌握重要的思政内容英文表达，将基于中国文化的内容潜移默化地融入听力教学中，建立学生的文化自信和文化认同（李弢，2019：61；朱芮，2019：60；孔标，2020：181）。在口语教学中，要求教师深度挖掘与思政元素相关的内容，引导学生积极参与讨论，开展相关话题的口语报告、演讲比赛、辩论赛等，使学生在提高口语水平的同时，提高自己的思想政治意识（孔标，2020：181）。在阅读教学中，教师可以选取有关中西文化对比、中国政治、经济等相关的英文版报纸和杂志等阅读材料，安排学生分别就《人民日报》（英文版）和《卫报》《纽约时报》等针对性地开展拓展阅读，使学生在提高阅读技能的同时，批判性地看待西方文化，培养学生的文化自信和民族自豪感（梅强，2018：59）。在写作教学中可以引导学生围绕“爱国主义的内涵”“中国梦”等含有思政元素的话题进行写作。在翻译教学中，帮助学生积累中国特色词汇的表达，选取具有中国特色的材料给学生做翻译练习。

四 高校英语教学进行“课程思政”改革的具体实践

国内许多学者以某一门英语课程为例，进行了该门课程融入“课程思政”的探讨和实践，如陈丽霞在《高校英语专业课程的思政价值内涵

与实现路径——以〈综合英语〉课程改革为例》这篇文章中，从《综合英语》这门课程的德育目标设计、教学团队建设、教学方法和模式改革三方面探讨了该门课程实现思政价值内涵的主要路径；王甲能等在《〈大学英语〉课程思政：课堂教学创新实践探索》中展示了两个英语教学和课程思政融合的生动案例，从教学目标方法、教学设计过程、教学反思与评价三方面对显性语言教学和隐性道德教育的有机融合进行了教学实践；童晓梅的《高职高专院校大学英语课程思政教育的设计与实践——以教材〈新编实用英语综合教程〉为例》从课前、课中和课后提出了将思想政治元素融入英语课程的实践策略。

还有一些学者以某门课程中的某一单元或某一篇文章为例，对如何在这些单元或文章教学中融入思政元素进行了较为细致的探讨，如王小玲的《新时代“课程思政”背景下高职英语课堂教学研究——以教学单元“Holiday Celebrations”为例》，从单元教学目标设计、教学实施过程、效果评价及反思这几方面探讨了“课程思政”在高职英语教学中的融入；郭凤青在《从教材视角论大学英语课程思政之教学方法——以〈大学英语精读〉中的〈礼物〉为例》这篇文章中探讨了通过了解教材的设计结构，找出融入课程思政切入点的方法。丁水芳在《协同育人：大学英语“课程思政”教学模式建构研究》这篇文章中，以全新版《大学进阶英语Ⅰ》综合教程第一单元“The Pursuit of Dreams”为例从课前导入、课中渗透、课后巩固三方面设计了渗透思政教育的大学英语教学活动。

这些具体英语课程或内容融入“课程思政”的改革实践为以后高校英语开展“课程思政”建设积累了经验，有一定的参考价值。但通过在知网上对相关文献的检索发现，此类研究相对较少，仅有35篇，占总数的11.63%。只有各级各类英语课程广泛开展课程思政的改革实践，才能推动高校英语“课程思政”建设真正落实，实现英语专业课程的隐性思政功能。

五 研究小节与未来展望

通过梳理高校英语教学融入“课程思政”的相关文献，我们可以发现，目前该领域的相关研究主要从某一类课程、某一具体课程展开，取得了比较丰硕的成果，为高校英语教学进一步深入推进“课程思政”的实施提供了有效的参考和借鉴。现有研究主要呈现三大特点：第一，研究主要探讨了英语教学融入“课程思政”的重要意义和实施路径，但付诸实践的实证类研究成果相对缺乏，未能深入探究高校英语教学融入“课程思政”的具体成效。第二，研究层次不够均衡。现有研究主要从宏观角度分析了英语教学融入“课程思政”的实施路径，且大部分是以论述为主，可操作性不强，真正适用于某一具体课程的“课程思政”研究相对较少。第三，针对高校英语“课程思政”实施的评价研究极度缺乏，仅阐述了如何对高校英语“课程思政”进行评价，但却鲜有研究探究其具体实施的效果。

展望未来，高校英语教学融入“课程思政”的研究可能有如下趋势：相关的实证研究可能会越来越多；对不同英语课程融入思政元素的具体实施路径、教学目标、教学方法、教学设计和教学过程的研究可能会不断细化且持续增加；实施效果评价的研究将受到重视。

参考文献

陈丽霞：《高校英语专业课程的思政价值内涵与实现路径——以〈综合英语〉课程改革为例》，《江西中医药大学学报》2019 年第 3 期。

陈雪贞：《最优化理论视角下大学英语课程思政的教学实现》，《中国大学教学》2019 年第 10 期。

丁水芳：《协同育人：大学英语“课程思政”教学模式建构研究》，《东华理工大学学报》（社会科学版）2020 年第 1 期。

杜刚跃、孙瑞娟：《高校英语教学“课程思政”有效策略研究》，《延安大学学报》（社会科学版）2019 年第 4 期。

郭凤青：《从教材视角论大学英语课程思政之教学方法——以〈大学英语精读〉中的〈礼物〉为例》，《海外英语》2020 年第 3 期。

胡恒：《远程英语教学课程思政的内涵指向及实践路径》，《湖北广播电视大学学报》2020 年第 1 期。

蒋婷婷：《基于混合式教学的大学英语“课程思政”模式建构》，《丽水学院学报》2019 年第 6 期。

靳秀莹：《大学英语教学“课程思政”实施策略探索》，《牡丹江教育学院学报》2019 年第 11 期。

孔标：《“大思政”格局下大学英语“课程思政”的落实研究》，《长春师范大学学报》（人文社会科学版）2020 年第 2 期。

李弢：《课程思政视角下“大学英语听力”课程教学模式新探》，《湖南科技学院学报》2019 年第 12 期。

刘瑛：《课程思政视角下商务英语专业教学改革的研究与实践》，《赤峰学院学报》(哲学社会科学版) 2019 年第 11 期。

卢军坪:《大学英语课程推进“课程思政”的可行性探索》,《上海第二工业大学学报》2019 年第 2 期。

梅强:《以点引线 以线带面——高校两类全覆盖课程思政探索与实践》,《中国大学教学》2018 年第 9 期。

陆道坤:《课程思政推行中若干核心问题及解决思路——基于专业课程思政的探讨》,《思想理论教育》2018 年第 3 期。

渠天花:《课程思政融入大学英语文化教学的策略》,《教书育人(高教论坛)》2020 年第 4 期。

童晓梅:《高职高专院校大学英语课程思政教育的设计与实践——以教材〈新编实用英语综合教程〉为例》,《新西部》2019 年第 36 期。

王甲能、郭宁、贾爱武:《〈大学英语〉课程思政:课堂教学创新实践探索》,《黑龙江教师发展学院学报》2020 年第 3 期。

王小玲:《新时代“课程思政”背景下高职英语课堂教学研究 ——以教学单元“Holiday Celebrations”为例》,《高等职业教育-天津职业大学学报》2019 年第 6 期。

韦金凤:《高校商务英语专业推行“课程思政”探析》,《高教论坛》2020 年第 2 期。

习近平:《在庆祝中国共产党 95 周年大会上的讲话》,人民出版社 2016 年版。

夏文红、何芳:《大学英语“课程思政”的使命担当》,《人民论坛》2019 年第 30 期。

夏元芬:《论大学英语课程思政的内在机理与实践路径》,《湖北经济学院学报》(人文社会科学版) 2020 年第 4 期。

杨琼:《基于课程思政的大学英语课程教学模式研究》,《教育教学论坛》2020 年第 2 期。

张巨武:《〈大学英语〉“课程思政”教学改革研究》,《西安文理学院学报》(社会科学版) 2020 年第 1 期。

张莹:《课程思政在高职英语专业中的实施路径——以天津职业大学为例》,《高等职业教育-天津职业大学学报》2019 年第 3 期。

周帆:《大学英语“课程思政”路径研究》,《吉林工程技术师范学院学报》2019 年第 9 期。

朱芮:《“课程思政”视域下的高职英语教学研究》,《辽宁高职学报》2019 年第 1 期。

A Review of the Studies on the Integration of "Ideological and Political Education" into English Teaching in Colleges and Universities

Abstract: Since the concept of "ideological and political education in all courses" was put forward, many scholars have carried out a series of studies on the integration of "ideological and political education" in college English teaching and achieved fruitful results. From different perspectives, the scholars have discussed the connotation of "ideological and political education in all courses", the feasibility and necessity of integrating "ideological and political education" into college English teaching, its implementation ways as well as the practice of specific English courses. Based on the review and summary of relevant studies, this paper finds that the empirical research on the integration of "ideological and political education" into college English teaching is relatively few, and the relevant research is comparatively macro and not easy to operate; the evaluation research on the implementation effect is scarce. The author looks forward to the research trends in this field, with a view to providing reference for advancing the reform of the integration of "ideological and political education" into English teaching in colleges and universities.

Key words: ideological and political education in all courses; English teaching in colleges and universities; review

中法 FLE 教材中词汇编写的比较与思考

王燕红*

摘　要：FLE 意为“法语作为外语的教学”。

在法国，关于 FLE 的教材、教学、实践以及理论等各方面的研究历史悠久，尤其是教材建设和研究代表着全世界基础法语教学教材的发展趋势，而在我国，无论是教学实践还是理论研究，起步较晚，其中教材建设也是长期受限于传统教学模式。

我们选取了中国出版的中国高校普遍使用的《新大学法语》和法国著名出版社 Hachette 出版的 *Alter-Ego*+进行了词汇、语法、文本材料、练习等各方面的比较。但本文仅对二者的词汇编写进行数量、表现方式及重复频率的比较，分析其优劣，希望通过这一对比分析对我国基础法语教材建设以及教材使用技巧提供有益的启示和参考。

关键词：法语；二外教材；比较；词汇

FLE 的意思是“法语作为外语的教学”。

近年来，随着我国国际地位的提升、参与国际事务的增加以及与法国和各法语国家的政治、经济、文化交流与合作的日益扩大和深入，我国对法语高级人才的需求与日俱增。目前，全国有一百多所高校开设了法语专业，开设法语第二外语的学校不胜枚举。同时，随着赴法语国家留学热潮的升温，各种法语培训也迅速发展。

在这种形势下，法语教学水平的提升，教学模式的转变，如何进行改革，培养高素质的具有国际视野的复合型高级法语人才等问题，都提到日程上来。

* 作者简介：王燕红，陕西师范大学外国语学院（Shaanxi Normal University）讲师。研究方向：法语语言与文化。

在法国，关于FLE的教材、教学、实践以及理论等各方面的研究历史悠久，而在我国，无论是教学实践，还是理论研究，起步都比较晚，而且发展缓慢，其中教材建设也是长期受限于传统教学模式，一直在寻求突破瓶颈的合理方法。法语教材既是教学的源泉，提供课程内容并规定教学方法，还是教学任务和目标的载体，其作用和重要性在教学中不言而喻，著名语言学家程晓堂也曾说过，“课堂活动和组织主要是建立在教材的基础上，要改善教学就要有理想的教材”（程晓堂，2005：57）。因此，对中法FLE教材的各方面进行比较研究，借鉴法国教材较为先进的编写理念和模式，分析二者之优劣，并依此对我国法语教材的编写和改革、对法语教师在基础教学中对教材的使用技巧提出一点建议，都是有积极意义的。如今，许多重要的出版社都在借鉴法语原版教材的编写模式，对我国法语专业或二外教材进行积极的改革。那么为什么要作出这样那样的改编，各种教材更适用的教学法是哪一种，国内外法语教材的优缺点又是什么？

我们选取了在中国高校普遍使用的法语二外教材《新大学法语》（高等教育出版社出版，李志清总主编，2011年版，共三册，“十一五”“十二五”国家级规划教材）和法国官方教学文化机构法语联盟普遍使用的*Alter-Ego+*（法国Hachette出版社出版，2012年版，共五册），对二者的词汇、语法、文本材料、练习等各方面的编写内容和形式进行详尽的比较，分析其优劣所在。本文是这一研究的一部分，仅涉及两种教材的词汇（语言的三大要素之一）内容编写的数量、表现方式及重复频率的比较，希望通过这一对比分析，对于我国基础法语教材在这一方面的建设以及教材使用技巧提供有益的启示和参考。

一　词汇的比较

词汇是语言的三大要素之一（语音、词汇、语法）。语言学家River认为：掌握足够数量的词汇是灵活运用一门外语的主要因素之一。一本教材的词汇数量因此也成为策略问题。在母语中，词汇是在日常生活活动中自然地、循序渐进地获得的；与之不同，外语词汇则是在确立某一目标后，通过系统和策略的学习获取的。那么该学哪些词，学多少，如何介绍这些词，这些都是教材编写需要注意的重要问题。

法国语言教材评估专家Anne-Marie Thierry在制定评估表格时，对词汇一项的基本要求是：词汇活跃度（重复使用情况）、形象易懂的表达、同义词、语言的层级等（Jean-Pierre Cuq，Isabelle Gruca，2003：257—258）。美国的 Skierso 在其 1991 年推出的教材评价标准中也提出有关词汇的标准：词汇数量是否适合学习者的需要，是否使用标准语言，难易度是否适合学习者的水平，词汇是否重复，词汇的介绍是否从易到难等（田炳姬，2011：18）。参考这些标准，我们将进行以下四个方面的比较。

（一）词汇数量的比较

考虑到教材的平衡性，我们选取前两册进行比较。

我们首先来看看两种教材中第一册和第二册各单元词汇数量的分布，如图 1、图 2 所示。

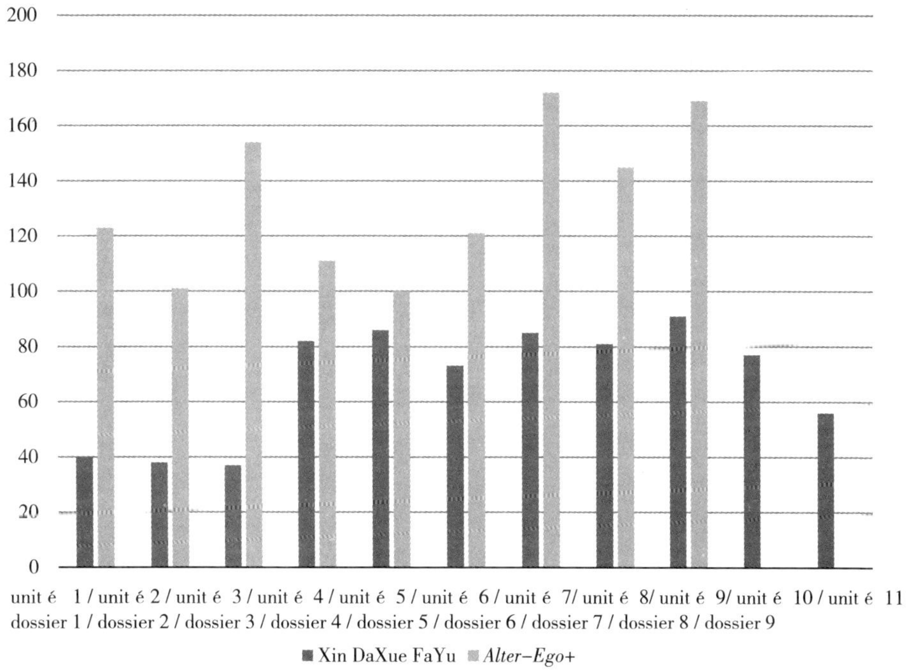

图 1　两种教材词汇分布（第一册）

从图 1、图 2 我们能很明显地看出，法国教材 *Alter-Ego+*词汇数量优于中国教材《新大学法语》。法国教材第一册包含了 1190 个词和词组，第二册为 1563 个，平均每单元为 161.9 个。我们有理由认为使用该教材的

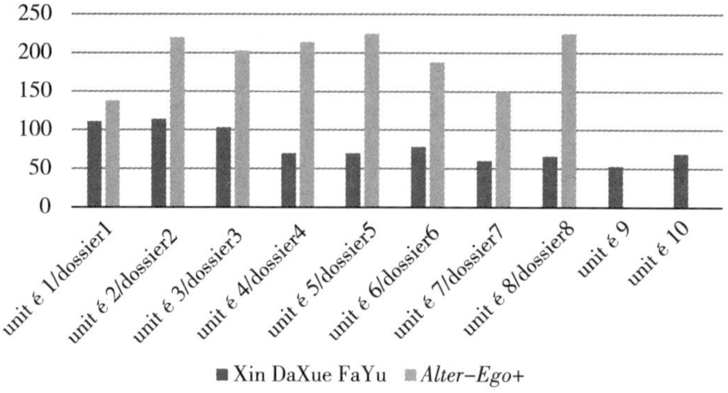

图 2　两种教材词汇分布（第二册）

学习者能有足够的词汇运用于日常交际。当然，这对于初学者来说是个巨大的挑战；且这些词汇是否能频繁使用而得到实际掌握也是个问题，这就对编排策略和使用技巧提出了很高的要求。

而在《新大学法语》中，第一册包含 746 个词和词组，第二册为 794 个，平均每单元 73.3 个。而根据 2002 年 1 月最新版大学法语教学大纲，基本要求为领会式掌握 2800 词，而我们教材中的词汇数量并不能满足这个要求；同时，这一版大纲较之以往的大纲还提出了新的教学目标：使学生能用法语交流简单的信息，提高文化素养并为进一步提高法语水平打下较好的基础。在长期教学中我们发现，使用该教材的高校学生并不能达到这一目标，即不能进行顺利的日常交流，除了教学方法、教学条件（班级人数、教学时数等）的限制外，词汇数量不够也是一个重要原因。这就造成了培养目标与教材短板之间的矛盾。

（二）词汇表现形式的不同

在《新大学法语》中，词汇列表位于课文之后，其排列既不按首字母顺序，也不以主题归类，所有词性的单词和词组按照它们在课文中出现的顺序排列，附汉语翻译。比如：superficie n. f 面积。单词和语法一样，是为课文服务的，每个单元基本按照主题功能划分，但是在单词表中各种词性的词混杂在一起出现，仅为理解课文服务，没有一定的系统性，不利于识记。更值得一提的是，名词只标明阴阳性，没有给出冠词，无法有效提示学生记忆的方法，使学生们习惯性地只识记单词，再单独去记忆其性数，这种方式非常抽象，导致大多数学习者认为阴阳性的记忆极其困难。

虽然该教材从大单元来看按照新的意念功能大纲编订，但是由于其更适用于传统的“语法—翻译”式教学方法，且词汇数量有限，而这种词汇编排更加阻碍了其功能的真正实现，即使用者学习完词汇后，对于大多数词，如果没有教师的补充和讲解，依然不知如何使用，因为它们都以独立的单词形式出现，没有用法也没有例句，如果让自学者使用，对词汇的掌握难度较大。另外，受到母语翻译的影响，许多词汇意思混淆，例如：“看”这个词，书中有：lire（看书，表示读），regarder（看，强调动作），voir（看见、看望，强调结果），admirer（欣赏地看），contempler（注视地看），observer（观察）等词；再如：“穿”有：mettre（vt. 穿上，表示动作），porter（vt. 穿着，表示状态），s'habiller（v. pr，不及物的代词式动词）。类似这样的情况不在少数，学习者总是搞不清楚它们的区别而使用错误，许多常用词汇不能达到复用式掌握的目的。好在第二册和第三册增加了“词和词组”专栏，对某些词进行详细讲解。

在词汇的使用上，每课课后配有一题相应的词汇辨析应用填空题，可帮助学习者在练习中再次了解某些词的用法、含义和与其他词的区别；同时，每一课新出现的不规则动词均列出其动词变位；并且在教材最后列有以首字母为顺序的总词汇表，便于查询使用。

而在法国教材中，在每课中没有完全的单词表，单词总表位于教材的最后附件中，按主题排列，例如：娱乐、运动、旅行、服装、人物描述、人的性格等，主题的形式更利于学习者系统记忆单词，对比使用，查阅起来也非常方便。在每一课里，设有一个或多个“帮助记忆”模块（*Aide-mémoire*），按实用功能组织了本课中最重要和常用的词组和表达方式，构成一个实用“词汇工具箱”，很少出现独立的单词，而是以语段的形式出现，即短语、表达、语段甚至句子，使用者可从中一目了然地了解该词或词组的功能及具体用法。每单元之后也附有相应的词汇辨析使用练习。此外，给出的词汇都给出相应的冠词，如：la superficie，un livre 等，提示学习者习惯性地把冠词当作名词的一部分记忆，学习起来更加有效，也减少了另外去记忆词性的困难。

另外，非常重要的一点是，在总词汇表中，大部分单词或词组都详细地标示出语言的层次（口头语、笔语、文学用语、俚语、俗语等），以及该词汇的同义词或反义词［例如：classique ≠ original，un boulot（fam.）= un travail，une boucherie：un（e）boucher（ère）…］。这就进一步扩大了词汇量，也有助于学习者更准确理解掌握该词，按照自己的学习需要选择记忆，扩大了教材本身的适用范围。使教材的词汇学习显得具有相当的系统性。

（三）词汇教学方式的不同

根据教学所适用的教学大纲的不同，词汇教授的方法也不同。

显然，《新大学法语》的整体内容和编写方式更适用传统的“翻译—讲解”教学法，在每课的单词表和全书的总词汇表中都只标注单词的词性和中文翻译。很容易引导教师也进行翻译式的讲解，一般在解释了单词的含义和常见的搭配用法，朗读之后便转入课文，对新词汇的重视度不够。

而 *Alter-Ego*+法国教材的文本内容和编写方式相对而言更加适用于交际教学法或任务式教学法，由于书中没有词汇翻译，所以为了使学习者认识每一个新单词和短语，都需要各种不同的教学手段和传达过程，包括图片、例句、手势、模仿、解释等，通过这样的方法讲解每一个单词或词组，学习者必然对每个单词或词组有较为清楚和直观的认识。

（四）单词重复状况的比较

说到单词的重复问题，左焕琪教授在他的一部著作中曾举过一个例子，“印度语言学家 Kachroo 曾在印度一所学校里做了一个关于词汇的重复率对于词汇掌握的影响的试验。他发现大部分学习者能熟练掌握在教材中出现至少七次的词汇，而他们很难记住那些由于缺少重复的词”。在同一部著作中他还强调：“某些学者建议一种‘4+1+1+1’的教学模式，也就是说一个新单词在教材中至少出现四次，并在之后的三天里每天至少重复一次，就算完成任务了。”（左焕琪 2002：189）在这种表述里，词汇重复频率的重要性也可见一斑了。

由于中国教材按照主题划分单元，每一单元中的每一课都有相同的中心，因此，词汇在同一单元的两篇课文、文档、对话及练习中多次重复。比如第一册第五单元，其主题是“季节与节日”，我们可以找到大量多次重复的词和词组，例如：saison，fête，printemps，été，automne，hiver，commencer，finir，il fait +adj.，il pleut，quel temps，ciel，Noël，等等。句型“ Il fait froid ”重复出现有五次：

（1）课文 A：**Il fait froid**，il neige，la terre est blanche.

（2）语法练习：I-9. **Il fait froid** dans la montagne.

（3）课文练习：II－1. En hiver, **il fait froid**. On fait du feu à la maison.

（4）课文 B：**Il fait froid**. Et il neige.

（5）课文 B 理解练习：

II-1. Il ne neige pas souvent à Avignon, mais aujourd'hui, la neige tombe, quel temps ! Ici, 《 quel temps 》veut dire qu' ________.

1. il fait beau B. il fait chaud C. il fait mauvais D. il fait froid

其他刚才提到的词也出现类似的重复，就第五单元而言，86 个词中有 53 个至少重复了两次。在该教材的其他单元中，重要的词汇重复也不在少数。在教学中，我们发现学生对这些重复足够的词汇掌握较好，容易记忆。

而在法国教材 *Alter-Ego+*中，一方面是由于大量新词汇的充斥，另一方面是教材单元按语用目标组织，每单元为达到一个交际任务往往需要学习多方面的主题，因此词汇的重复率明显不足。虽然教材的同一主题在不同的单元有可能重复出现，但由于是螺旋式地上升，重在添加更深层次的内容，所以对以往词汇重复不多，无法弥补这一问题的缺憾。

举个例子：在教材第一册的第六单元第一课中，其主题也是“季节”，在这一课的 66 个词和词组中，只有 6 个重复超过 4 次，为：printemps, été, automne, hiver, chaud et frais。该单元的第二第三课主题完全不同，没有重复这一课的词汇。同时，这也是该教材更重视表达多样化的结果，同样的意思使用不同的表达方法或同义词代替，当然从另一方面来讲这也是教材的优势。

通过以上四个方面的静态比较，即文本比较，我们还进行了动态比较，即对使用过这两种教材的 50 位学生和 7 名教师进行了问卷调查和访问，得到关于以上四个大问题的一些看法，总的来说：8%的学生认为《新大学法语》能帮助他们**有效**掌握法语词汇，40%认为**基本**有效，52%认为**很难**有效掌握；而对于 *Alter-Ego+*，这三个数据分别为 40%、56%和 4%。总体看来，学习者对法国教材的词汇编排有较高的满意度。

最后我们把动态和静态比较的结果置于表 1 中。

表 1 两种教材的词汇比较结果

	《新大学法语》	*Alter-ego+*
词汇数量是否足够	-	+
是否介绍了日常生活中最常用的词汇	+	+
词汇学习是否具有系统性	-	+
词汇编排对于教学是否方便有效	-	+
是否配有词汇使用练习	+	+
词汇重复率是否足够	+	-

表格各项中，“+”表示表现良好，“-”表示表现不足。

二 教材词汇编排的优劣、思考和建议

（一）两种教材词汇编排的优势和劣势

通过上一部分的比较，我们可以看出中国教材《新大学法语》的词汇不够丰富。尽管三册书的总词汇数量基本接近大学法语教学大纲的要求，但并不能满足学习者的实用目标和真正学习需求。孤立的单词表现形式使学习者很难真正掌握词的用法，也不利于记忆。但是词汇的重复率充分，这部分地弥补了教材词汇编排的不足，也帮助学习者有效地记忆和掌握这一部分词汇。

法国教材 *Alter-Ego+*的词汇量非常丰富，总词汇表按主题来组织，便于记忆；语段和例句的表现形式便于学习者真正理解词的意义，掌握词的用法；同义词和反义词更加扩大了词汇，也使词汇学习更加具有系统性；词汇的不同教授方法也使词汇教学变得丰富和更具有趣味性。但是词汇的重复性表现不充分，不利于记忆；另外，词汇从数量上来说难度较大。

（二）对于教材编写在词汇上的启示

从以上比较和总结中我们可以看出，我国 FLE 教材中词汇部分编写依然处于相对老旧的状态，而法国教材从 20 世纪 80 年代以来已经更新换代，经历了各种编写模式后达到一种较先进、更实用有效的状态。我们在这一部分的变革也势在必行，编写时应该摒弃老教材的劣势，借鉴法国教材的先进之处，结合我国的实际，既考虑教师的需求，也考虑学习者的学习目标以及教材更广泛的适用性，以教学大纲为指导，在开发新教材时提高词汇部分的编写水平，开辟新的编写模式，使 FLE 教材建设更符合

“思想性、发展性、科学性、趣味性、灵活性”（程晓堂，2002：86—88）的编写原则。同时，只有教材的编写改进，才能促进教师们采用更加先进的教学方法。为此，本研究提出以下可供参考的一些建议：

在考虑到学习者实际学习需要和可接受的难易度的前提下，尽可能提供丰富的词汇。改变原有教材中清一色的标准词汇，可以在除了精读课文外的其他阅读材料中让学习者了解其他语级的同义词，并明确标示。在词汇表中提示可供替换的同义词或反义词，扩大词汇量，学习者可以根据自己的需要来选择掌握。

为了使词汇的学习更具有效性和趣味性，尽量多地提供语段、词组而非孤立的单词；也可改变教学策略，提供例句或小对话、小短文，由学习者自行总结、领会重要词汇的含义和用法，通过这个主动总结的过程加深对词汇的印象；为了配合词汇的这一改革，可以把包含新词汇的千篇一律的课文，改成其他的各种真实语篇的形式，如邮件、明信片、通知、广告、报纸杂志片段、情景对话等，既可以提高教材的趣味性、真实性，也可以使学习者避免在大篇幅的课文中迷失，难以抓住重点。

继续重视词汇的重复性，保证学习者对重点词汇有效掌握。

在总词汇表中，改变以往的按首字母顺序排列的固有模式，尝试按主题排列，使词汇的学习更具系统性，也便于整体记忆。

此外，也可以为教材增加一些色彩来吸引学习者，甚至帮助记忆。

（三）对于教师课堂教学词汇教学技巧的建议

教材的改革需要长期的努力，也并非一朝一夕能够改变，那么在现有教材的使用上，教授者就应该具备一定的教学技巧，以扬长避短，帮助学生最有效最灵活地掌握词汇。本研究也提出一些具体建议：

在教授词汇时，在时间允许的情况下扩充词汇，讲解必要的同义词、反义词、同根词、同族词等；强调词性的重要性，记忆名词时要同时记忆其阴阳性；传授“学习怎样学习”的策略，要求记忆语段、例句、固定表达等，而非独立的单词。

增加听写练习，帮助学生准确掌握词的发音和拼写；增加复习环节，提高词汇的重复率，以帮助学生巩固记忆。

另外，也可以根据学生的学习目标和实际需求，补充一些趣味性词汇活动。在 *Alter-Ego+*教材的配套练习册中有大量的填词游戏、词语使用的交际练习，而《新大学法语》没有配套练习册。在使用中式教材时可以借用法国教材的练习册达到这一目标。把两种教材有机结合在一起使用也是一种可以尝试的教学手段，但是对教师教学能力的要求比较高。

三 结语

总之，我们知道，《大学法语（二外）教学大纲》最新版已经提出了新的学习目标要求：使学生能以法语为工具，获取所需的信息。而我们的教材依然处于相对老旧模式，词汇部分的编写也是如此，改版更新却没有改变编写策略，已经无法完全满足大纲的新要求，也无法满足对学生的培养要求。我们的法语教材建设需要合理借鉴法国 FLE 教材的先进编写模式，同时也要考虑我们的实际使用情况，在词汇这一模块上有所突破，既能够应对法语公共四级、法语 Tef、Tcf 等考试，又能有利于学生在实际应用中的词汇使用，为培养更好的法语人才，作出积极的转变。

参考文献

程晓堂：《英语教材分析与设计》，外语教育与研究出版社 2002 年版。

Jean-Pierre Cuq et Isabelle Gruca -*Cours de didactique du français langue étrangère et seconde*, Presses Universitaire de Grenoble, 2003.

Pierre Martinez-La didactique des langues étrangères, Puf, 2002.

Christian Puren-Histoire des méthodologies de l'enseignement des langues, Clé International, 1988, Paris.

关晓红：《中法 FLE 教材对比研究及启示》，《科技文汇》（上旬刊）2011 年第 5 期。

周雪林：《浅谈外语教材评估标准》，《外语界》1996 年第 2 期。

大学法语教学大纲修订组：《大学法语教学大纲》，高等教育出版社 2002 年版。

左焕琪：《外语教育展望》，华东师范大学出版社 2002 年版。

李志清：《新大学法语 1》《新大学法语 2》，高等教育出版社 2011 年版。

Catherine Hugo et d'autres-*Alter-Ego+*, Hachette, 2012.

Comparison and Reflection on Vocabulary Compilation in Chinese and French FLE Textbooks

Wang Yanhong

Abstract: FLE (Français langue étrangère) means teaching French as a foreign language. In France, there has been a long history of teaching materials, teaching practice and theory of FLE. In the field of development and research of the teaching material, the French academia has been leading the trend of French teaching materials development all over the world. Nevertheless, related studies in China started late both theoretically and practically. Among those studies, the construction and development of French teaching material is also restricted to the traditional teaching mode for a long time.

Two French teaching materials are employed as samples in the current study: the frequently used *New College French* in China and the *Alter-Ego+* published by Hachette. A comparison has been carried out between their vocabulary, grammar, texts and exercises. This paper mainly focuses on the comparison of their content capacity, presenting approaches, and repetition rates. Based on that, the pros and cons of these two textbooks are analyzed, in order to provide some enlightening insights for the development of basic French teaching materials and the use of teaching materials in China.

Key words: French; FLE textbooks; comparison; vocabulary

日本历史文化教学的设计与开展

——以日语专业《中日关系史》课程的信息化建设为例

许赛锋*

摘　要：在传统的日语专业本科教学中，语言类课程是教学内容的主流，日本历史文化类课程只是作为辅助陪衬而存在。然而面对社会的发展变化，将语言技能与历史文化教学紧密结合，同时融入一定的实践性和科研性，是今后日语专业课程改革的一个重要发展方向。本文以《中日关系史》课程的信息化建设为例，分析类似课程在资料运用、教学组织等方面的信息化实现途径，对课程建设与运行过程中出现的一些问题进行探讨和反思。

关键词：日语专业；历史文化知识；教学改革；信息化

引言

如众所知，成长于信息化时代的大学生，逐渐习惯了数字化的学习模式，更倾向接受形式多样、简洁易懂、集知识与趣味于一体的信息。如果教育者仍坚守传统的教学模式，用陈旧、刻板的理念教授知识，势必会造成“教”与“学”的矛盾，难以收到良好的教学效果。另外，就日语专业本科教学而言，像教育部制定的《高等院校日语专业基础阶段教学大纲》也指出，外语教学要在有利于语言运用的前提下，适当加入社会文化的内容，培养学生兼备语言运用能力和社会文化理解能力。也就是说，通过四年的大学课程学习，日语专业学生应该具备日本社会、政治、经济、企业文化等方面的诸多相关知识，在一定程度上了解日本人的历史文化和行为传统。

* 作者简介：许赛锋（1981—　），男，陕西师范大学外国语学院副教授，研究方向：日本近代史、中日关系史。

近几年的调查数据显示，日语语言基本功扎实，具有历史、经贸、法律等专业知识和国际视野的复合型日语人才备受青睐。为此，国内很多大学的日语专业，开始尝试摆脱纯语言技能的教授框架，逐渐导入了将语言教学建立在某个学科或主题上的“内容依托式教学模式”（CBI，Content-Based Instruction）。孙敏（2017）通过抽样统计指出，目前中国日语课程的内容依托式教学中，历史学领域的课程处在第三的位置，其中《中日关系史》为许多大学日语专业普遍开设的课程。在这一背景下，对该课程进行信息化建设和教学模式改革，无疑具有良好的带头和示范作用。自2016年《中日关系史》课程获得陕西师范大学信息化项目建设立项后，课题组成员在相关的课程建设、课程运行过程中积累了一些经验和体会，谨在此进行分享和探讨。

一　课程的前期信息化建设

中国和日本是一衣带水的邻邦，两国交流的历史源远流长。《中日关系史》课程，主要聚焦于中日两国从古代至近代的文化交流史和政治关系史，通过铺叙基本的历史事实，点描在双方关系史上有过重大影响的历史人物及其事迹，阐述各个阶段中日关系的主流和特点，使学生对中日关系的发展历史有一个基本了解，能够在今后的实际工作、生活中，正确对待和处理所遇到的相关问题。

我们认为，在课程资源信息化及教学方式信息化方面，课程内容是连接老师和学生的重要桥梁，也是教学中的核心元素，课程内容的信息化程度及信息化方式，会直接影响到信息化教学的效果。因此，将原有的纸质课程内容进行数字化处理，进而设计教学方案，加入相应的素材（教学文本、文献记述、文物图片、音频视频、习题练习等），无疑是课程在信息化前期建设中必须完成的任务。

需要注意的是：首先，课程脚本不等同于教案，应该包含详细的教学用语讲稿、教学实施方案、教学方法设计以及画面效果设计，同时主讲教师还要配合技术人员的工作，跟进教学讲稿的后期制作、编辑，以确保内容的准确性。当然，所谓的“信息化”，并非任何内容都要生搬硬套地搞成电子形式，而是要根据内容本身的特点和性质，看是否需要信息化和怎样信息化。必要时，未曾电子化的书籍、文献等具体实物，也可以适当配合使用，一本古色古香的线装书，留给学生的记忆也许会更加深刻。其次，授课视频是信息化课程的重要主体，需要呈现关键的教学过程。已有的研究告诉我们，一个人在45分钟的时间内，通常只有15分钟可以注意力高度集中，所以课程视频的时间最好限定在 10—15分钟左右，同时尽量保持生动性和趣味性。而且正如赵继政（2006）所指出的那样，“任务式教学”会对学习者的注意力产生重要影响，故而视频的主题性必须突出，要围绕具体的历史事件或历史人物，传递出明确的识记要点或思考任务。最后，将课程资源上传至网络学习平台（目前使用的是Blackboard平台，简称BB平台）后，最好先面向课程组以及部分学习者开放，经测试无问题后，再面向全体学习者开放。

此外，保持教学内容及资料的真实性和准确性，是历史学科的基本要求。一般而言，为了提高学生的能动性，就必须让学生成为资源的建设者，让其自己寻找与学习活动紧密相关的资源，真正参与到学习情境中来。但由于网络上的资源纷杂凌乱，教师必须要帮助学生从中“去伪存真”“排杂留优”，担当电子资料导引者的角色。例如目前能够进行OCR处理的文本，基本都是普通的横排版本，但中日文古籍均为竖排书写模式，故而经常会出现识别错误，而且中日古籍文献中没有标点符号，电子版的扫描识别会出现错误断读现象，从而造成输出信息的错乱。

更为重要的是，牢记历史教育本身所具有的严肃性和政治性，对《中日关系史》这门课程尤为重要。当前全球信息化的迅速发展，促进了世界各国在政治、经济、文化等方面联系的密切度，但外文资料中夹带的各种价值观念、意识形态以及表述立场等，给大学生历史观的教育实施带来了许多严峻的考验和难题。更有甚者，由于近代中日之间是“侵略受害者”与“侵略加害者”的角色关系，因而还使得一些学者和媒体，有时会把爱国主义的政治情感与民族主义的政治思潮等同起来，使人陷入盲目排外、狭隘自私的极端民族主义或狭隘民族主义误区。职是之故，在资料信息化的前期建设中，针对学生在寻找和接受各类资料时可能出现的问题，需要详细考量相应的应对措施和方案。只有这样，庞杂的信息资料才能得到规范和梳理，相关的信息化资源才能符合课程的需要，从而真正为教学育人服务。

二 课程的框架设定与组织开展

（一）课程的框架设定

近些年来，各种新型的教学模式，都开始从强调“教”，转变为强调“学”，即从“以教师为中心”，转向“以学习者为中心”。依据这一方针，为使《中日关系史》课程的教学模式从“知识传授型”转向“能力获得型”，让学生从“学会”变为“会学”，本课程组在“课前准备”“课中教学”“课后拓展”三个环节进行了一些改变和尝试。

正如目前很多一线教师所感受到的那样，当前的大学生，某种程度上的确缺乏学习的主动性，而且学习的有效性较低，对课程的投入度较差。因此，针对这一现象，课程组从认知因素、情感因素和制度行为因素等角度，努力尝试着提高学生的学习热情。例如，在课前准备环节，首先要求学生在每次上课前的三天内，通过 BB 平台了解学习任务，查看教师提前录制的授课视频及相关音视频资料，了解下次上课时讲授的内容及重点。其次，根据教师提供的相关中日文资料，自我进行“中→日”及“日→中”的语言对照和理解。（考虑到上课学生的实际日语能力程度，其中日文资料以现代文版本为主，字数控制在 2000 字以内。）学生在完成这种类似“阅读理解”的文献阅读能力训练后，需要在 BB 平台上完成 10 题左右的客观题测试，以验证其对历史资料的理解程度和掌握程度。

一般而言，不同的专业课程，会有不同的授受特点，因此教学设计应当有所差异，要根据具体课程的特点因地制宜地去进行，只有当教师完全了解了所教课程的认知规律之后，才能选择出适当的教学内容和教学方式。《中日关系史》课程的信息化建设，在“课中教学”中突出学以致用的开设理念，根据中日历史的不同发展阶段，设计了相应的教学标的和讨论专题。正如周恩来曾概括的那样，中日两国是“两千年友好，五十年对立”，因此古代部分应尽量以相关历史人物的生平、相互交往活动为重点，近代部分尽量以政治、军事的交涉或冲突为主线，同时辅以中日重要人物在其中的作用及影响，使学生在学习过程中形成深刻的宏观印象和应有的历史责任感。举例来说，古代中国是东亚文明的中心，在政治、经济、军事上都占据绝对的优势，日本全力学习大陆文明，留下了浓重的中国文化痕迹，这一阶段的讲授，就应注重中日文化交流的相似性和差异性。在中日关系史的近代部分，日本通过明治维新，国力开始超过徘徊不前的中国，两国地位发生逆转，随后日本不断向外扩张侵略，引发两国长达半个多世纪的矛盾和敌视。此阶段的讲授，要以中日关系中的重大历史事件为主线，辅以相关的影像资料和实物，通过课堂上互动讨论、自由发言等形式，促进学生对该时期学习内容的掌握。同时，教师可以结合学生较为感兴趣的中日关系实例，调动学生的学习积极性，有意识地锻炼其发现问题、解决问题的能力。像针对中日甲午战争中清朝的失败，可以导入“唐日白村江海战”“蒙古入袭日本”等历史事件进行对比教学，鼓励学生从不同角度对同一问题进行研究，探讨其中不同结果产生的原因。

（二）课程的组织开展

基于上述理念，本课程非常重视信息化与实践考察环节的结合。众所周知，陕西师范大学所在地西安，古代曾长期是中国的政治文化中心，也是日本人来华时的重要滞留地，遗存有很多中日交往的相关史迹。为了能让学生对历史有直观和切身的感受体验，我们根据相关史迹的重要性和实际的可操作性，设置规划了八个专题考察地点和考察内容，即：1 青龙寺——空海，2 兴庆公园——阿倍仲麻吕，3 环城公园——吉备真备，4 香积寺——日本净土宗，5 西北大学博物馆——井真成，6 陕西历史博物馆——唐三彩、奈良三彩，7 大明宫遗址——日本平城京，8 八路军驻西安办事处——抗日战争。鉴于《中日关系史》目前的开课时间为一学期（36 学时），加上连休放假、期末考试等客观因素，以上 8 个专题可以按两周一次的频次展开。在每学期的第一周，学生根据自己感兴趣的地点（选择不均衡时，由教师进行调控），自由组合成考察组开展考察。（通常的自然班约有 25—30 人，因此每组以 3—4 人为宜。）

在这一环节中，为了提高学生的考察质量，要求学生事前从 BB 平台下载“《中日关系史》实地考察报告表”，按照表格的各项指引和要求完成考察任务。其中，需要填写的主要内容包括“调查目标的基本情况”“调查过程和方法”“调查收获心得”“未解决的问题及思考”等几个板块。核心部分的“调查过程和方法”，要求学生独立、主动地收集材料，对相关历史中的问题提出自己的认识与观点，而且允许以文字、图片、视频等多种介质组合完成。随后，当课程授课进度到达相关内容及知识点时，由学生对其考察情况进行报告，发表时间为每人 10 分钟左右，使用语言尽可能为日语。教师及其他学生对其报告进行点评、提问。最后，该组学生汇总各方意见对自己的报告进行修改，将报告表扫描上传至 BB 平台，作为平时成绩的评定参考。

拓展环节方面，本课程的尝试在于“日本实地考察模式”的推行。近几年来，陕西师范大学日语系学生赴日交换留学、带薪实习的人数逐渐增多，借助 BB 平台教学，无疑可以较好地解决此类学生不能在校上课的问题。进而，我们根据赴日学生的所处地点，会适当地为其安排对应的实地考察对象。譬如，居住在京都的同学，可以指导其前往岚山，考察周恩来的题诗碑；位于奈良的同学，可前往当地的“林神社”，考察元代宁波人林净因将“馒头”传入日本的事迹。这些学生同样需要根据要求来完成考察报告，并将自己的发表内容录制成视频上传 BB 平台，供教师和同学观看、评价。由于每年学生所去地点都有所不同，其发表内容通过 BB 平台的保存积累后，将会逐渐形成一个中日对比研究的“资料群”，不但可以为本课程的后续学生提供更加丰富的知识素材，也可以为日语专业大四学生撰写毕业论文提供有益的切入视角和启发点。

此外，本课程的另一重要思路还在于，希望能进一步扩大《中日关系史》课程的学习人数，努力将该课程建设成为具有通识性质的公选课程。迄今为止，由于语言能力的限制，该课程只对陕师大日语专业的本科生开设，受教人数每年始终停留在 30 人左右。而另一方面，同校的历史专业却因缺乏相应的师资力量，未能开设日本近代史、中日关系史等方面的课程，造成这一重要学科领域的教学一直处于空白状态。本团队希望借助信息化课程的建设和开展，变动教材及授课的使用语言（即由以日文为主中文为辅，转换为中文为主日文为辅），形成“历史+日语”的教学模式，鼓励本校其他专业的学生学习该课程，使其在理解相关历史知识的同时，可以学习和掌握一定程度的日语能力。

三　教学成果与教学反思

（一）教学成果

1. 加强了课程教学内容的深度、广度、密度

2012 年，教育部颁布了《教育信息化十年发展规划（2011—2020 年）》，设定目标“用十年左右的时间初步建成具有中国特色的教育信息化体系，使我国教育信息化整体上接近国际先进水平，推进教育事业的科学发展”，此后经过多年的信息化发展，中国整体的信息化教学水平有了大幅度的提高。在本课程的建设中，教师通过多媒体网络技术，利用影

像、图片、声音等将一些抽象的历史知识和复杂的历史事件，变成立体的、声情并茂的直观影像，为学生提供了丰富的学习内容。在教师提供的信息化学习资料帮助下，学生可以多遍学习知识要点、自由记录学习过程中的感受联想，并且通过网络平台完成学习自测题，整理和归纳该阶段的学习内容，同时将产生的问题传递给教师。随着课程的推进，学生的知识面不断扩大，视野进一步拓展，对教师的依赖性呈逐渐下降趋势。

2. 提高了学生的学习动力和评价准度

现代心理学理论认为，学习动力基于个体学习行为价值判断的动力系统而发生，主要由学习动机、学习兴趣和学习态度等构成，是激发大学生学习积极性、挖掘学习潜能、影响教育质量的关键因素之一。可以看到，相比传统的课本和 ppt 教学，在本课程中实践的这种自主学习、合作学习、探究学习模式，使学生的学习热情和兴趣有了明显的提升，自主学习的意识也不断得到了强化。

另外，学生在 BB 平台上的学习活动，可以清晰地表现出其参与程度与能力状况，这使得学生在被评价的同时，产生了较强的自我监督、自我督促动力。而授课教师，也可以通过客观测试、互动问答、作业提交等方式，对每个学生的学习状况有更好的了解，在期末总评的时候获得可靠的裁判依据。当然，必须要指出的是，核心素质的培养所强调的是品格与能力的培养，而不是知识与技能的堆砌，因此在运用结果评价时，应该相对弱化评价的甄别功能，避免干扰学生对课程学习的专注度和投入度。

3. 促进了学生的实践能力和研究能力

陕西师范大学日语专业的学生，有很大一部分在毕业后前往日本攻读研究生学位，而如众所知，日本作为教育发达国家，近年在已有的教育改革成果基础上，提出了以“自立”“协作”“创造”为终身学习基础的教育理念，将“思维能力”置于核心地位，注重发现和解决问题能力、创造和批判思维能力，对人才培养提出了更新、更高的要求。（李婷婷、王秀红，2019）因此，在中国大学本科阶段的素质培养，将是其后期国外专业学术生活的重要前期积淀。《中日关系史》信息化课程开课几年来，学生通过学习与锻炼，实践能力、思考能力和研究能力都有了明显的提高。像在 2017 年度，部分学生就先后成功申请了陕西师范大学的勤助科研项目“中日三彩瓷器差异与日本奈良时期的社会特征”和大学生创新创业项目“中日古都历史文化资源优势在城市建设中的转化研究及其借鉴意义”。这些成果在体现出学生个人能力的同时，也在一定程度上反映了本课程在其中发挥的促进作用。

（二）教学反思

1. 信息化的自身短板

正如很多教师已经指出的那样，在一些教育领域，教学重心不断地向信息技术方面倾斜，教学从以前的“人灌”，变相地沦为某种程度的“机灌”。像热门的MOOC学习模式，在值得肯定其价值及作用的同时，也不可忽视其完课率低、最终学习成效差的缺点。（祝智庭、刘名卓，2014）事实上，信息化教学的确容易出现资料大量堆积、利用低效的情况，像有些教师只是将相关史料资源进行简单的罗列，没有对无关信息进行过滤和剪切，这非常容易造成学生学习的碎片化和无序化，学习效果也未必比传统的学习模式有多少提高。即便教师对资料进行了整理，但大量的图片、链接文本和视频资料，依然会超量占用学生的时间，令学生在课前、课中、甚至课后不停地忙于接受。最后只见学习动作的热闹，却不见对历史事件、历史人物的真正解读和反思，信息化教学不知不觉陷入了形式上的俗套。

2. 所需费用及安全等问题

在信息化课程里，学生需要通过电脑、手机等电子产品来完成相应的学习任务，教师对信息化课程的构建，无疑都是事先建立在学生已经拥有此类产品的前提下，并没有考虑到部分家庭经济困难学生的实际状况。此外，在实践考察环节，虽然本课程已将对象地点限定在学生所处的周边地区，但相关的出行费用，对经济拮据的学生来说也会成为一种负担。而且，在安全保障方面，由于学生外出考察都在课余（甚至国外），授课教师不可能次次同行，其间发生的意外事故该如何处理，也是事关学生人身安全的重要问题。我们认为，作为开设课程的学校一方，如果能针对上述问题完善制度建设和后勤保障（如提供一定的交通、伙食和保险等补助），无疑可以更好地提高教师的安心度和学生的参与度，保证相关学习活动能更加规范、有序地进行。

结　语

信息化教学模式在诸多大学的实践表明，其相比传统的教学模式，更能有效地提高人才培养的质量。但毫无疑问，在日常的教学过程中，最重要的仍是要致力于培养学生的思维能力和实践能力，课堂教学的创新切忌舍本逐末，要避免陷入“样样求新”和“为新而新”的认识误区。其实，只要坚持以学生为本的第一原则，不断探索促进学生全面发展、符合教学规律要求的道路，任何教学方法都会取得丰硕的成果。

参考文献

窦心浩：《我国高校日语专业社会文化类课程开设现状》，《日语教学的本土化研究——2011年度上海外国语大学日本学国际论坛纪念文集》，华东理工大学出版社2012年版。

杜芳：《对信息化历史课程资源有效利用的思考》，《中国电化教育》2009年第4期。

孙敏：《内容依托式教学下的日语专业课程设置探索——以国际关系学院日语系为例》，《教育现代化》2017年第21期。

赵继政：《注意力研究与任务设计》，《天津外国语学院学报》2006年第3期。

李婷婷、王秀红：《日本新一轮基础教育课程改革新动向——文部科学省“学习指导要领”（2017）述评》，《外国教育研究》2019年第3期。

祝智庭、刘名卓：《“后MOOC”时期的在线学习新样式》，《开放教育研究》2014年第20卷第3期。

王秀文：《日语教育改革与人才培养模式的构建》，《贵州民族学院学报》（哲学社会科学版）2007年第1期。

袁平华：《大学英语教学改革与以学科内容为依托的语言教学模式》，《外语界》2010年第3期。

Design and Development of Japanese History and Culture Teaching

—Informatization Construction of "History of Sino-Japanese Relations" Course in Japanese

Xu Saifeng

Abstract: Among the traditional undergraduate teaching courses for Japanese major, Japanese language courses play a dominant role, which are supplemented by some courses on Japanese history and culture. However, social development and changes make it necessary to closely integrate language skills with contents of history and culture, and to make courses of Japanese major more practical and scientific. Taking the informatization construction of "History of Sino-Japanese Relations" course for example, this paper analyzes the informationization approaches of similar courses in data application, teaching organization and others, discusses and reflects on some problems arising in the curricula construction and operation.

Key words: Japanese language; history and culture; teaching reform; informationization

俄语语法教学反思与设想

王　翠*

摘　要： 在缺乏俄语语言环境的情况下，俄语语法教学要充分考虑到语法学科的性质。我们应区分语言学习中的正迁移与负迁移，将语法教学与词汇学习相结合。提高语法技能还要与结构语言学、功能语言学、语义学、认知语言学等各语言学理论相结合。借助网络资源和计算机手段，建构丰富且生动的语料库。我们还应完善教学方法和手段，按认知步骤，有计划地培养或提高学生的语法技能。

关键词： 语法教学；语法技能；教学方法；语言学理论

我国零起点学习俄语的俄语专业大学生在俄语专业学习的初期必须同时学习语音、阅读、听说、词汇、语法和精读等多门课程，面临没有大量的词汇储备，尚未掌握完整的语法体系，不能或错误地表达思想等困境。这种状况下俄语语法教学面临许多困难，为了提高学生的语言综合能力，俄语语法课在教学模式方面应有所反思和创新。

一　俄语语法课的学科特点

对外俄语教学中语法教学具有极强的实用性。俄语语法课可以帮助学生正确组织自己的言语，监督话语的正确性。俄语学习过程中必须要掌握一定的语法知识，以保证教学情景中和现实情境中的正常语言交流。学生对俄语语法的学习同时具有两面性：其一，了解并掌握语法形式意义；其二，理解言语中具体语法形式的功能性。俄语语法教学过程的任务主要是

---

* 作者简介：王翠（1976—　），女，陕西师范大学外国语学院副教授，研究方向：俄语语法学。

使学生以书面和口头话语为材料，激活并完善自己的语法技能；形成系统的语言知识体系，能够正确地进行书面和口头表达；在阅读和听力练习中能正确辨别出各类语法现象。具体包括一定的构词知识、语法形式、语法概念的知识、根据言语作出相应的反应和行为。

初级阶段的语法教学主要是让学生掌握一系列基本的词法知识。俄汉语言体系在此过程中会相互干扰，产生正迁移或负迁移。在此过程中最大可能地使用正迁移效果，通过对比汉俄语言的同异，解释负迁移的本质和原因。克服负迁移的主要途径是在巩固语言材料的初级阶段尽量少用逐字翻译练习；使用以重复某结构为基础的训练；翻译练习用于复习和检查学习效果；使用情景练习训练语法形式和规则的掌握；如果俄汉语之间的某语法现象差别较大，则需增加相关练习，如二者之间差异小或几乎没有差异，则可减少相关的练习。

二　语法与词汇的相互作用

话语的形成除了具备一定的语法结构，还必须选择使用相应的词汇。语法与词汇之间存在紧密的联系，二者不仅在理论方面相互依赖，例如佐洛托娃（Г. А. Золотова）、卡拉乌洛夫（Ю. Н. Караулов）、加克（В. Г. Гак）等人的论著，也在语言实践方面存在密不可分的联系。根据言语活动的不同类型和体现，以话语为基础，完善言语交际技能过程中，要同时掌握词汇和语法材料。话语或语篇的选择应符合所教授的语法主题，其词汇则是对句法结构的填充，以便引入一定的形态—句法规则。词汇学习过程中学生应该理解和记住俄语单词的语义、发音和书写；在具体的语境中为完成特定的交际任务会使用这些词；会使用词汇组合。通过一系列的学习，学生能认知、思考、总结和使用语法知识与规则。

关注语法结构中的词汇填充，要特别注意话语或语句的信息性，这些话语所表达的情景、所反映的语言图景。虽然俄语的时态只有三个，但是动词的体对此做了极大的补偿，词汇、句法语义成为句子模态意义的重要成分。说话者的立场，说话者与受话者的相互关系不仅是词汇性的，而且还是句法结构性的。

言语技能的培养以情景主题方法为主。因为具体的情景可以提供词汇选择，反之也决定了句法结构的选择和不同的词汇填充。词汇中心方法中语法发挥着辅助的作用，可用于言语生成过程中。因此在教学中既可从形式出发选择相应的语法结构和词汇单位，也可从意义出发寻找恰当的表达手段。语法与词汇的关系反映了语言与语篇、语言与功能和语法体系相关的多维性特性。

三 语法技能及其培养

语法技能是一种综合行为，指在既定情景下选择适合言语任务的模式，形成正确的各级言语单位，且该行为符合技能参数，是完成言语活动的条件之一。语法技能的形成始于理解，体现于言语中。（Пассов，2002：20）根据休金（А. Н. Щукин）的观点，语法技能的形成具有阶段性，共分四个阶段：了解和初步巩固、训练、使用、检查。

第一阶段的目的是让学生了解语法单位，以便于形成使用语法单位的技能。教师在这个阶段要让学生理解语法材料。为此，教师需要确立新语法材料的功能方向；将使用语法结构的情景模式化，让学生从视觉和听觉上理解新结构；通过俄译汉练习予以检查。

第二阶段的目的是在特定的言语情境中发展准确理解语法单位的能力，根据交际条件的变化提高构建准确话语的能力。

第三阶段的目的则为从形成语法技能转变为具体的使用能力，不用经过提示就能使用新的语法技能。具体手段可以通过（1）独白或对话中激活并使用新的语法现象；（2）转述或陈述；（3）针对读过或听过的文章进行讨论；（4）进行多种角色游戏。

第四阶段的目的是检查新语法技能，这种检查可以在言语活动中进行，也可以通过各种语言和言语练习实现。首先，通过提出问题型任务，让学生展示新语法现象的重要性，作出示例，让学生通过语言现象的特征认识具体的语言现象。其次，再现所学语法现象的练习，为表达思想掌握必需的语法结构，包括句子及其各组成部分。最后，通过翻译练习，汉译俄练习促使学生更好地理解新的语法材料，提高学生的兴趣和学习动机，发展语感。

学生在学习俄语的过程中要培养并形成两种语法技能：语言语法技能（交际条件之外运用语法材料的技能）和言语语法技能（在口语和写作过程中保持正确地运用语法现象的技巧）。

这些言语练习的目的是形成和发展学生为完成交际任务而必需的言语技能，沙季洛夫（Шатилов，1986：63）提出以下类型的言语训练：

（1）模拟练习，指针对语法结构明确的单结构语法材料，无须改变便可以重复练习。多次听读、重复和抄写此类语法例子和语法单位。（2）语法演练，其目的是巩固语法材料，形成类似情景中自动使用语法结构的能力。此类练习中允许有提示。这类练习中学生不仅要组建类似的句子，还要选择恰当的语法形式。（3）转化练习，包括组合、扩展和缩小语法结构的能力。以多种方案表达不同情景中的报道内容。这些练习的选择和使用取决于具体的交际任务。（4）再现练习，学生独立再现新的语法现象。上述四类练习形成一套组合训练，通过记忆、模拟、演练和再现，将知识抽象化、概括化，构成新语法形式的模型。

四 理论与实践相结合的教学方法

俄语语法教学可以与语言理论研究相结合。弗谢沃洛多娃（Всеволодова，2000：3-4；2000：16-18）指出，目前俄罗斯形成了两种语法，即以邦达尔科（А. В. Бондарко）和佐洛多娃（Г. А. Золотова）为代表学者的学术理论语法，以及缘自俄语语言教学实践主要是实用和教学使用的学校语法。从学术和实践角度看，功能语言学的许多理论都可以应用于语法实践教学中。这两类研究可用于描述表达不同语义场、语义或情景范畴或结构的语言手段、以功能为基础对比不同语言的特点；从掌握语言的难点入手分析语言手段并对此作出解释。弗谢沃洛多娃（М. В. Всеволодова）在《交际功能句法理论》（2000：97）中提及俄语教学问题，通过大量的例证，表明不同语言中相同的意义可借助不同层面的语言手段表达，这些语言手段被归为不同的功能语义场结构，教学过程中需要考虑俄语与学习者母语的语义场相互对应关系。这种观察和比较可以使学习者更加系统性地看待所学习的语言内容。

当前的外语语言教学往往已超出单纯的语言结构范围。功能语法、交际语法、认知语言学等理论为语言学习者打开了新的语言空间和完善语言水平的可能性，使我们也有可能将语言形式表达与内容融恰地统一于话语中。俄语语言教学一直与寻找有效的教学方法紧密联系。整合性的语法教学具有明显的优势：可以全面评价话语表达手段，从而加快和简化对语言单位的选择使用，使话语表达更符合特定的情景。

对功能主义的广泛理解可以从交际角度入手。使用交际方法教授语法的目的不是传授语言的形式概念，而是交际单位的概念。这需要在教学过程中给予完全相符的科学描述和解释。

首先需要区分语言表达和交际能力的概念。语言表达的一般概念包括存在/不存在，现实/非现实；空间方位或坐标；运动；时间；性质和属性；数量；情感意志与智力活动；联系与关系。这些范畴都可分为不同的次范畴。教学中除了要学生掌握表达这些范畴的语言手段（句法结构、词汇要素、熟语），还要熟悉从意义指向形式，即为了表达某语义功能，使用必需的语言手段。为此需要发展各种不同的能力。各级别的语言知识与言语技能的对应关系如下：语音知识及语音规则→理解及产生语音，音的组合、韵律；词、词组的知识→理解并使用词和熟语；词形变化、构词及句法规则→构成正确的词形和句子；句子的构成规则→理解并构成正确且连贯的语篇和对话；词汇单位的联想和伴随意义→理解并使用词汇单位的转义；社会规则知识→话语符合不同的条件和情景；社会文化知识→交际中使用社会文化知识。由此可以看出，成功的交际需要各类语言知识及相应的技能。

功能方法强调对语言的创造性使用。如果学生不能创造新的恰当的表达手段，只囿于课本和教学过程中已学的语言手段，则不具备这种创新能力。从功能角度入手进行语法教学需要关注两个主要问题：教什么，如何教。教什么指确定教学内容和范围，限定各层面的基础知识和范畴，判断需要呈现和激活的语法手段。如何教包括呈现教学材料、制定练习和上课。帕尔梅诺娃（Парменова，2002：36-39）指出，形态和句法的传统教学中补充同义或近义的多种表达手段是极有益的。

目前根据科斯托马洛夫（Костомаров，1988）、阿基希娜（Акишина，2002、2012）、休金（Щукин，2003）等人的观点，РКИ 理论以功能交际法为特色，主要由交际性、充分顾及学生的母语特点、顾及所学语言国的语言国情三大内容构成。РКИ 理论的核心是强调语言的交际性，培养学生的实际语言交际能力。РКИ 理论原则大致包括以下内容：针对各国国情和外国人特点，区别对待，方法各异；重视培养外国学生的联想能力、构词能力、遣词造句时的搭配能力，同义词表达能力及排除本族语干扰的能力；注意语言单位的出现频率和使用场合；注意教学和教材的系统性、多样性、知识性、趣味性，使之融为一体，互为补充；注意在基础阶段推行强化教学；教学过程中重视学生的心理因素；强调情景教学。（周民权，2009：78）

五　合理利用现代化多种资源辅助语法教学

当前在信息资源极大丰富的情况下，我们可以利用计算机技术辅助俄语语法教学，使学生掌握俄语语法范畴及其规律、规则以及相互关系，准确且熟练地运用于言语交际之中。通过语法教学活动的创新，研究新的语法教学模式，提高教学效果。根据不同的语法主题，选择建立相应的俄语语法题，以多种灵活的形式帮助学生深刻理解俄汉语言体系的同异，准确且迅捷地使用具体的语言手段，掌握和提高运用俄语的技能。将俄语语法教学理论与教学改革实践紧密联系，探索俄语语法教学创新。

具体的教学实施可以分为初级俄语语法教学阶段和高级俄语语法教学阶段，语法规则、词汇、练习等不同领域的语法教学内容。

（1）初级语法教学阶段的教学步骤为针对每节课的语法知识点进行讲解、练习、使用和巩固。在讲解及练习部分增加语法学理论为基础的语言现象分析，以俄语环境中的真实语料为讲解对象；在语法和语言知识的教授过程中穿插国情文化知识。语音、词汇、语篇等方面都蕴含着语法内容，借助语法理论和语言知识进行深层分析，详细阐释，可以帮助学生快速记忆、理解和掌握，自觉与自己的母语进行对比，并在自己的表达中再现这些知识。高级语法教学阶段则将语法延伸至语篇，从形式结构扩展到功能，甚至是认知的阐释，语法与修辞、话语等学科相结合。

（2）语法规则的教学是语言学习的基石。语法规则教学要进行区别对待。“基本规则要讲透，并让学生熟练掌握，尤其是泾渭分明的地方，不容含糊。”（杜彦玲、许凤才，2012：65）记忆和使用语言规则要经过相应的训练，某些学生对该过程某种程度上感到艰巨而又枯燥，因此教学过程中可以借用俄罗斯中小学的PPT、小视频、图画等教学材料，也可以根据内容搜索相关材料，使教学内容生动形象又趣味横生，使学生便于记忆又印象深刻。

（3）语法教学与词汇教学密不可分，词汇量是俄语学习的重要突破口径和基础。词汇学习不仅是综合俄语、俄语阅读和听说活动中语言素材的重要来源，更是口头和书面表达中必不可少的部分。词汇量的大小直接影响语言表达的准确性、丰富性和生动性。通过学习构词知识，对词进行分解、重组、对比、造句等可以帮助学生很好地区分同义词、近义词、形近词、同形异义词。词汇材料来源于俄语国家语料库和学习网站，通过限定条件的搜索，可以查询到相关的例句，通过对不同子语料库的筛选，分别抽取不同语体的例句进行分析，不但能深化对词汇的掌握，也可增加对功能语体差异的切身感受，培养学生对语言现象的辨析力。

（4）从语法角度分析语篇。通过词汇联想，形成不同的语义场，借助语篇中的词法、语义、修辞手段，从衔接与连贯角度，分析语篇的情境结构、主题的分化等。这既是对各语法点的融会贯通，也是语篇组织能力、阅读能力和翻译能力的综合训练。在该阶段我们将学生分成不同的小组，各小组从不同角度对同一语篇进行分析，教师在学生讲解之后进行点评，这既使学生开阔了视野，加深了对文章整体的理解，也对自己的写作有所启发。

（5）语法练习部分的讲解对于消除学生的疑惑，养成良好的语言表达习惯有着重要的指示作用，“重在思路、方法上的指导归纳，引导学生对知识点进行总结、分类，并进行一题多变的练习，培养学生的创新能力”（李岩、王琳，2011：49）。在该阶段除了教师的讲解，利用各类语言书籍，做详细的补充说明之外，还可以选择使用网络上恰当的句子等表达。因为以往语法参考书上的例句有的带有较明显的历史痕迹，有的例句并不符合实际的交际情景。因此，针对这种现象我们需要寻找更贴合现实交流场景的语言表达。

（6）改革俄语语法课的考查方式，让学生重视平时练习的完成情况。平时的练习内容针对性强，小测验的内容覆盖面则较广泛，既包括基础题型，也包括提高和扩展题型。针对每次作业的测验的错题进行讲解，启发和引导学生自己寻找对答案的合理解释，鼓励学生提出质疑、发展自我查阅的能力。

利用计算机技术辅助俄语语法教学对于教师的教和学生的学都极有益处，但是该过程中应注意以下几个问题：

（1）教师备课必须充分，课前不仅要熟悉教学内容，语法规则，还要借助计算机寻找大量相关的语料并上传至教学平台，对比分析，提出相关的问题和解答。对于学生可能产生的疑问也可有所准备，针对易混淆的内容还可以组织学生进行课堂讨论。

（2）教师在备课中要针对教学难点精心设计互动话题。在讨论环节教师要作出示范和指导及解释，使学生各抒己见，言之有物，言之有据。循序渐进，培养学生思索、提问、查阅的能力。

（3）语法教学目的是提高学生在具体语境和交际情景中的语言应用能力，在基础阶段必须要推行强化教学，掌握课本内容为主，同时还要重视学生的心理因素，强调情景教学。

（4）为了充分调动学生积极性，发展学生全面的语言综合运用能力，今后教学过程中可以增加口头和书面作文的环节，让学生注意在语篇中运用语法知识，使表达恰当合理。让学生在学习平台上传口头或书面作业，教师分别进行相应点评。

总之，作为对外俄语教学组成部分的俄语语法教学在缺乏俄语语言环境的情况下，要充分考虑到语法学科的性质，将语法教学与综合提高词汇量、丰富语言表达相融合，结合结构语言学、功能语言学、认知语言学等理论知识，全面深刻地分析各类语言现象，辅助计算机和各类网络资源，拟定生动且切合实际生活的习题，提高学生书面和口语的语言技能，按照不同的阶段培养学生的语法技能、语言表达的创造性，为顺利完成言语交际奠定扎实的基础。

参考文献

Всеволодова М. В. *Теория функционально-коммуникативного синтаксиса: фрагмент прикладной (педагогической) модели языка.* М., Изд-во МГУ, 2000.

Парменова Т. В. Что может дать функциональная грамматика практике преподавания языков Русский язык как иностранный: теория, исследования, практика. Вып. 5. СПб.: Сударныня, 2002.

Пассов Е. И. *Методология методики: теория и опыт применения.* Липецк: Изд-во Липецк ГПУ, 2002.

Шатилов С. Ф. *Методика обучения немецкому языку в средней школе.* М.: Просвещение, 1986.

杜彦玲、许凤才：《俄语规范的演变与俄语语法教学》，《中国俄语教学》2012年第1期。

李岩、王琳：《基于自主学习平台的〈基础俄语语法〉课程教学模式探讨》，《中国俄语教学》2011年第4期。

周民权：《РКИ理论对中国俄语教学的影响》，《中国俄语教学》2009年第1期。

Reflections and Ideas on Russian Grammar Teaching

Abstract: In the absence of the Russian language environment, the nature of the grammar subject must be fully considered in the course of Russian grammar teaching. We should distinguish between positive and negative transfers in language learning and combine grammar teaching with vocabulary learning. The improvement of grammar skills should be combined with structural linguistics, functional linguistics, semantics, cognitive linguistics and other linguistic theories. With the help of network sources and computer means, construct a rich and vivid corpus. We should also improve teaching methods and means, and systematically develop or improve students' grammar skills according to cognitive steps.

Key words: Grammar teaching; grammar skills; teaching methods; linguistic theories

基于 BP 辩论模式培养学生思辨能力的大学英语口语课堂设计研究[*]

王　挺[**]

摘　要：思辨能力是当今高等教育重点培养的技能之一，然而思辨能力较弱，甚至是思辨缺席广泛地存在于大学英语学习者中，而且引起了国内外广大学者的广泛关注。本文将从思辨能力入手，通过分析英语基于辩论模式的口语教学与学生的思辨能力培养和发展的关系，进而探讨了公共英语口语教学中通过引进辩论模式培养和发展学生思辨能力的有效途径。

关键词：辩论模式；思辨能力；大学英语口语课堂

引言

思辨能力发展是我国高等教育的核心目标之一。《国家中长期教育改革和发展规划纲要（2010　2020 年）》明确提出，教育的长期发展需要“促进学生全面发展，着力提高学生服务国家服务人民的社会责任感、勇于探索的创新精神和善于解决问题的实践能力”，“倡导启发式、探究式、讨论式、参与式教学，帮助学生学会学习”，“营造独立思考、自由探索、勇于创新的良好环境”。由此可见，培养和发展学生的思辨能力不仅是教育工作者义不容辞的职责，同时也是国家长期发展的战略任务。然而，长期以来我国学生在分析、推理、评价、综合、辨析等思辨能力方面的表现不尽如人意。黄源深（1998；2010）指出，这种能力的缺失可谓“思辨缺席”。造成“思辨缺席”的原因众多，作为我国高等教育重要组成部

＊　本论文是陕西师范大学教师发展中心项目“基于 BP 辩论模式培养学生思辨能力的大学英语口语课堂设计研究”JSJX2019Z07 的阶段性成果。

＊＊　作者简介：王挺，陕西师范大学外国语学院 College of International Studies Shaanxi Normal University 陕西师范大学外国语学院 15332396192wltj310@ 163．com。

分的大学英语教学对学生思辨能力关注力度不足是其中原因之一。鉴于此，应以思辨能力培养为导向，构建大学英语教学思辨能力培养模式，将我国的大学英语教学改革推向纵深，培养出英语技能和思辨能力俱佳的有用人才。

一 理论框架

1. 思辨能力

思辨能力源自英语"critical thinking skills"，在我国学界也常被译成"批判性思维"。这些年来，学者们也越来越关注大学生思维能力的理论与实践研究，涌现出了一批成果（如钱坤强，1996；高一虹，1999；文秋芳，1999；罗清旭，2001；殷晓芳，2004；刘艳萍，2009；文秋芳等，2009；潘红，2010；韦晓保，2012 等）。在理论研究方面，殷晓芳（2004）提出了文本思辨创新式阅读教学模式，顺应了大学英语教学从技能型向思辨型转变这一形势的要求。李莉文（2011）分析了英语专业技能课程与批判性思维能力培养的关系问题，探讨了以批判性思维能力培养为导向的英语专业写作评测模式。孙有中（2011）认为要使英语专业摆脱目前在大学学科体系中的弱势地位，必须以培养学生的思维能力为导向，全面推进培养目标、培养模式、课程设置、教学方法、测试方法、教材编写和师资发展等方面的改革。在实证和实践研究方面，高一虹（1999）、文秋芳（1999）、文秋芳和刘润清（2006）等分别从演讲、口语和写作等诸方面揭示了英语专业学生思维水平低下的事实。文秋芳等（2009）为了解我国外语专业与非外语专业文科学生在思辨能力上是否存在差异，构建了大学生思维能力测量量具。文秋芳等（2010）还进行了我国首个大规模文科类大学生思辨能力的调查研究。

2. 口语教学中引入辩论对培养学生思辨能力的可行性

口语是利用语言表达思想，培养学生进行口头交际的能力。英语口语教学主要是加强培养及训练学生语言知识转换能力。其宗旨是要学生通过读和听获得知识、信息和语言，经过思维，在原有知识及语言的基础上对获得的内容和语言加工和重组，并赋予新的内容，然后输出语言，完成教学整个交际过程。口语教学的目标，毫无疑问应该是培养学生学会用英语来表达思想，进行交流。为了达到这一目标，采取什么样的教学方法和手段就显得非常重要。但是事实上，在实施口语教学时，许多教师往往采用的是与思想脱节的机械训练，要求学生去模仿一些刻板、机械、无意义的句型或场景会话，或者背一些会话课文。致使学生缺乏积极性和主动性，只是为应付老师才开口。研究表明，学生只有在有交流意图时，才会去开口说话，而且学生的口语能力只有在将自己的思想转换成语言时才得以表现出来。所以要提高学生的口语交流能力，首先必须要激发他们的交流意图和说话动机，使学生愿意开口讲话，积极使用英语来表达思想。

传统的口语教学模式多局限于演练日常生活中常见话题的表达，重点演练交际用语，这并没有真正培养学生用英语进行批判性思维的能力，也无法帮助学生表达更深刻，更有内涵的观点。我们经常在课堂上看到学生们就某一话题发表观点时词穷，觉得无从下手，或内容不够深刻，逻辑性欠佳，缺乏思维的深度和角度。这反映出我们在口语课堂上只注重培养学生的语言交际能力，而忽略了发展学生的思维能力。如何有效地培养学生的思维能力是值得探讨并解决的问题。同时，在外语班型较大的情况下，教师很难兼顾到全部的学生，确保每个人都积极参与口语活动。而学生之间由于口音重或发音不够标准，经常存在互相之间听不懂的情况，这也影响学生参与口语活动的积极性，英语课堂存在费时低效的问题。

《国家中长期教育改革与发展规划纲要（2010—2020年）》明确提出“适应国家经济社会对外开放的要求，培养大批具有国际视野、通晓国际规则、能够参与国际事务和国际竞争的国际化人才”的教育目标。辩论活动因其辩题覆盖面广、语言能力要求高、逻辑思辨能力强而逐渐成为培养我国大学生上述能力的重要手段。

2010年第14届外研社杯全国大学生英语辩论赛首次使用英国议会制辩论模式（British Parliamentary Style Debate），辩题涉及政治、经济、文化、法律、环境、医学、国际关系等众多国际性和地区性的话题。自此发起了全国范围内对英国议会制辩论的研究和学习。部分学者和教师逐渐尝试将此模式应用于英语口语教学当中，提出了教师应灵活运用BP辩论赛制规则，根据课程设置组织辩论活动，并建议高校教师要充分对学生进行培训，使其了解BP辩论的规则和流程，应结合学生的实际水平确定辩论发言的时间，使全班同学参与到辩论当中。在此背景下，在口语教学中使用英国议会制（BP）辩论模式（以下简称为BP辩论）并尝试使用立论和驳论的演讲式辩论模式，旨在锻炼学生的思辨能力和国际化人才的英语能力。

在西方，辩论的最早也是最负盛名的开拓者莫过于伟大的哲学先贤苏格拉底。此后，经过柏拉图、亚里士多德等人的不断继承和发扬，到中世纪时，辩论已经发展成为七门大学文科中的一门，谓之论辩学（Forensics）。所谓论辩学，即运用逻辑学、修辞学、美学、哲学、心理学、社会学、传播学、文学、口才学、演讲学的基本原理对人类的争辩论证行为进行综合研究的理论概括。现如今这门课程已经成为现代西方教育体系中非常重要的一门必修课。除此之外，很多高校还成立有专门的辩论协会，定期开展校内或校际间的各种联赛。在此背景下，很多辩论理论、技巧的研究著作应运而生。如 John Meany 的《艺术，论据，争辩》（2002）详尽阐述了议会制辩论的程序流程，辩手的职责意识和辩题的辩驳技巧，并附录了辩论的具体辩词样本。其另一本书《就该观点：议会制辩论入门》（2003），着重分析了如何准确地理解定义辩题，如何有效快速地记录笔记，如何公正科学地裁决，如何提出含金量较高的质询等议会制辩论的相关具体技巧。Sue Kay 编著的《实用辩论技巧》（2006）是一本阐释英语辩论实战技巧的手册，对于英语辩论实战具有非常强的指导意义，但缺少对辩论理论和辩论赛赛制的研究。Steven L. Johnson 所著的《赢在辩论》（2009）一书，为读者详细讲述了“英国议会制”辩论赛的具体形式和国际标准，为读者提供了英国议会制辩论的理论基础，实战策略和如何获胜的实用方法。此书在中国接受度非常高，更被誉为辩论界的“红宝书”。

在中国，春秋战国时期，辩论就曾经蔚然成风，辩士大量涌现，诞生了很多新颖睿智的观点，开创了“百家争鸣”的局面。除了春秋战国时期，中国历史上还出现了很多经典的辩论，如“白马非马”之辩、“鱼乐之辩”、“鹅湖之辩”、“两小儿辩日”，等等。在我国，虽然从古到今人们都很重视口才、演讲、辩论，但对英语辩论的研究却起步较晚。虽然近几年国内英语辩论赛非常风靡，影响逐步扩大，但由于赛事的相关培训仅限于辩手和带队教师之间，国内对英语辩论、议会制辩论的相关研究仍处于初级阶段，相关的学术研究和著作都不多。不过令人欣喜的是，国内已有学者（孙利民，2007；任亮娥，2008；万江波，2010；金烁锋，2013）认识到英语辩论及辩论赛在英语教学中的重要作用，并从不同方面进行了不同程度的研究。就目前国内高校课程设置和教学实践方面的情况而言，我们必须承认英语辩论所占的比重极小。虽然随着“外研社杯”全国大学生英语辩论赛的大力推广，部分大学开始尝试把英语辩论引入口语教学，陆续开设英语辩论课程，催生了一种全新的“以竞赛促教学，以教学推竞赛”的教学模式。但从实际来看，这些学校即便开设了该类课程，也大多只是面向高年级学生作为选修课，或简单地把英语辩论课等同于高级口语课或英语演讲课，缺乏专门的课程设置。在教学上，很多老师也仍以介绍赛制，传授语言知识为主，或许也强调听说，但对英语辩论核心层面的逻辑推理，论据评价等方面鲜少涉及或流于形式，其结果往往是过分强调应试性，不利于学生创新批判能力的培养和语言交际能力的充分发挥。因此，针对所有学生的英语辩论课的设置势在必行。

二　基于BP辩论模式培养学生思辨能力的大学英语口语课堂设计

由于笔者所在学校的公共英语课的班型都比较大，所以本研究是基于BP辩论模式的渐进式口语教学模式，即第一阶段结合教材主题进行自由辩论练习；第二阶段进行小组式思辨情景训练；第三阶段进行简化版议会制辩论。基于文秋芳的外语类大学生思辨能力层级理论模型，初步探讨了该教学模式体现学生思辨能力的三个主要认知技能：分析技能、推理技能和评价技能。英语演讲口语课程的教学目标不仅仅是提高学生的语言表达和运用能力，我们应该把培养和发展学生的思辨能力作为该课程的一个重要的显性目标。很多学生在选择这门课程时，首先是把提高自己的英语语言表达能力和辩论技巧作为学习目标。因此，为了充分的发挥学生思辨能力层次理论模型中最高层次的“元思维能力”，即自我调控能力，教师应在开课之初就向学生明确培养思辨能力是英语辩论课程的重要学习目标，让学生在学习的过程中有意识地计划、监控和评估自身的英语辩论技能和思辨能力，从而既能有效地提高学生的英语辩论能力，又能提高他们的思辨能力。

1. 教学设计的特点

将BP辩论作为一种口语教学模式应用于大学英语课堂，能够有效提高口语教学质量。再者辩论不仅能够提高学生语言能力的发展，而且有助于学生的批判性思维、团队合作精神以及观点表达等语言能力的全面发展。由于辩题涉及范围十分广泛，学生在准备辩论的过程中需要查阅大量资料，因此有助于帮助他们开阔视野，提高对社会的关注。此外，在辩论过程中批驳对方观点、维护己方观点的锻炼，使学生的批判性思维能力和心理素质都得以加强。具体如下：

1.1 帮助学生陈述自己的观点

在帮助学生陈述自己的观点的口语课堂活动中，要有阶段，有步骤地进行，先易后难。可以引导学生从一些最基础的话题如：自我介绍，体育运动，起居饮食，校园生活开始。因为这些话题和学生的生活息息相关，所以学生则有话可说，并能让每一个学生都能参与活动。其活动主要是在教师的指导下，由学生自主地完成。教师应该明确自己的角色功能，在教学活动中，教师应该是学生在活动过程中的指挥者——让学生明白活动的内容，指导学生积极有效地练习；组织者——组织学生的活动，让学生在各自的学习小组中积极开动脑筋，热烈而有秩序地投身于活动；监控者——监控整个教学过程，看学生是否按教师所设计的计划进行；刺激者——使学生与学生之间，学生和教师之间相互作用，以促进积极的教学双边活动；示范者——提供新的语言输入并给学生示范怎样使用语言；纠错者——当学生在语言练习中出错时，纠正什么，纠正多少，何时纠正以及怎样纠正；帮助者——当学生需要帮助时，及时给以帮助。同时，教师要控制好时间，在时间允许的情况下，活动最好控制在半分钟，5 分钟到 10 分钟为宜，也可以让学生准备所需要的时间大致和让学生在班上陈述的时间相当。在学生陈述时，教师要策略地诱导学生，拓宽话题，逐渐加深议题的深度，加快表达的速度，精练表述的质量。当然，学生在进行表述活动时应该是脱稿，不能把事先准备好的稿件在班上照本宣科。陈述完毕之后，各小组成员中就议题互相提问。这样的活动可以在一个课时中进行一至两次，待时机成熟时，拟出不同难度的议题，根据学生的个体差异，让学生根据自己的情况选题。这时，教师可以将该活动延长至 30 分钟，让那些想说的学生尽量把话说完。这种活动的目的主要是帮助学生在语言活动中保持浓厚的学习兴趣，同时也让那些缺乏自信心的学生在活动中找到自信。

1.2 帮助学生设立正反议题

设立正反议题涉及很广的范围和形式。教师要有目的、有计划地按步骤进行。首先教师要拟定好题目，题目要有中心，辩论要有意义，问题要有可辩性。议题提出以后，教师就要积极地鼓励学生参与对该议题在全班范围内进行争论，同时注意搜集不同的观点。对一些稍难点的议题，教师先给学生以启发性和诱导性的示范。教师在拟定议题时一定要根据学生的实际，从易到难，循序渐进，千万不要好高骛远，对一般性的正反议题最好是在两个为一组的学生中进行。在开始正反议题辩论之前，学习小组先进行讨论，然后再表述。其次在学生表述中，教师要强调要求学生有逻辑地在极短的时间内快速简要地陈述自己的观点，就各自对该议题的观点进行反证以丰富语言的内容，加大语言的输入和输出量。对程度好的学生，教师可以采用稍有挑战性的辩论方式，将学生编为三人一组，就有关课文的议题开展辩论。在某一特定的情节中，三人之间互相转换议题，这样会增加辩论的难度。最后在学生具有一定的表述能力以后，教师可以组织学生就课文的某些观点进行复杂的辩论。其组织形式仍然是三人为一组，程序仍然和上述相同。当一个学生提出问题，其他两个进行反驳，然后再交换角色。

1.3 学生创造性表述的能力

指导学生从简单的句型表述到复杂的、具有创造性的表述是整个口语活动的目的，它是一个语言处理的过程，而不是一个单纯的语言活动，该过程只有在课文结束后的前提下才能进行。完形心理学派的创立者威台海姆在《创造性思维》一书中明确指出：严格的训练会使学生的思维麻木不仁，唯有引导学生自由地探索、灵活地思考，才可进行创造性地发展。在课堂教学中，教师要组织全体学生进行双向或多向性交流，广泛交换意见，营造一种宽松和谐的语言学习气氛，全方位地开动脑筋，发挥学生的主观能动性，养成逆向思维的习惯，激发学生的创新意识。在句型控制练习中，学生进行创造性的表述时可能会为了加快语速而摆脱“正确”语法和“范例”的束缚，产生语言表述的错误，这是难免的，也是可以谅解的。但随着学生反复地练习，加上教师策略地指正，学生会在短期内有效地提高语言的准确性及表述的质量

2 课堂教学环节

2.1 英国议会制辩论简介

英国议会制辩论（以下简称为 BP 辩论）主要模仿英国下议院的辩论模式，是目前国际校际英语辩论赛通用的一种模式。每次可参与 8 人，更适合应用于班型较大的大学英语课堂。

2.2 BP 辩论流程

BP 辩论由正反双方组成，每方有两队，每队两人，正反方队员交替发言。正反方的一队均负责开篇陈述，二队均负责总结陈词。每位选手都

有明确的称呼和职责。正方一队一辩的职责是展开辩题，并给具有特殊意义的词汇下定义。正反方一号之后的辩手都要延伸之前辩手的观点，正反方的最后一位辩手称为党鞭，其职责是总结己方观点，驳斥对方观点，不能提出新的立论点。

2.3 BP 辩论规则

BP 辩论的辩题在辩论开始十五分钟前公布，各队当场抽签决定各自的立场，辩手们在十五分钟内利用纸媒资料准备发言内容。每位辩手有七分钟的发言时间，其中二至六分钟内，对方辩手可以要求质询（POI），正在发言的辩手可以接受或回绝质询。如果接受质询，提问辩手有十五秒钟时间质询，提问与回答的时间均计入发言辩手的七分钟。POI 是 BP 辩论的一个重要环节，每位辩手在 POI 中的表现均被列入裁判员的考量范围，是辩手们展示个人风采的最佳时机。也是 BP 辩论过程中最有乐趣的部分。

而在最后两轮的总结陈词发言期间，不允许对方提任何 POI。比赛中发言时间受到严格控制，不允许超时发言。另外，发言的辩手有权拒绝对手的 POI，但是不可以全部回避。POI 的提出者一定要在 15 秒之内结束发言，提出时间也严格限制在前四轮陈述的允许时段。

2.4 活用议会制辩论规则

一场完整的英国议会制辩论需要 40 分钟，再加上公布议题和 15 分钟的准备时间，大概一个小时就过去了，对于英语口语课堂来说，这将意味着在一整个课时的时间里全班除了 4 名辩手外，其他同学都不得不保持沉默，充当听众。因此，为了满足更多同学参与辩论的愿望，同时提高口语课堂的教学效率，教师必须灵活运用议会制辩论的规则，合理分配时间，在辩论实践之外，还有必要加上讨论和讲评环节，及时给学生辩手提供反馈意见，以鼓励他们更有激情地按照议会制辩论规则去参与辩论。关于如何灵活使用议会制辩论规则，教师在组织课堂时可从下面几个方面入手：

A. 培训辩手。教师就议会制辩论的规则 、评判标准和辩论技巧对学生进行全面培训，可参照往年的全国大学英语辩论赛实况录像，通过讲解和评析，让他们更直观地了解议会制辩论。等学生明白每个辩手的主要任务和发言顺序后，可把学生分成小组，选择简单辩题组织辩论实战演习。这个环节需要教师及时发现并纠正学生辩论中出现的错误，并提示学生完成自己的任务。

B. 提前布置辩论任务。在熟悉辩论规则和技巧之后，教师开始组织课堂辩论。但是辩题的公布时间不能太晚，可考虑提前一周公布，给学生充分的思考时间，查阅资料，以增加课堂辩论时的信心和对话题展开的广度和深度。考虑到提前公布话题可能导致部分学生准备得“过于充分”，以至于在实际辩论中出现“读稿”的现象，教师可以提前公布话题（general topic)，然后在课堂辩论前 15 分钟公布具体辩题，组织辩论。比如，教师可提前一周安排学生查阅有关安乐死（Euthanasia）的相关资料，然后在课堂辩论前 15 分钟公布当天的辩题为“Euthanasia is not only fair but also reasonable.”

C. 压缩发言时间。比较简便的做法是把每场辩论的时间减半，也就是把每一轮发言的时间限定在原议会制英语辩论发言时间的一半，这样只需 20 分钟就能进行一场形式完整的辩论。当然，辩论时间可以灵活掌握，根据情况适当增减。

D. 增加辩手。为了满足更多学生参与课堂辩论活动的需要，教师可以控制时间，给每名辩手相同的时间发言，要求做一个结构完整的辩论演讲，有驳论还要有立论。教师甚至可以把全班同学分成两大组，正方和反方，除了选出的一辩和最后做总结陈词的辩手之外，每组其他同学均可以自由决定谁来发言、何时发言。增加辩手之后教师一定要保证在辩论过程中正反方轮流发言，最后双方都要总结陈词。

E. 小组辩论口语课堂的辩论活动必须分组进行。按照辩论规则的要求，可把学生分成四人小组，每次以自主决定或抽签的形式分成正反两方，就给定辩题首先进行小组内的辩论练习，然后教师再从不同的小组中随机抽出一支正方队伍，和一支反方队伍，让他们为全班做一场 20 分钟的模拟辩论。辩论结束后教师组织学生分小组讨论，然后各组选出代表汇报讨论结果。最后教师做总结性点评，肯定学生的进步，指出表现突出之处，当然也要简要概括缺点和不足。

F. 同级评价。在选出四个辩手做模拟辩论的环节，教师有必要要求其他学生认真倾听，做笔记，并为每个辩手打分，这样既可以帮助学生专注于正在进行的演讲，又能为之后的讨论做好准备。课后教师还可以把学生的笔记和打分收上来，作为课堂考评的依据。考虑到英语辩论要求学生具有较高的英语表达能力和思辨能力，并要求掌握一定的信息量和知识体系，笔者适当引入辩论形式，尝试从简单的辩题入手，第一学期开始做辩论规则和思维方面的培训。第二学期的口语课则以辩论为主，展开不同形式和规则的辩论活动，以此锻炼学生思维，培养口语表达的能力，提高口语教学的效果。

总之，辩论是语言的艺术、思想的交锋，智慧的较量。作为传统课堂的一种很好的补充，辩论为语言的使用营造了真实的环境，便于“师生”和“生生”交流，实现交际性教学的目标，并且给他们提供个性发展的机会，提升他们的综合素质和能力。

三　基于 BP 辩论模式培养学生思辨能力的口语课的启发

BP 辩论作为一种方兴未艾的英语口语竞技形式，也可以作为一种教学模式应用到我们的英语课堂中来发挥其压倒性的优势，完善口语教学。它既可以解决大学英语课堂费时低效的问题，又可以培养学生语言与思维的全面发展，提高学生的综合素质。

1. BP 辩论的辩题往往是当今社会人们关注的话题，学生们在准备辩论的过程中必然要想方设法收集相关信息，关注社会现状，开阔视野，改变他们以往“两耳不闻窗外事”的状态，促使学生积极主动地储备知识。对于每个辩手而言，发言的过程是他们在所准备材料的基础上进行的即兴演讲与即兴辩论完美结合的过程。POI 是 BP 辩论的亮点，要求辩手倾听、听懂发言辩手的观点并及时作出反应，或驳斥，或质询。而发言的辩手也必须及时回应，这要求辩手具有即兴演讲的能力。每个辩手的发言都是一次演讲，这要求辩手们掌握演讲的要素和艺术，展示个人风采与良好的风度。辩手之外的学生可以作为裁判来参与辩论过程。与传统的辩论不同，BP 辩论的裁判们不仅仅是坐在那里旁观，他们要记录每位选手的观点并点评，作出的裁判要有理有据。裁判们实际上是整场辩论中最辛苦的参与者，对学生的听力和速记都有很高要求，因此 BP 辩论可以让全班同学积极主动地参与其中。POI 和评委的工作均要求学生之间互相能够理解对方的发言，这有助于学生们学会认真倾听，适应不同口音的英语。同时，在 BP 辩论的评判标准中，辩手的观点内容要比语音面貌更重要。这会激发学生提高他们的思维框架，促进他们思维的深度和角度，考虑问题更加深刻。

2. 在教学实践中应用 BP 辩论，经过一个学期的培训与演练，为 BP

辩论改变了他们的思维模式，他们分析问题更具有条理，不再拘泥于单一的角度，并且一改过去无话可说的局面。在经过学习之后，学生们可以滔滔不绝地对给定话题发表观点。对语言内容的重视也激励语音面貌差的学生积极参与进来，他们不再为自己的语音语调或口音感到自卑，不再像过去那样安静地听其他同学发言。有了发言的意图，他们更加关注思维能力的培养和观点的表达，提高了学生们在口语活动中的参与度，激发了学生们的学习热情。

3. 辩论本身的对抗性、挑战性和竞争性满足了学生个性化需求和展示自我的愿望，激发他们更大的勇气，增强信心，学会用自己的智慧和思考去克服困难，取得胜利。同时议会制辩论严格的规则和评判原则可使学生在教学中受到严格的训练，长远来看，这必将影响他们的职业发展和人生态度。

4. 辩论的过程离不开辩手之间的互助合作，没有良好的分工合作就无法呈现精彩的辩论过程，这是培养学生们团队合作能力和塑造班级凝聚力的良好机会。在激烈辩论的同时保持理性，时刻做到有风度、有礼貌，从而提高学生们的心理素质。

四　结语

在教学实践中应用 BP 辩论，经过培训与演练，BP 辩论改变了学生们的思维模式，他们分析问题更具有条理，不再拘泥于单一的角度，并且一改过去无话可说的局面。在经过学习之后，学生们可以滔滔不绝地对给定话题发表观点。对语言内容的重视也激励语音面貌差的学生积极参与进来，他们不再为自己的语音语调或口音感到自卑，不再像过去那样安静地听其他同学发言。有了发言的意图，他们更加关注思维能力的培养和观点的表达，提高了学生们在口语活动中的参与度，激发了学生们的学习热情。辩论本身的对抗性、挑战性和竞争性满足了学生个性化需求和展示自我的愿望，激发他们更大的勇气，增强信心，学会用自己的智慧和思考去克服困难，取得胜利。同时议会制辩论严格的规则和评判原则可使学生在教学中受到严格的训练，长远来看，这必将影响他们的职业发展和人生态度。辩论的过程离不开辩手之间的互助合作，没有良好的分工合作就无法呈现精彩的辩论过程，这是培养学生们团队合作能力和塑造班级凝聚力的良好机会。在激烈辩论的同时保持理性，时刻做到有风度、有礼貌，从而提高学生们的心理素质。

参考文献

黄源深：《英语专业课程必须彻底改革——再谈“思辨缺席”》，《外语界》2010年第1期。

孙有中：《突出思辨能力培养，将英语专业教学改革引向深入》，《中国外语》2019年第3期。

文秋芳等：《评述外语专业学生思辨能力的发展》，《外语学刊》2006年第5期。

文秋芳等：《构建我国外语类大学生思辨能力量具的理论框架》，《外语界》2009年第1期。

文秋芳等：《我国英语专业与其他文科类大学生思辨能力的对比研究》，《外语教学与研究》2017年第5期。

任文：《再论外语专业学生的思辨能力：“缺席”还是“在场”》，《中国外语》2013年第1期。

刘艳萍：《英语演讲教学与思辨能力的培养》，《外语艺术教育研究》2009年第3期。

李传玲：《英语演讲教学对大学生思辨能力培养的作用研究》，《淮海工学院学报》2012年第10期。

卢杨、何璇：《公共英语演讲课程与思辨能力培养》，《开封教育学院学报》2014年第8期。

杨晓青：《论英语辩论在大学英语课堂中的应用》，《中国教师—高等教育》2016年第8期。

Cultivation of Critical thinking skills through Debate-based Oral English Class

Abstract: Critical thinking skill is one of the skills that are emphasized in today's higher education. However, the weakness and absence of critical thinking skills widely exist in college English learners. Many scholars at home and abroad pay much attention to the cultivation of the critical thinking skills. This paper starts from the connotation and theoretical models of critical thinking skills, and, through analyzing the relationship between the English debate teaching and the cultivation and development of critical thinking skills, and explores the effective ways of training and developing students' critical thinking skills through teaching public English debate in oral English class.

Key words: English debate teaching; critical thinking skills; college oral English class

中国英语在高校英语专业教学中的重要性探析

祁喜鸿[*]

摘　要：中国英语是一种英语语言变体，是世界英语在中国社会文化环境中的本土化形式。中国英语不仅符合英语语言规范，而且具有鲜明的中国文化特色，具有记载和储存中国社会文化内容的作用。英语专业学生肩负着传播中国文化、促进中外交流、提升中国国际影响力的历史使命。在高校英语专业教学中重视中国英语相关内容不仅能帮助学生更好地学习英语语言文化知识，提升其跨文化交际能力，还可以帮助其更加有效地进行对外文化传播。

关键词：中国英语；中国文化；英语专业教学

一　引言

当今世界，国与国之间在政治、经济、文化、社会生活等各个方面的交流越来越频繁，呈现出了前所未有的繁荣景象。在此全球化的大背景下，英语作为使用率最广、普及率最高的国际通用语，发挥着举足轻重的作用。同时，由于不同国家文化之间频繁的交流互动，英语也在不断地经历着继承、创新和变化。“英语在国际化过程中与使用国特有语言和文化充分接触、融合，其必然结果就是英语的本土化（nativization），形成各种使用型变体（performance variety）”（刘祥清，2005：72）。英语的本土化发展已经打破了以英国英语和美国英语为中心的一体化格局。中国英语（China English）作为英语变体的一种，不仅是一个单纯的语言演变现象，其背后还隐藏着更深层次的文化政治问题。本文通过探讨中国英语的客观存在，肯定中国英语对当前我国英语专业文化教学的积极意义，强调

---

* 作者简介：祁喜鸿（1976—　），女，陕西师范大学外国语学院讲师。研究方向：英语教学。

在高校英语专业教学中应该重视中国英语。

二 世界英语说与中国英语

对英语变体的研究可以追溯到20世纪七八十年代，当时出现了一些针对英语功能、类别和分布多元性的分析，其中以印裔美国语言学家Kachru提出的世界英语说（World Englishes）最具影响力。Kachru（1982/1992）将全球的英语变体划分为三层同心圆，其中内圈（Inner Circle）是本族语变体，如英国、美国英语；外圈（Outer Circle）是制度化的非本族语变体，即传统上作为第二语言的英语变体，如印度、新加坡英语；扩展圈（Expanding Circle）是使用性变体，即传统上作为外语的英语，如日本英语、中国英语等。此后世界英语说及卡式路径（Kachruvian Approach）成为热门的研究领域和视角。随着各国学者从语音、词汇、句法、语篇、语用、态度等不同方面对各类英语变体展开的诸多研究深入进行，世界英语说已经成为国际语言界研究的热点。世界英语说的提出颠覆了标准英语与非标准英语、本族语者与非本族语者的权力结构和二元对立，使英语成为可以由不同国家和民族使用以表述各自文化与身份的语言，对于打破英美英语的霸权地位及建设多元的全球语言环境起到了巨大推动作用，具有革命性的意义。

“中国英语”（China English）是英语全球化和本土化过程中产生的众多英语变体中的一种。国内有关“中国英语”的概念最早由葛传槼（1980）于20世纪80年代提出。进入90年代以后，学界对“中国英语”这一说法展开了广泛的讨论。诸多研究以分析“中国英语”的特点，区别“中国英语”和“中国式英语”入手，就“中国英语”的定义和性质进行了讨论（汪榕培，1991；李文中，1993；谢之君，1995；贾冠杰，向明友，1997；杜争鸣，1998等）。“中国英语”的概念被越来越多的学者接受和认同，成为一种以规范英语为依据，通过音译、译借及语义再生等创造性手段来传达中国特有文化、事物或观念的具有中国特色的英语变体。尽管英语在中国还是被看作是使用性变体（performance variety），在英语教学中英国英语和美国英语还是作为英语教学的规范，但是随着英语学习者和使用者数量不断增多，以及以英语为媒介的对外交流活动日趋频繁，具有民族文化特色的中国英语显现出了前所未有的重要性。一方面，中国人在使用英语时努力遵循标准英语的规范以保证交流的可理解性；但另一方面，在用英语讨论中国的事情时，英语使用者的社会文化特征不可避免地反映在其所使用的语言中，促进语言的变革和更新，从而使中国英语呈现出常用常新的发展态势。

三 中国英语与中国文化

就目前来看，英语是向全世界传播中国文化的主要语言工具。中国本土文化想要实现全球化，必须借助英语这一重要媒介。在世界多元文化格局中，只有通过英语向世界讲述中国的本土文化，才能让世界听到更多的中国声音。而中国英语就是表述中国文化的最佳英语载体。

语言是文化的载体，同时也是文化的写照。一个民族的物质文化和精神文化都必然会反映到该民族所使用的语言中。作为世界英语在中国社会文化环境中的本土化形式，中国英语和中国社会文化环境相融相生。中国英语“既有标记语言使用者社会文化特征的功能，又是语言使用者实现不同交际目的的有效工具”（胡晓丽，2008：14）。

中国英语作为一种语言变体，依赖着中华民族的独特文化而存在。中国英语具有记载和储存中国文化信息或内容的作用。由于词语是语言最积极、最活跃的部分，中国英语的文化内涵在词汇层面的特征最为明显。与历史上其他语言中的词汇进入英语词汇的途径相似，汉语中的大量词汇用语也通过借词（borrowing）形式进入英语词汇。汉语借词主要通过音译和译借手段（包括直译和意译）产生的大量音译词语和译借词语（句）进入英语，形成中国英语。中国英语借助大量音译词和译借词将中国特有的语言、文化、思想等传达给世界，最大限度地保留了中国文化的底蕴和中国语言表达的特色，具有充分的可理解性和交际功能，同时在全球范围内弘扬中国文化，标志着中国人的文化身份（胡晓丽，2008：15）。中国英语中耳熟能详的音译词语有 jiaozi（饺子），kungfu（工夫），guanyin（观音），qipao（旗袍），mahjong（麻将），hutong（胡同），fengshui（风水）等；还有以音译词语+英语词语的方式形成的词语，诸如 Peking Opera（京剧），the Tang Dynasty（唐朝），Shenzhou Ⅵ spacecraft（神舟六号飞船）等；以及按汉语表达直译过来的借词和语句，诸如 spring rolls（春卷），a land of fish and rice（鱼米之乡），Four Books and Five Classics（四书五经），One Country，Two Systems（一国两制），He who has not scaled the Great Wall is not a man（不到长城非好汉）等。除此之外，还有通过意译形式产生的反映中国独有文化内容的借词和语句，例如 the Summer Palace（颐和园），Dragon Boat Festival（端午节），place equal emphasis on material progress and ethical and cultural progress（两手抓，两手都要硬），等等（李涤非，2006：84-85）。

在语篇层面，中国英语在 China Daily，China Today，China Periodical，Beijing Review，CCTV International 等国内媒体报纸杂志的报道中有充分的表现，此外以林语堂、胡适等为代表的当代中国作家、学者创作的介绍中国文化的小说、散文、杂文等各类英语作品，以 Pearl S. Buck，Edgar Snow 为代表的外国作家、记者创作的反映中国社会不同历史时期状况的各类英语作品以及由国内外一流翻译家（国内如杨宪益和 Gladys Yang 夫妇、许渊冲；国外如 D. Hawkes、H. A. Giles、A. Waley 等）翻译的中国文学作品的英文版等，都是中国英语文本类型（李涤非 2006：85）。

毋庸置疑，这些中国英语的词汇语句和语篇不仅符合英语语言表达规范，同时反映了中国社会文化、政治经济制度、自然地理环境、本土生活方式、传统习俗、伦理道德价值观念等中国文化独有的方方方面，彰显了中华民族的文化个性。

不可否认，英语在当今世界各国间的交流中占据着主导地位，相比之下，汉语在国际交流中依然处于劣势。要想实现让“中国文化走出去”的愿景，我们必须借助中国英语这一烙有明显中国文化印记的语言形式，才能让外国人获得理解中国社会和文化的一个内部视角，更好地传播和弘扬中国文化。

四 中国英语在英语专业教学中的重要性

由高等学校外语专业教学指导委员会英语组起草、外语教学与研究出版社和上海外语教育出版社于 2000 年出版发行的《高等学校英语专业英语教学大纲》（以下简称新《大纲》）明确指出，英语专业的培养目标是“培养具有扎实的英语语言基础和广博的文化知识并能熟练地运用英语在外事、教育、经贸、文化、科技、军事等部门从事翻译、教学、管理、研究等工作的复合型英语人才”。在附录Ⅰ“英语专业课程描述”中，新《大纲》对文化教学的课程设置及授课内容做了详尽的描述，并特别要求英语专业学生要“对中国文化和社会经济发展有一定的了解，提高对外介绍能力”。同时新《大纲》在附录Ⅱ“英语专业学生阅读参考书目”中还特地列出了英文版的中国文化阅读书目。由此可见，英语专业大纲要求英语专业学生不仅要具备扎实的英语语言知识和技能，同时还要具备对外介绍能力，运用英语向外国人介绍我们自己的社会生活和文化。在中国文化“走出去”战略背景下，英语专业学生肩负的传播中国文化、促进中外交流、提升中国国际影响力的历史使命尤为艰巨。

但是长期以来我国的专业英语教学过分注重目标语和目标语文化的输入，忽视了母语文化的注入，在英语专业学生中出现了“去中国文化”现象和“中国文化失语”现象（周红，2015：97-98）。英语专业的学生将主要精力放在了英语语言以及与之相关的英美文化上，从而忽视了汉语及其文化的学习。加上英语专业的教材内容往往是以英美文化为背景，用英语介绍中国文化的内容寥寥无几，久而久之，学生对中国文化反而陌生了起来。在跨文化交流中，“当遇到要用英语表达反映中国文化特色的内容时，学生们往往词不达意，让听者不知所云”（陈建平、杜军，2008：56），出现了中国文化“失语症”。与此同时，由于在英语学习过程中接触了过多的西方文化和意识形态，英语专业学生的文化价值取向也受到了严重的影响，学生缺乏文化全球化意识，对外传播中国文化的意识薄弱。上述英语专业教学中的文化失衡现象不仅制约了学生跨文化交流能力的提升和整体英语语言水平的提高，而且背离了我国培养英语专业人才的目的，不利于英语专业学生树立对我国文化的自觉和自信，应该引起高度重视。

要想提高英语专业学生的英语整体水平和跨文化传播能力，真正实现英语专业的人才培养目标，为中国文化“走出去”作出应有的贡献，高校的英语专业教学不仅要重视学生英语语言知识技能的强化和训练以及英美文化内容的介绍，同时还要强调对中国文化内容的英文表达和探讨。中国英语就是在英语专业教学中实现中国文化内容和谐融入的一个有力抓手。

从之前的探讨可以看出，中国英语作为英语在中国文化土壤环境中的一种使用性变体已经是一种客观存在，而且已经成为一种无法忽视的语言现象。对于中国的英语学习者来说，了解、掌握并主动运用中国英语，可以在很大程度上增强其跨文化交流能力以及文化自觉和自信。对于英语专业学生来说，尤其如此。因此，高校英语专业教学中应该包括中国英语内容，在英语语言教学中同步进行中国文化教学，帮助语言专业学生更好地理解中国文化，学习中国社会现象和文化内容的英语表达方式，全面提高其英语语言运用能力和跨文化交际能力。

具体来说，中国英语在高校专业英语教学中的重要性表现在以下几个方面。

首先，中国英语是英语专业语言文化教学的重要组成部分。产生于英语全球化和本土化过程中的中国英语遵循了规范英语的语法规则，具有“可理解性”（intelligibility）、“可接受性”（acceptability）和“适宜性”（appropriateness）（周宣丰，2017：49）。作为世界英语的重要组成部分，中国英语是在中国文化背景和汉语语言环境下发展起来的，是对英语的有利补充和发展。中国的社会文化特点体现在中国英语的词汇、句子和篇章等诸多方面。表达得当的中国英语在表达中国特有事物时起着独特作用，是英语专业学生学习的重要内容。新《大纲》在其附录Ⅱ“英语专业学生阅读参考书目”中特地列出了英文版的中国文化阅读书目，以期督促英语专业学生更好地了解中国文化。这些阅读书目诸如 The Spirit of the Chinese People，Peasant Life in China，My Country and My People 都是中国英语的典型例子。因此，中国英语是英语专业语言文化教学中不可或缺的重要内容。高校英语专业教学中，不仅需要加强学生英语语言知识技能的训练和英美文化内容的介绍，同时应该重视中国英语中包含的有关中国社会文化生活方方面面的内容，将其作为英语专业教学的重要部分。

其次，中国英语有助于英语专业学生跨文化交际能力的培养和提升。语言教学离不开文化因素，英语语言教学的目的之一是让学习者能够运用英语进行交际，即具有交际能力。新《大纲》在教学原则中也特别提出，要“注重培养跨文化交际能力。在专业课程的教学中要注重培养学生对文化差异的敏感性、宽容性以及处理文化差异的灵活性”。英语专业学生将来要成为在不同工作岗位工作的复合型英语人才，对他们来说，仅仅具备用英语表达英美文化内容的能力远远不够。他们还必须深刻了解本国社会生活文化的方方面面，并且掌握用英语表达中国文化的能力，才能在跨文化交流中发挥应有的作用。在很大程度上，没有用英语表达中国文化的能力就无法进行跨文化交际。作为国际使用型英语变体，中国英语集语言工具性和文化性于一体，在跨文化交际中发挥着重要的作用。因此，在高校英语专业教学中包含中国英语相关内容，可以更好地培养和提升英语专业学生的跨文化交际能力。

最后，中国英语是英语专业学生用来传播中国文化的重要工具和桥梁。英语专业学生作为本国文化与外国文化的接触者，承担着向外传播中国文化的历史使命。我国在《“十一五”时期国家文化发展规划纲要》和《文化产业振兴规划》中提出了中国文化“走出去”的国家战略方针。英语专业学生应该积极响应这一战略，通过各种渠道和方法向外国人介绍优秀的中国文化。“中国英语是世界了解中国社会和文化的主要渠道，也是中国向世界传播中国文化的主要载体”（李涤非，2006：85）。通过学习和使用中国英语，英语专业学生可以获得一个了解本国社会文化的外部视角，驱使他们不断调适中国文化和英语文化的关系，加深对语言和文化关系的理解，对中国文化有进一步的认识和了解。同时，中国英语还可以帮助外国人“直接接触和体验原味的中国文化，改善和重构国家形象，还原一个更为真实的中国”（周宣丰，2017：50），推动中国文化更为有效地“走出去”，增强中国文化在国际舞台的影响力和辐射力。因此，中国英语是英语专业学生进行对外文化传播的有力工具和有效途径。

五 结语

作为世界英语在中国社会文化环境中的一种本土化形式，中国英语的存在已然是一种无法否认的事实。中国英语具有标记中国文化身份的重要功能。在高校英语专业教学中包含中国英语相关内容，不仅有助于英语专业学生提高英语语言知识技能，提高其跨文化交际能力，而且可以产生文化导向作用，帮助学生更好地了解中国文化，增强其文化自觉和自信，从而为促进中国文化“走出去”作出应有的贡献，因此具有重要的实践价值和战略意义。

参考文献

Kachru, B. The Other Tongue: *English across cultures*. Urbana: University of Illinois Press, 1982/ 1992.

陈建平、杜军：《英语专业教学不可忽视的一课：中国文化》，《成都大学学报》（教育科学版）2008 年第 7 期。

杜争鸣：《中国英语问题及其他》，《外语教学》1998 年第 3 期。

高等学校外语专业教学指导委员会英语组：《高等学校英语专业英语教学大纲》，上海外语教育出版社 2000 年版。

葛传椝：《漫谈由汉译英问题》，《中国翻译》1980 年第 2 期。

胡晓丽:《中国英语之功能研究》,《外语与外语教学》2008年第11期。
贾冠杰、向明友:《为中国英语一辩》,《外语与外语教学》1997年第5期。
江晓红:《跨文化交际中的中国英语》,《四川外语学院学报》2001年第17卷第6期。
李涤非:《中国文化、中国英语与文化教学》,《广州大学学报》(社会科学版) 2006年第5卷第8期。
李文中:《中国英语与中国式英语》,《外语教学与研究》1993年第4期。
刘祥清:《"中国英语"研究与英语专业文化教学》,《天津外国语学院学报》2005年第5期。
商叙明:《全球化背景下英语专业学生中国文化缺失调查及其对策》,《语文学刊》(外语教育教学) 2013年第10期。
汪榕培:《中国英语是客观存在》,《解放军外语学院学报》1991年第1期。
谢之君:《中国英语:跨文化语言交际中的干扰性变体》,《现代外语》1995年第4期。
于万锁:《中国文化失语症对英语专业跨文化交际能力培养的负面影响成因与对策》,《中北大学学报》(社会科学版) 2016年第32卷第4期。
郑德虎:《把"中国英语"融入高职高专英语教学的实证研究》,《当代外语研究》2012年第7期。
周宣丰:《后现代语境下中国英语的文化政治意义》,《外语与翻译》2017年第24卷第2期。

The Importance of Including China English in English Language Teaching for English Majors in Chinese Colleges and Universities

Qi Xihong

Abstract: China English is a performance variety of English. It has come into existence as a result of the nativization of World English. China English not only abides by the norms of standard English, but records and stores Chinese social culture as well. English majors hold the responsibility of spreading Chinese culture, promoting the exchange between China and foreign countries and enhancing China's international influence. To attach importance to China English in English Language Teaching for English majors in Chinese colleges and universities will help English majors better learn English language and culture, improve their intercultural communicative competence and enable them to spread Chinese culture to other countries more effectively.

Key words: China English; Chinese Culture; English Language Teaching for English Majors

叙事的多维转向与应用*

——从会话叙事的高校课堂实践谈起

朱冬怡**

摘　要：20世纪90年代以来，后经典叙事的研究对象一再扩大，叙事研究也因此产生了多个转向。新的叙事转向逐步迈至人类日常性和生活化的交际世界之中。以此为切入，会话叙事研究沿袭但又修正了叙事在文学探究中的分析脚本，得出了会话叙事所具有的和经典叙事结构完全不同的特点，即结构性碎片化、连贯性不充分、叙事维度多样性、切入主题多变化的话语特点。本文将借此以会话叙事在高校课堂中的应用为例，探析叙事多维转向过程中的日常偏向和高校课堂应用，以期为叙事的日常交际和分析使用提供借鉴，同时也表明课堂会话叙事互动是调度学生话语思辨能力的有效途径。

关键词：叙事研究；会话叙事；英语专业课堂；英语词汇学

1. 引言

20世纪90年代以来，后经典叙事学的研究对象从单一的文学叙事扩大到影视、新闻和日常会话等多种叙事类型（赵玉荣，2014：93），叙事学从文学幕后逐渐走入日常台前，而以此引介的叙事研究，无论是作为一种认识论或方法论，抑或是称之为一种学术范式，已深刻影响了过去几十年的社会科学发展，推动了文学、语言学、教育学、传播学、文化学、艺术学、社会学、地理学等不同领域学者对故事及其社会文化功能的关注和思考，形成了蔚为大观的“叙事转向”（侯松等，2017：38）。在此叙事

---

* 本文是陕西师范大学2019年“教师教学模式创新与实践研究”专项基金项目：“课堂会话叙事视野下的语言教学探讨（JSJX2019Z18）”的研究成果。

** 作者简介：朱冬怡，女，陕西师范大学外国语学院讲师，研究方向：会话叙事、话语分析。

转向上，关乎人类日常生活的不同于宏大叙事的小故事事件日益走上舞台，以互动性、散装性的小故事为基础（Georgakopoulou，2006；朱冬怡，2019），一种“新”的叙事转向逐步踏入探究领域，以期打开叙事学日常性与生活化的新局面。

“新”叙事转向的提出为日常会话交际叙事提供了探析脚本。会话叙事是源于日常交际的一种语体。不同于文体，语体是说话的一种体式，是话语交际的“体”，或称之为“方式或结构系统”。简单来讲，会话叙事指的是日常会话交际中的故事讲述活动。会话叙事最初是作为自发性会话的次级活动类型出现的（赵玉荣，2013）。Fludernik（1996：13－19）曾采用“自然叙事”这一说法，指出在正常的、日常交谈中自然而然发生的一种自然叙事非常值得研究，这种“自然的会话叙事”常用来区别未经考虑而作出的叙述和有“构建性”的人物且出现在具体讲故事语境中的叙述。她特别强调了个人直接或间接的经验性故事讲述活动，并指出经验性会话叙事是自然叙事和其他一切叙事的叙事原型。在此之后，Norrick（2000：27）将“会话叙事”作为术语并进行了一系列研究，他将会话叙事定义为“不同于文学叙事文本的自然叙事，是一种出现于日常自然会话中的叙事，具有面对面互动交际，话题动态发展，话轮转接没有固定次序和长度限制的叙事特点”。这个定义在概念上基本等同于Fludernik所提到的个人的经验性会话叙事。会话叙事在新的叙事转向中介入至语言的教育应用是叙事多维转向中的“小范式，大作用”。下文便从此转向下的会话叙事入手，探析叙事的新转向在高校课堂语境中的角色扮演和文学启发。

2. 高校课堂语境下的会话叙事初探：相融还是交锋？

以笔者所在高校的英语专业来看，英语专业课堂上的教与学围绕着教师与学生在跨语言的桥梁上对目的语言的文化、文法与文学语境的观念互动、知识互动与思想互动。近年来有越来越多的专家和学者对我国英语专业的学科和课程定位建言献策，批判申辩，归纳而言，我们将其总结为“三个定位”的思考：其一是在学科划分层面的“人文学科”的以人文通识教育为主的学科定位（胡文仲、孙有中，2006；孙有中，2017；顾悦，2019）；其二是在专业内容层面的“均衡的言语技能+均衡的语言文化”的以学生输入为主的内容定位（何其莘等，1999；汪榕培，2000；张冲，

2003)；其三是在培养目标层面的“纯熟的语言能力、自如的语文转换、深度的专题研究”的跨语言文化的专门研究人才的培养定位（张冲，2003：11）。从备课环节到教学实践，从师生互动到教学反思，笔者对“三个定位”的切身思考是：如何在真实的课堂语境中实现对上述“三个定位”的探究，具体而言，是否可以从英专课堂的真实语境中于启迪学生人文素养的同时，以语言技能的考量为手段，和学生在课堂语境中共建一个微观性的思辨性语境，使教师在教学细节过程中与学生建立起师生互动，生生互析的课堂局面？

以此为切入，这一思考中的局面不仅涉及课程设置和教学方法，更为核心的是在培养目标定位中，如何使纯熟的语言能力、自如的语言文化切换和深度的专业课话题析辩相结合的教学目标转化为真实的教学实践，对于一线教学的笔者来说，这是一种深切的课堂实践企盼，更是一种针对教学方法的尝试和挑战。英语系学生自然是英语专业课堂的主体，而以教师为主导的课堂教学自然应就这一所期的课堂局面上下谋略，以期课堂主体能够在此种局面中具有脑有所想，口有所言，理有所据，使课堂主体真正主动地对课堂主题进行参与、分析、思考、言说，而不至于在被动的环境中造就“思辨的缺席”（黄源深，1998：1），成为教师课堂展示中的陪读者。结合“三个定位”的思考，本文在积累了近三十段课堂教学语料的基础上尝试性地探究了基于会话叙事视域下的一种英语专业教学方式，以此对“英语词汇学”课堂语境中会话叙事的类型进行界定和功能探讨，是为针对课堂会话叙事视野下对教学方法或方式进行的创新实践思考。

那么，从会话叙事的概念管窥课堂中或曾出现的自然会话或会话叙事，笔者不妨将其称为“叙事互言”的一种过程体现，其特点主要表现在：师生以及生生之间的“面对面互动交际”，话题通常由教材主题或学生自拟所定，话轮转接的次序和长度限制则由叙述者（通常是课堂主体中的学生）和受述者（通常是课堂引导者—教师以及其余受述者—学生）共同决定。然而，传统英专课堂以教师设定为主的课堂主体教学模式中，话轮转接的次序和长度更多由教师为教程的设定与计划所定，话轮转接次序单一，更多的是从教师的课堂“独白”向“自问自答”行进，类似的课堂模式是单一型教学到复合型教学的英语专业教学改革所迫切需要转变的内容之一，金衡山（2019）就此指出：

“在过去的二三十年里，中国的英语教学经历了几次上上下下的变化过程——从单一型教学到复合型课程设置再到实用性人才培养……而此次新一轮的英语专业教学改革则是倾向于回归英语语言文学教学的本体，同时强调人文思想的教育和思辨能力的培养。这个过程表明中国高校英语专业的很多教师在经历实用主义大潮的‘洗礼’后开始认识到英语专业人才培养的本质问题，即如何在英语本身上倾注足够的注意力……因此，如何真正融通语言学习与文学和文化的学习，则成了英语专业文学教师亟待思索的问题，而其中的要素则是如何在教学过程中体现人文思想的渗透与学生思辨能力的培养和提高。”

如金文所言，在教学过程中渗透人文思想并着手培养和提高学生的思辨能力是英专课堂教学主体所应思索并当以多样化探索的重要议题。课堂语境中“叙事互言”的过程，在具体教学过程中体现为以学生为参与主体的主观经验分享。以笔者的一线教学实践为例，笔者从事的“英语词汇学”的教学目的是引导学生探索现代英语词汇在语篇中的使用规律，在此基础上，结合具体的章节讨论话题，通过开放型的课堂句子分享(sentence sharing)① 找到恰当的视角切入课程主题，从话题的开放性到探寻学术理论的切入过程，是对学生语言组织能力和主题思辨能力的一种尝试，亦是对上文所探讨的“三个定位”思考的一种教学实践尝试。在探索这一模式的过程中，笔者发现参与学生的句子分享主题大致围绕人生哲理、友谊、爱、生命探索四大类主题进行。而教师在其句子分享和会话叙事行进的过程中，得到了充分观察和体悟其语言能力与语文转换能力的机会，关于学生产出了何种分享、学生是否从此环节中产出了可供受述者师生探讨的议题、学生从此议题中切入了何种课程主题等，正是此种教学实践中师生以及生生之间对语言的文化性、语用的知识性和针对具体话题的思想性的一种“言以致用”。以一段语料为例：

语料（1）

01 S1：Hello everyone，today I want to share with you a sentence：<u>Every person need a friend to make them laugh when they think they will n-</u>

---

① “句子分享”环节通常设立在进入课堂主题内容之前，该环节持续十分钟，句子的具体内容由学生自己根据其所熟悉的英文文学作品、谚语或报刊阅读等途径获悉，分享的环节学生具体集中在“Why I want to share you with such a sentence?”这样的问题，在其分享之后，其余学生可依据其所谈及的语篇进行评价、反馈和探讨。参与该门课程的所有学生均被鼓励参与此环节。

ever smile again. I got this sentence from one book I had read when I was a freshman, unfortunately I just wrote this sentence down on my notebook but forgot its origin. I think I am really a (0.2) such a lucky dog maybe, in every stage of my life. Eh … there are such person with me. Eh, maybe (0.1) they are not very perfect maybe, but they are very important person in my life. In high school, I have a good friend (0.1) named Guo Xiang. Yeah, it's Guo Xiang. Eh, and… both of us love to, eh, laugh very much. And even, actually I have laughed to vomit with her ↑ #笑到吐# (0.2) Eh, at that time, eh, in our high school, the classroom, and, the distance from the classroom to our dormitory (0.2) it's about 10 minutes' walk. And we laughed all the way. Maybe others think we are very ridiculous but we actually do that. And then, in the summer, our dormitory is in the… on the six floor. And we took off our shoes. And then (0.1) we went on…went up our floors, just bare foot. And (0.1) we just laugh, laugh, laugh. But we don't know we really laugh about what. But we, actually, only laugh. And then, when I got my dormitory, I just vomit (略)

02 S2: (raise hand to interrupt S1's narrative)

Actually I do have the same experience, ah…as you and your friend, as what you've said, laugh to vomit, but this closed ones is not a same-age peer, but is my mom (0.2) I still remember that is…ah (略) was for my dad, he got his trousers teared but he even not knew that, (略) you know, we can see his pants inside:: My mom and I saw him with that tore cloths, haha…you know, we cannot sit down inside the sofa anymore, we laugh at him, really, eh, as you say, to vomit. We really had a very high time for that night, and of course, it already be one of my warmest memory (0.1) eh, in my mind.

03 S1: Thank you so much for your sharing of your stories upon my sentence. And also, your story reminds me to get the synonymous but more formal saying of #笑到吐#, I don't know whether we can say "have a high time" or what any other expression? I think I want to get things about synonyms and the related lexicons.

课堂的句子分享作为开启课程新内容的一项引入环节，其用意在于激发、保持并促进学生下意识使用恰切语境词汇的心理过程，使他们形成一种熟练、自如、可复制与可迁移的自主思辨型学习模式。笔者的课程便是以类似的开放型会话语篇展开，句子分享环节学生的自由讨论通常为开放型，班级整体的参与度随着学生叙述者对话语以及叙事事件的深加工而逐步增加。从学生所分享的主题句子入手，其口头产出话语的过程中，生生之间均倾注了更多的注意力和认知投入（Craik，2002）。“叙事互言”过程本身是对学生语言能力的隐性考验，而生生之间的互动则逐步调动了其对语言内容和语境的敏感度。正如语料（1）中 S1 同学对主题分享句的解读引入了自己的叙事阐述，这种叙述形式也是 Toolan（1988）以及 Cohan 和 Shires（1988）对会话叙事最简形式的解读，即叙述者从主观经验层面入手对于非随机相连的一系列可被叙述和感知的事件的叙述排列和组织。S2 对 S1 的叙事回应产生叙事共情（Siroma，2012：525），其对共享句子的情感和态度促进了会话叙事的发展，并在下一话轮转接过程中，促使 S1 对“笑到吐”以及其所言的“laugh to vomit”的语言形式的恰当与否进行了思考，进而使 S1 切入至当节课堂中词汇“语义理据”以及“语义分类”的课程主题。

诚然，英语专业课堂中教师在学生进行开放型的会话叙事过程中同时以受述者和引导者的身份出现。正如 S1 在话轮结尾处切入了其对自身叙事过程中产生的语言内容与语用内容匹配与否的问题，这是学生通过自主的会话叙事参与之后主动将课堂的整体知识点引导和思辨交互于教师的一种主动行为，而对于教师而言，接过学生话轮，新的会话叙事的阐述，尤其是对词的理据性、词与词之间的同义关系的表达以及英语俚语的简要介绍①等专业内容的分析引导和探讨，则形成了新的课程主体内容。

综上来看，英语专业课堂语境下以句子分享为导入形式的“叙事互言”的会话叙事过程，对学生在词汇文化理解和社会文化融合方面产生了积极的推动。英语专业学生在中国文化和价值观所构筑的价值

---

① 教师之所以会引入俚语的引导与介绍，在于语料中学生所表达的“笑到吐”或称“laugh to vomit”一说，与英语俚语“laugh one's ass off”的语义对等性问题，借此将成为师生对英语俚语的语义统一性和结构固定性特征问题的俱佳引导切入。

体系背后，因其专业的特殊性，不断地更新负载有更多西方文化体系及价值观的话语表达和言语表述，这一更新、融合、吸收和博弈的现象本身，也是学生进行文化自觉和语言自觉的梳理过程。诚如费孝通先生（1997：22）所言，“文化自觉需要生活在一定文化中的人对其文化有自知之明，明白它的来历，形成过程，所具有的特色和它发展的趋向”，对于英语专业学生而言，语言自觉则需要我们加强对语言表述的文化转换能力，取得决定适应不同语境，不同时代时语言选择的自主地位。

英专课堂语境下的会话叙事，是从学生的语言表达技能入手，其间调动了学生透过句子探寻丰富文化或价值观的表述能力。在此基础上，叙述者和受述者的听、说过程以此成为其敏于探究的根本途径，叙/受述者对于句子分享主题的会话叙事过程本身，则是师生以及生生群体对叙事事件暗涵的社会文化性质、口头语汇的特征阐释与关联课程的思想联结的多重相融的过程。而此种相融的过程充分调动了学生的情感态度表述能力与语言认知产出能力，正如孙有中（2015：22）所言，包含了情感态度和认知技能两个层面的思辨能力的培养，也是英语专业课堂所应呼吁有之的一大目标。

3.《英语词汇学》课程的实践与启示

从宏观知识层面来看，“英语词汇学”属于具体的语言学范畴，侧重于分析研究现代英语的词汇现象，揭示现代英语词汇规律，特别是其在语篇中的使用规律（陆国强，2009：1）。“中国最早于 20 世纪 50 年代从苏联引进了英语词汇学，而如何把词汇的知识用于教学和科研，尤其是帮助学习者习得词汇，得到了国家的重视，词汇学被视为一门重要的、大有发展的学科。”（班柏、汪榕培，2017：116）而随着现代词汇学的发展，其已逐渐脱离了局限于研究词的形式、内容、发展变化以及各种词汇之间的相互变化关系的传统研习层面，如陆国强（2009：1）所指出的：“传统的词汇学学习局限在词、短语和句子层次上的孤立的、静态的”研究层面，“现代英语词汇学应突破原有的框架，着重探讨词汇在语篇中体现的语义特征和语用特征”。

以上提到，笔者从事的“英语词汇学”的教学目的是引导学生探索现代英语词汇在语篇中的使用规律。以此为目标，结合学生于每节课主题导入之前的句子分享语境，找到合适的视角切入“词汇学”已学、已预习或即将展开的课程主题，学生之间进行会话或叙事互动，共同探讨会话语篇中潜在的词汇学问题，产出自己的观点。本课程为二年级下的英语专业本科生开设，学时为18周，共36学时，每周会进行一个词汇学主题论述，并就该主题进行分组讨论。笔者就所录制的28段课堂语料，分析了学生在话语产出中的内容、结构和话语形式，同时对课堂会话叙事互动进行了界定、识别和析取。从笔者的课程主题安排到支持学生内部的会话探讨过程，主要发现了此门课程中师生以及生生之间的会话叙事互动特点，以及会话叙事在推进词汇学课程主题过程中的表现和功能。

笔者首先对词汇学课程中的会话叙事互动话语的特征进行了分析。和Labov（1972：362）提出的经典叙事的“完整形式”的六要素，即摘要、介绍、复杂行动、评价、解决和尾声不大相同，课堂上的会话叙事互动通常由学生叙述者使用“典型的”介绍和评价要素，以这些结构从基本的过往经验中构成故事（朱冬怡，2017：51）进行叙述，基于课堂上的自然会话语境，笔者将28段课堂语料划分为三类，即讲述叙事、趣事叙事和例示共享叙事，并根据Plum（1988）、Eggins和Slade（1997）、Georgakopoulou（2007）等文献以及本研究中的语料数据确定了不同类型的课堂叙事话语，并对其表现和功能加以描述。具体内容如表1所示：

表1　　词汇学课程中会话叙事互动详析表

叙事类型	数量	表现	功能	对词汇学课程的推进
讲述叙事	16	叙述者主要围绕分享句子而进行的关于其自身过往经历的叙述； 叙述者主体为学生；	分享、举例、说明、阐释； 以自身经历阐释分享句子；	导入词汇意义、语法意义及语境意义的区分辨识； 明晰词的理据性常识；
趣事叙事	10	叙述者以分享句子为主进行的关于他人/物所遇事件的态度观点叙述； 叙述者主体为学生；	举例或说明，以他人/物的经历阐释分享句子； 引用或类比，以他人/物的事件阐释分享句子；	推动学生对词汇的词义广度以及产出性语用规则知识的理解；

续表

叙事类型	数量	表现	功能	对词汇学课程的推进
例示共享叙事	2	叙述者围绕分享句子以阐明其对叙/受述者共知事件的主观评价叙述； 叙述者主体为教师。	举例或说明，以叙/受述者所共知共晓的事件阐述分享句子； 利用集体叙事建立共同的认知基础（张庆华，2018：5）。	导入词汇与西方文化信息知识； 提高学生对词汇语义场的敏感性。

笔者在观察课堂会话叙事中叙/受述者言语表现及言语内容的基础上，对每段语料的话语语境做了详细的记录，包含学生的话语停顿、手势语、重音和轻音、以及语码转换等叙事互动因素。下面仍以语料（1）为例，对叙事类型和表现、功能及其对词汇学课程的推动性作一阐释。

（1）讲述叙事

在语料（1）中，S1 由其所分享的句子引发叙述了其过往经历，说明和阐释了她对这个句子的感受。从自身经历出发的阐释型叙事意在通过叙述者自身的言语例举达到其叙述者身份的标示，"为其自身创造探究未知世界的机会、构建新的身份认同和实践方式"（Early 和 Norton，2012：199），以此推进受述者对叙事的接纳。然而 S1 在对"笑到吐"进行话语表述的过程中出现了直译性表达"laugh to vomit"，也正由于此表述，由当下受述者 S2 抢过话轮，进行了新的叙事阐述。事实上，在第 3 话轮处，S1 对其第一话轮的表述进行了修正，并提出了"synonym"的词汇学概念。值得一提的是，该节课的课程主题是"词的联想与搭配"探讨，而"synonym"作为已进行过的"词的语义分类"的讨论篇章，对学生来说不仅对已有知识进行了回顾，对词的联想和应用讲解也起到了自然的推进作用。又如下例：

语料（2）

01T：If life is divided by two，the former is "no hesitation" and the latter is "no regret". The reason why I chose this sentence as my sharing today is that when making choices，I am not a resolute and determined person，so I would like to use this sentence as a warning to my future life.

→Two weeks ago, I was booking the house for summer travelling with my friends. We wrote down our requirements, typed them into our phone and searched. Then we had a lot of options, but we faced a dilemma as well-if we wanted to be closer to our destination, the prices were pretty higher. We did not want to spend a lot of money on that, nor live far away, so we just delayed this plan (.) Finally, after some days, when searching for houses on my phone again, I found that most of the houses we had seen before were booked. Besides, there were a rise on the prices of some houses left. Finally, all of us felt regretted and upset, thinking that if only we had booked the house the first time, we searched it, the situation would be better.

→Perhaps, it is not an interesting story, but I do have learned something from it- when making choices, don't delay it to next minute because whenever it is, we have to make the final decision, but if we do that by now, it will definitely save us more money, time and energy. Also, this principle "no hesitation, no regret" can be applied to our future life. That is to say, when facing crossroads in our life, we need careful thinking, but we never need hesitation.(略)

该语例中的讲述叙事穿插在会话主题介绍之后，学生在故事讲述过程中对 dilemma 的阐释及后续的故事引申，对于课堂中涉及词汇的使用及词汇的语用理据性（motivation）具有良好的示例作用。从自身经历入场的讲述叙事对于学生在词汇学课程中自测语言的恰切表达与词汇的认知选择与产出起到了直接的引介作用，以此也促进了学生对于话语表达中词的词汇意义、语法意义以及语境意义的区分与辨识。

（2）趣事叙事

语料（1）中的第 2 话轮处，S2 接过第 1 话轮，对叙事主题进行了补充阐述。S2 以其家庭中发生的一段趣事为例，叙述了一件让其“laugh to vomit”的故事事件。和 S1 不同，S2 在话语表达中修正了“笑到吐”的表达，并产出了“have a high time”描述了其和家人共有的一段开心趣事事件。第三话轮处 S1 因此也重新审视了“笑到吐”与“have a high time”以及其他相关表述，使学生自身意识到其认知中单词的词义数量所构成的词义广度（马广惠，2009），这从语言技能方面促进了学生从词汇的接受性常识到其产出性规则知识的发展，提升了学生对诸如包括了词汇的一词多义、同义、反义、上下义以及语义场等语义关系的理解，能够利用这些语义关系理解上下文；在自然会话叙事语境下，学生对于运用词汇的曲折或派生等变化规则，以及应用所知词汇的语用规则（马广惠，2016：40），得体地产出交际话语。因此，课堂语境下的趣事叙事多以叙事回应话轮的形式出现，学生在趣事叙事过程对词汇运用所涉及的词义广度和语用规则产生了更为深切的理解。

（3）例示共享叙事

为便于此处分析，笔者将接续语料一向下进行的教师教学话语，即第4话轮，编码为语料（3）：

04T：Okay. Thank you ↑ for your sharing with us your sentence and stories. You have thrown your question to me，of course，I will answer it and let's try to get our understanding of the word synonym ↑ and English slang together. Firstly，the sentence from S1 tells us that to have a friend who can make you happy is actually a very important thing.（略） But I don't think you will vomit when you have so much happy time right ↑::But when we say：every person need a friend to make them laugh when they think they will never smile again，obviously，→when S1 had recalled so many good memories from，eh（0.2）（略），they had spent，I see，a whale of big，or high time ↑. And also，we might not really vomit when we are spending a happy time with our friends. This reminds me the week before last，we had discussed the onomatopoeic motivation between English and Chinese，I remember most of you had done a wonderful job by imitating the animal sounds，and you all said that you had spent a high time for that class，as S2's memory of his family a high time.（略） Yet，we had not vomited right ↑ →Actually I had to recall my days at America，I'd made some very good friends and one day we have…ah…we had talked about a funny academic poster（略） I will show you next time，one of my friend exclaimed that OMG，this really laughs my ass off ↑ I think it's necessary for us to get definition and ideas about "slangs" ↑ of laughing expressions…

教师在此话轮中对学生针对分享句子中提出的语言技能方面的问题进行了解答，如教师间接回复了上面三个话轮中 S1 与 S2 对于“笑到吐”或其所引申的“共度快乐时光”的确切表述形式，在提及其恰切与否的同时，教师叙述了其在过往课堂上对于学生展示汉英“拟声理据”讲解时的课堂状态，以所有学生为叙事整体进行了彼此共知的对已知事件的集体叙事共享，以此向学生阐释上述短语的恰切性。其后的二次叙事互动围绕着“笑到吐”所对应的英语俚语表述，在课程推进过程中展开了涉及词汇与文化（如英语俚语中和人体部位相关的俚语表达）以及词汇语义场（如和“笑”有关的俚语、习语或俗语表达等）的课程知识讲解。因此，例示共享叙事是教师在课堂语境中为唤起受述集体所使用的惯常叙事手段，这是由于教师在教的过程中对课堂的整体把握与知识点调控具有更为灵活的安排，使其知晓所能够产出的用以唤起学生集体认知基础的小故事事件。而师生互动过程中语言教育、语言学习和教育反思在此过程中渐为一体，形成了教与学的能动性循环。

笔者从词汇学课堂中的会话叙事互动得到了这样的启发：从一个细微的句子分享活动进入词汇学课堂，学生善于并乐于分享其从句子中经过思辨性的例举和阐释所产出的叙事活动。会话叙事的过程从表面看来虽然仅表现在学生语言能力的开展，但却不是纯粹的针对词汇或话语的语言技能训练，而是在特定的课堂文化语境中，即师生互动，生生之间贴近其学业生活的会话与“小故事”的讲述过程，嵌入式地对学生的语言能力、认知思维能力和文化阐释力产生了积极的影响。正如 Moore（1988：248）提到了教学实践中的叙事行为本身也是人类交际中显著模式的一种具体语境输出，是不同语言文化的载体，可以说是一种意义丰富的且具有深远影响的教育方法论。

4. 结语

本文以笔者所从事的“英语词汇学”教学语料为案例，阐释了词汇学课堂中通过学生的句子分享环节引发的课堂会话叙事互动对词汇学课程本身所具有的积极影响。通过上文分析我们发现：

首先，从英语专业学科实践层面来讲，会话叙事互动打破了课程设置的边界，使得教学过程中师生互动、生生互动成为语言学习和教育反思共为一体的教—学铺设。我国语言教育专业的课程设置主要包括语言基础课、语言学习与教学理论课、教育理论课、教育实习四大模块（侯松、吴彬芳，2017：42）。本文所析语料发生在英语词汇学课堂上，属于语言学习与教学理论课模块，而会话叙事主要调动了学生在语言基础模块的言语能力，课程设置的边界因此被模糊化，但教学实践证明，会话叙事与语言理论学习的情境相互融合，课程设置的边界也在学生之间被充分调动了主观能动性进行的叙事互动中被补偿并超越。

其次，从英语专业学科内容的层面来讲，会话叙事互动以语料为导向，以经验文化为框架，为学生和教师铺就了一条从被动的受述者到主动的叙述者的“叙事互言”之路。实践语料中得出的讲述叙事、趣事叙事与例示共享叙事是师生以及生生之间以经验文化为框架而产出的多样化的叙事类型。以词汇学课程为例的探索中我们或许仅仅观察到学生以及师生在其叙事互动中得到的关于构词法、语块、语义、语用以及语境的叙事视角切入，也正是由于语料所限，我们相信在更多不同课程设置的课堂语境下，我们或许能够探究出更多的对学科内容带来良性启发的叙事互动类型。

最后，从英语学科的培养目标定位来看，课堂语境下的会话叙事互动调度了学生丰富的情感表述和自由的思维切换。本文所探究的叙事互动始终建立在“学生句子共享—会话叙事互动—词汇学理论切入”的多面角度课堂情境之中，从学生所分享的具有多元化的句子主题，到其主动回述经验事件叙事，最终从自身的话语产出中思考并辨析真实生活叙述与话语产出中暗涵的词汇学理论。笔者在实施这一过程的教学过程中，深切体会到了教学过程中学生层面的会话叙事所内化的语言与思想、语言与内容的关联与影响，如庄智象和陈刚（2018：1）所言：“我们呼唤语言与内容、语言与文化的更深度融合，使语言教学和研究更富于内涵，有更广阔的空间，具有更丰富的知识性、文化性和思想性。”

确定会话叙事互动在英语专业课堂上的内涵和功能，将是我们在后续教学实践和反思过程中持续思考的一个课题。本文仅以笔者的教学实践语料为例梳理了一个实践想法。就英语专业课堂的创新实践而言，如何突破课程设置边界是关键，而其中最重要的因素是课程教学中教师如何调动学生对人生经验或经历进行思辨性思考和表达，使其内化为语言输出过程中的言语习惯，这既需要教师具有仰望星空的前瞻性，更需要学生脚踏实地的运行语言思维的体操。

参考文献

Cohan, S. & Shires, L. M. *Telling Stories: A Theoretical Analysis of Narrative Fiction*. New York: Routledge, 1988.

Craik, F. I. M. Levels of processing: past, present…and future?. *Memory*, 2002 (10): 305 - 318.

Early, M. & Norton, B. Language learner stories and imagined identities. *Narrative Inquiry*, 2012 (22): 194-201.

Eggins, S. & Slade, D. *Analyzing Casual Conversation*. London: Cassell, 1997.

Fludernik, M. *Towards a "Natural" Narratology*. London: Routledge, 1996.

Georgakopoulou, A. Thinking big with small stories in narrative and identity analysis. *Narrative Inquiry*, 2006 (16): 122-130.

Georgakopoulou, A. *Small Stories, Interaction, and Identities*. Amsterdam: John Benjamins, 2007.

Labov, W. *Language in the Inner City: Studies in the Black English Vernacular*. Philadelphia: University of Pennsylvania Press, 1972.

Moore, M. Narrative Teaching: An Organic Methodology. *Process Studies*, 1988 (17): 248-261.

Norrick, N. R. *Conversational Narrative*. Amsterdam: John Benjamins, 2000.

Plum, G. *Text and contextual conditioning in spoken English: A genre - based approach*. University of Sydney, 1988.

Siroma, M. Resonance in conversational second stories: a dialogic resource for stance taking. *Text & Talk*, 2012 (32): 525-545.

Toolan, M. *Narrative: A Critical Linguistic Introduction*. London: Routledge, 1988.

班柏、汪榕培:《英语词汇学及其新进展：汪榕培教授访谈录》,《大连海事大学学报》(社会科学版) 2017 年第 4 期。

费孝通:《反思·对话·文化自觉》,《北京大学学报》(哲学社会科学版) 1997 年第 3 期。

顾悦:《回归人文学科：英语专业的学科定位与发展路径》,《外语教学理论与实践》2019 年第 1 期。

何其莘、殷桐生、黄源深、刘海平:《关于外语专业本科教育改革的若干意见》,

《外语教学与研究》1999年第1期。

侯松、吴彬芳:《基于“小故事”的语言教育研究:国际视野与本土探索》,《山东外语教学》2017年第4期。

胡文仲、孙有中:《突出学科重点,加强人文教育:试论当前英语专业教学改革》,《外语教学与研究》2006年第5期。

黄源深:《思辨缺席》,《外语与外语教学》1998年第7期。

金衡山:《“文学教学”特别专栏》,《外语教学理论与实践》2019年第1期。

陆国强:《现代英语词汇学》,上海外语教育出版社2009年版。

马广惠:《英语专业学生二语限时写作中的词块研究》,《外语教学与研究》2009年第1期。

马广惠:《英语词汇教学与研究》,外语教学与研究出版社2016年版。

孙有中:《外语教育与思辨能力培养》,《中国外语》2015年第2期。

孙有中:《人文英语教育论》,《外语教学与研究》2017年第6期。

汪榕培:《面向21世纪的我国高等外语专业教学》,《外语与外语教学》2000年第2期。

张冲:《关于英语专业定位的思考》,《外语界》2003年第4期。

张庆华、杨鲁新:《基于课堂叙事话语的英语教师实践性知识研究》,《外语与外语教学》2018年第4期。

赵玉荣:《自然会话叙事中话语意义的建构与认知过程》,《外语教学》2013年第4期。

赵玉荣:《自然会话叙事中主体间性的意义资源与认知识解模式》,《外语学刊》2014年第4期。

朱冬怡:《自然会话叙事标记语“然后”构建的语义缺省》,《外语学刊》2017年第5期。

朱冬怡:《自然会话叙事中投射映现的散装故事分析》,《重庆第二师范学院学报》2019年第2期。

庄智象、陈刚:《外国语言文学一流学科建设呼唤深度融合》,《外语教学理论与实践》2018年第4期。

Multidirectional Trends of Narrative: A Conversational Narrative Practice in College Class

Abstract: The 1990s has witnessed a multidirectional post-narrative turn that promotes interactive and daily communication research in the academia. This research takes a view from this turn and tries to focus on conversational narrative, which refers to the storytelling activity occurring in everyday conversations or talks. The present study bases its analysis on English-majored sophomores' class from "Modern English Lexicology", and has observed a "classroom inter-narratives" mode. It is from this mode that three types of classroom narrative have been concluded, i. e. recounting narrative, anecdote narrative and exempla narrative. Types and functions of these narratives help to elucidate and develop a way of rendering the curriculum provision, from which can be an effective method to motivate discourse critical capabilities for English-majored students as a whole.

Key words: Narrative study; Conversation narrative; English - major class

英语词汇知识广度和深度的现状和差异研究

范　娜*

摘　要：本文研究了中国中西部四所大学419名非英语专业二年级学生的英语词汇知识广度和深度的现状和差异。我们采用了广度测试工具VST和深度测试工具WAT来评测中国英语学习者接受性词汇知识水平，并使用Coh-Metrix分析了419份英语作文中体现出的多维度的产出性词汇知识，如具体性、意象性等。研究发现：（1）学生的词汇量为6494词族，这一结果高于其他相关研究；（2）学生的接受性和产出性词汇深度和其他相关研究相比存在差距；（3）学生的词汇量在性别、专业和英语水平三个因素上存在显著差异；（4）学生的接受性词汇深度在专业和英语水平上存在显著差异；（5）学生的产出性词汇深度仅在英语水平上存在显著差异。本文最后探讨了研究发现对词汇教学的启示。

关键词：词汇广度；词汇深度；个体差异

1　引言

二语词汇研究者大致认为词汇知识是由词汇广度和深度两部分组成的（如：Read，1998；Schmitt，2010）。在这一领域，学者对学习者词汇广度进行了广泛探讨，并开发了一些词汇量测试量表（如：Meara & Jones，1988；Nation，1990；Nation & Beglar，2007）。同时，一些学者对词汇量进行了实证性研究，如Hirsh & Nation（1992），Hu & Nation（2000）以及Nation（2006）等探讨了英语阅读和听力所需的词汇量。然而，只关注

* 作者简介：范娜（1985—　），女，陕西师范大学外国语学院讲师，研究方向：二语习得，语言测试。

词汇量并不能完全了解学习者词汇知识的全貌，因为词汇深度也是词汇知识的一个重要组成部分。自20世纪40年代开始，国外学者开始研究词汇深度，开始构建词汇深度理论框架（如：Dale，1965；Meara，1982；Nation，2001；Richards，1976；Wesche & Paribakht，1996），开发词汇深度测试（如：Ishii & Schmitt，2009；Paribakht & Wesche，1993；Read，1993、1998；Schmitt，1998），以及进行有关词汇深度的实证性研究（如：Nassaji，2006；Qian，2002）。国内学者也对词汇广度和深度进行了研究，比如席仲恩（1998），周大军、文渤燕（2000）以及邓昭春（2001）调查了中国英语学习者的词汇量；吴旭东、陈晓庆（2000），刘绍龙（2001）以及谭晓晨（2006）探讨了中国英语学习者词汇深度的发展；崔艳嫣、王同顺（2006）调查了词汇量和词汇深度的发展及其相关性；吕长竑（2003）和李晓（2007）探讨了词汇量、词汇深度与语言综合能力关系。虽然国内外研究者在二语词汇知识研究方面取得了丰硕的成果，但是也存在一些不足之处。首先，大部分词汇深度测试（如：Ishii & Schmitt，2009；Schmitt，1998；Schmitt & Meara，1997；崔艳嫣、王同顺，2006；刘绍龙，2001；谭晓晨，2006；吴旭东、陈晓庆，2000）存在的共同不足之处是这些量表所测单词数量非常有限并且只能考察词汇深度有限的维度；其次，国内词汇量研究（如：崔艳嫣、王同顺，2006；邓昭春，2001；李晓，2007；吕长竑，2004；席仲恩，1998；周大军、文渤燕，2000）通常采取不同测试工具，由于统计标准不同，结果存在较大差异。随着二语词汇量测试的发展，我们需要采用最新的测试工具来重新评测中国英语学习者词汇量水平；最后，词汇广度和深度与学生性别、专业及英语水平之间的关系有待进一步研究。鉴于此，本研究具体探讨以下三个问题：

（1）中国非英语专业大学生英语词汇广度现状如何？

（2）中国非英语专业大学生英语词汇深度现状如何？

（3）中国非英语专业大学生英语词汇广度和深度是否在其性别、专业和英语水平因素上存在显著差异？

2 文献综述

2.1 词汇广度及测试量表

词汇广度是指学习者所知道的单词数量，或者说学习者至少知道这个单词的某方面意义（Nation，2001）。从 20 世纪 90 年代起，为了确定二语学习者词汇学习的长期目标，研究者对英语本族语者的词汇量进行了探究。结果表明，英语总共包括大概 54000 词族（Nation & Waring，1997），其中教育程度比较好的本族语者大概掌握 17000 词族（D'Anna *et al.*，1991；Goulden *et al.*，1990）。词族是指学习者知道单词的基本形式以及了解这个单词的衍生词和派生词（Bauer & Nation，1993）。另外，一些研究探讨学习者完成不同的英语任务所需要的词汇量（Hu & Nation，2000；Nation，2006）。Nation（2006）发现二语学习者需要掌握 6000 到 7000 词族才能很好地理解英语日常口语；学习者需要掌握 8000 到 9000 词族才能流利地阅读英文原版读物。

为了探讨二语学习者的词汇量，国外研究者开发了一些词汇量测试工具（如：Meara & Jones，1988；Meara & Milton，2003；Nation，1983、1990；Nation & Beglar，2007）。其中最有影响力的应当是以下三个词汇量测试工具：Vocabulary Levels Test（VLT）（Nation，1990），Eurocentres Vocabulary Test（EVT）（Meara & Jones，1988）和 Vocabulary Size Test（VST）（Nation & Beglar，2007）。相比 VLT 和 EVT，VST 有很多优势。首先，VLT 和 EVT 的目标词均选自 Thorndike 和 Lorge（1994）所列的基于词条的词汇列表，这个列表相对简单并已经过时。VST 目标词选自基于词族的英国国家语料库（British National Corpus）。Nation 和 Beglar（2007）认为以词族为单位的测试更适合测试接受性词汇量，因为有一定词汇水平的学习者会掌握一部分词缀和单词的构成规律；其次，VST 包括 14 个词频组，涵盖 1000 到 14000 词频，从而能够更全面地测试学习者的词汇量；再次，这个测试中一些备选项单词的意义比较接近，因此受试者要选出正确的选项，需要非常清楚目标词的意义；最后，VST 有较高的信度值，Beglar（2010）发现其信度值高达 0.96—0.98（Rasch Reliability）。Nation 和 Beglar（2007）采用 VST 作为词汇量测试工具，发现二语本科生的词汇量大概在 5000—6000 词族之间，非本族语博士生的词汇量大概为 9000 词族。另外 Nguyen 和 Nation（2011）发现英语专业本科三年级的越南学生平均词汇量为 6661 词族。基于对以上三个词汇量测试的对比分析，本研究采用 VST 来测试学生英语词汇量。

2.2 词汇深度及测试量表

目前学界对词汇深度理论框架的认知主要有三类：第一类认为词汇深

度是由不同成分组成（the dimensional approach）（Nation，2001；Richards 1976）；第二类把词汇深度看作连续体（the developmental approach）（Dale，1965；Paribakht & Wesche，1993；Schmitt & Zimmerman，2002）；第三类认为词汇深度是词汇之间的关联（the association approach）（Meara，1982）。持有第一类成分法观的研究者认为词汇深度是指了解词汇知识的各个方面。Richards（1976）提出了词汇知识的七个方面：词频、语用限制、句法形式、词汇基本形式和衍生词、词汇关联、语义特征以及一词多义。虽然这一词汇深度理论框架相对比较全面，但是它没有包括词汇拼写和发音。Nation（1990、2001）进一步发展了词汇深度理论框架，他提出词汇知识包括接受性和产出性词汇知识，并且接受性和产出性词汇知识分别包含词汇形式、意义和用法。词汇的形式包括其读音、书写和词汇组成部分。词汇意义包括形成和意义，概念和所指以及词汇关联。词汇用法包括词汇的语法特征、搭配和语用限制。Nation（1990，2001）的词汇深度理论框架被大多数学者所接受和应用，是目前比较系统的理论框架（Schmitt，2010）。但是 Nation 的理论框架并没有涵盖 Richards（1976）提出的词频、一词多义以及语义特征。鉴于此，本研究采用的词汇深度理论框架综合了 Nation（2001）和 Richards（1976）的两个框架。

在词汇成分法观（Nation，2001；Richards，1976）的理论框架下，很多学者（如：Ishii & Schmitt，2009；Read，1993；Schmitt，1998）设计了词汇深度测试。其中最有影响力的是 Read（1993，1998）设计的 Word Associates Test（WAT）。WAT 的最新版本（Read，1998）包含词汇深度的两个方面：（1）词汇意义，主要是多义词和同义词；（2）词汇搭配。所有的目标词都是形容词，选自 Barnard 两千和三千词汇列表（Nation，1986）。虽然 WAT 被研究者广泛用来测试二语词汇深度，这个测试也有其不足之处，比如 WAT 目标词全部是形容词，而不包括其他词性的单词。另外，WAT 只考察了词汇深度的某些方面，如词汇搭配和同义词。即便如此，这个测试仍然是目前使用最多的词汇深度测试之一。

另外，Ishii 和 Schmitt（2009）、Schmitt（1998）以及 Schmitt 和 Meara（1997）与国内一些学者（如：刘绍龙，2001；吴旭东、陈晓庆，2000）设计了一系列词汇深度测试来考察词汇知识的各个方面。Ishii & Schmitt（2009）的词汇深度测试包含多义词、衍生词、同义词、词汇搭配以及语域特征等。虽然这些测试涉及词汇深度多个方面，但是也存在共同的不足之处：首先，这些测试比较耗时，而且考察的目标词相对较少；其次，评分标准繁杂，不便于研究者和教师操作；最后，部分信度值不明确。为了克服这些不足，Crossley 等人设计了可以测试作者英语写作中的词汇知识以及其他各种语言和语篇特征的计算机文本分析工具 Coh-Metrix（Graesser *et al.*，2004）。Coh-Metrix 可以测试词汇知识的多个方面，包括词频、词汇多样性、上位关系、多义性、语义相似性、词汇意义性、词汇具体性、词汇熟悉度和词汇意象性。基于这些词汇指示值，Crossley *et al.*，（2010）建立了一个词汇水平模型。他们发现在对学生作文的测评中，词汇多样性、上位关系值和词频可以解释 44% 的由人工测评得出的词汇水平结果。Crossley *et al.*（2011）还探讨了用这些词汇指示值来划分二语学习者英语水平的可能性。结果表明，这些词汇指示值可以准确地把 70%的文本划分到不同的英语水平组。以上这些研究表明，Coh-Metrix 可以作为很好的工具来测试二语学习者产出性词汇知识，同时也可以用来划分二语学习者的英语水平。通过对以上词汇深度测试对比分析，本研究使用 Coh-Metrix 来测试学生产出性词汇深度，同时使用 WAT 来测试学生接受性词汇深度。

3 研究方法

3.1 研究对象

本研究招募了来自中国大陆四所大学的 419 名非英语专业二、三年级本科生。其中，三所大学是国家重点本科院校，一所是普通院校。根据他们的四级成绩，学生被划分为高中低三个水平组。高水平组包括四级分数高于 550 分（口语测试分数线）的学生，低水平组包括四级分数低于及格线 426 分的学生，而中水平组包括四级分数等于或者高于 426 分但是低于 550 分的学生（426≤中水平组<550）。参与学生的基本信息详情请见表 1。

表 1 参与者基本信息（$N=419$）

分类		n	per cent（%）
性别	男	176	42.00%
	女	243	58.00%
学科	人文社科	220	52.51%
	理工科	199	47.49%
英语水平	低水平	46	10.98%
	中水平	324	77.33%
	高水平	49	11.69%

3.2 测试工具

3.2.1 词汇量测试（VST）

本研究采用 Nation 和 Beglar（2007）开发的 Vocabulary Size Test（VST）作为词汇量测试工具。这个测试包含十四个词频水平涵盖 1000 到 14000 词频，每个词频水平上有 10 个测试题目。每个题目有四个选项，受试者需要从四个选项当中选出一个和目标词意义相近的正确选项。每个题目是 1 分，测试总分为 140 分。以下是该测试题目的范例，受试者需要选出一个和目标词“saw”意义相近的选项：

The ysaw it.

a. cut

b. waited for

c. looked at

d. started

VST 在本研究中通过 Kuder-Richardson Formula 21（K-R 21）计算得出的信度值为 0.70。因为 K-R 21 通常提供比较保守的信度估计值（Anderson *et al.*，1995），所以这个信度值处于可接受范围。

3.2.2 词汇深度测试（WAT）

本研究采用 Word Associates Test（Read 1998）来测试受试者的接受性词汇深度，以下是该测试的一个范例：

sudden

beautiful quick surprising thirsty	change doctor noise school

受试者需要从两个方框内选出四个与目标词有关系的单词。左边方框包含可以解释目标词意义或者和目标词意义相近的单词，而右边方框包含可以和目标词搭配的单词。在上述例子中，左右方框中各有两个正确的选项。但是对于该测试的其他题目，左边方框可能包含一个正确选项，右边方框包含三个正确选项，或者相反。该测试信度值较高能达到0.93（Read，1998）（Rasch Reliability），0.91（Qian，1999）（Spearman-Brown split-half）和0.88（Qian，2002）（Cronbach Alpha）。在本研究中，通过K-R 21计算得出的WAT信度值为0.87。

3.2.3 英语作文

为了研究学生的产出性词汇深度，受试者需要写一篇300字左右的限时英语作文。作文题目是"Developing countries should open their doors to foreign companies to open offices and build factories. Do you agree or disagree with the above opinion?"。选择这个题目有两个原因：第一，这个问题在中国是备受争议的话题，学生应该对这个题目比较熟悉；第二，大学英语四级和雅思作文题目大部分属于议论文范畴，所以学生应该对这类作文类型比较熟悉。基于这两方面原因，本研究采用以上题目作为学生作文题目。

3.3 数据收集过程

本研究在四所大学分别进行数据收集。在进行测试之前，我们告知学生测试将不会影响他们课程成绩，测试结果将被严格保密。为了避免测试时间过长对学生造成过度疲劳，这些测试分两个阶段完成。在第一阶段，学生需要在50分钟内写一篇300字英语作文。学生实际完成作文的时间为30—50分钟。所有学生的作文输入电脑后使用计算机软件Coh-Metrix进行文本分析。在第二阶段，学生需要完成词汇量（VST）和词汇深度（WAT）两个测试，时间不受限制，但是不允许查字典。

3.4 数据分析过程

本研究用计算机软件Coh-Metrix分析学生的作文，然后将结果输入SPSS 21进一步分析。本研究采用的主要分析方法包括描述性统计分析和单向多变量方差分析（one-way multivariate analysis of variance）。描述性统计分析用于描述学生的英语词汇广度和深度现状，单向多变量方差分析用于探讨学生的词汇广度和深度在性别、专业和英语水平因素上的差异。

4 研究结果与讨论

4.1 中国非英语专业大学生词汇广度和深度现状

表2描述了学生接受性词汇量（VST）和接受性词汇深度（WAT）分数。

表2　学生接受性词汇量和接受性词汇深度描述性统计（$N=419$）

	Total Score	Min	Max	*M*	*SD*
VST	140.00	34.00	116.00	64.94	10.51
WAT	160.00	24.00	136.00	98.07	16.97

研究结果表明学生VST平均分为64.94，这个数值乘以100得到学生的平均词汇量为6494词族。Nation（2006）发现二语学习者需要掌握9000词族从而流利地阅读英文原版小说，8000词族阅读英文报纸，7000词族理解英语口语中大部分单词（包括专有名词），以及6000词族理解儿童电影中大部分单词。另外Nation和Beglar（2007）指出，掌握8000词族是二语学习者能够很好地理解真实的英语口语和写作文本的最低要求。基于这些标准，本研究学生在理解真实英语口语和写作文本时可能会遇到一些困难。在以往研究中，Nation和Beglar（2007）发现二语本科生的词汇量大概在5000—6000词族。另外Nguyen和Nation（2011）发现英语专业本科三年级的越南学生平均词汇量为6661词族。相比较，本研究学生的平均词汇量高于Nation和Beglar（2007）研究中二语本科生词汇量，同时和Nguyen和Nation（2011）研究中英语专业本科三年级越南学生词汇量相近。

关于接受性词汇深度，本研究学生WAT的平均分数为98.07，达到WAT总分数的61.29%。Qian（1999）发现中国二语学习者WAT平均分数为118.24，韩国学生为120.54，本族语者为148.62。与Qian（1999）研究中二语学习者相比，本研究学生的接受性词汇深度存在较大差距。另外，与本族语者接受性词汇深度相比，本研究学生存在非常大的差距。

表 3 描述了基于 Coh-Metrix 分析的学生英语作文中产出性词汇深度指示值。

表 3 基于 Coh-Metrix 的学生英语作文中词汇知识指示值描述性统计（$N=419$）

词汇指示值	Min	Max	*M*	*SD*
词汇多样性（MTLD all words）	31.42	141.49	67.68	18.64
词频（CELEX mean for all words）	2.73	3.40	3.03	0.09
上位关系（nouns and verbs）	1.16	2.69	1.78	0.21
词汇多义性（content words）	3.42	6.07	4.65	0.51
语义相似性（LSA，adjacent sentences）	0.04	0.60	0.20	0.09
词汇意义性（content words）	383.97	504.69	443.23	15.14
词汇具体性（content words）	323.30	443.89	376.95	18.74
词汇意象性（content words）	360.60	441.18	402.77	14.52
词汇熟悉度（content words）	552.64	597.67	577.23	5.31

本研究主要通过与基于 Coh-Metrix 的相关研究对比分析学生的产出性词汇深度。本研究学生词汇多样性平均分数为 67.68。González（2013）研究发现参加美国大学英语预备课程的二语学习者词汇多样性分数为 69.12。与 González（2013）的结果相比，本研究学生作文词汇多样性较低。CELEX 词频分数分布从 0 到 6，分值“0”代表英语中最不常见的词，而“6”代表最常见的单词（Baayen *et al.* 1995）。本研究学生作文词频的平均数为 3.03。González（2013）发现学生作文词频数值为 3.09，相比较，本研究中学生比 González（2013）中学生在作文中略多使用低频词。其他词汇指示值如词汇意象性、词汇意义性、词汇熟悉度和词汇具体性介于 100 到 700 之间。数值越高代表学习者使用的词汇有更高的意象性，与其他单词有更多联系（意义性），同时词汇熟悉度和词汇具体性更高。在本研究中，词汇意义性平均值为 443.23，词汇具体性为 376.95，词汇意象性为 402.77，以及词汇熟悉度为 577.23。Crossley *et al.*（2011）发现在参加美国大学英语培训课程的二语学习者作文中，低水平学生的这些词汇指示值高于高水平学生，也就说低水平学习者用的词汇有更高的意象性、熟悉度、具体性以及和其他单词有更多的联系。Crossley *et al.*（2011）发现随着学生英语水平的提高，实义词熟悉度平均值从592.13下降到585.13。本研究学生词汇熟悉度的平均值为577.23，这说明本研究学生比 Crossley *et al.*（2011）中学生在英语写作中用到更多熟悉度比较低的单词。这个发现和上面探讨的学生作文中词频发现大体一致，也就是说参与本研究的学生相比其他相关研究的学生在英语写作中倾向于使用略多低频词和熟悉度较低的单词。词汇上位关系值"1"表示最抽象的词，数值越大表示词汇具体性越高（Crossley *et al.*，2009）。本研究中词汇上位关系平均值为1.776。Crossley *et al.*（2009）发现经过52周的英语培训，二语学习者的词汇上位关系值从1.44下降到1.05，说明当学习者水平提高时，他们会使用更多抽象的单词。与 Crossley *et al.*（2009）相比，本研究中学生在作文中倾向使用更多比较具体的单词。另外，句子语义相似性（语义衔接度）的指示值介于0到1之间，"0"表示最低的语义相似性，"1"表示最高的语义相似性。本研究中语义相似性的指示值为0.20，表示本研究学生作文的语义衔接度较低。

4.2 中国非英语专业大学生词汇广度和深度在性别、专业和英语水平因素上的差异

我们采用一组单向多因素方差分析来探索学生接受性词汇广度和接受性词汇深度在性别、专业和英语水平上的差异。两个因变量分别为学生的接受性词汇广度（VST）和接受性词汇深度（WAT），自变量分别为学生性别、专业和英语水平。在做单项多因素方差分析之前，我们对初步假设进行了检验，比如正态分布、异常值、线性和方差协方差矩阵均匀性等分析。因变量中六个异常值（multivariate outliers）被排除在数据分析外。

表4表明接受性词汇广度和接受性词汇深度在学生性别［F（2，410）= 3.46，p = 0.032*；Wilks'Lambda = 0.98；Partial Eta Squared = 0.017］、专业［F（2，410）= 6.06，p = 0.003*；Wilks'Lambda = 0.97；Partial Eta Squared = 0.029］以及英语水平上均存在显著差异［F（4，818）= 15.85，p = 0.000**；Wilks'Lambda = 0.86；Partial Eta Squared = 0.072］。

表 4　　学生的接受性词汇广度和接受性词汇深度在其性别、专业和英语水平上差异的多因素方差分析结果

	Wilks'Lambda	F	Hypothesis df	Error df	p	Partial Eta Squared
性别	0.98	3.46	2	410	0.032*	0.017
专业	0.97	6.06	2	410	0.003*	0.029
英语水平	0.86	15.85	4	818	0.000**	0.072

* $p<0.05$，** $p<0.001$

在区分接受性词汇广度和接受性词汇深度（VST 和 WAT）两个因变量之后（见表 5），并且把 Bonferroni adjusted alpha level 设置为 0.025（0.05 除以因变量数量），本研究发现男女学生之间仅在接受性词汇量［F（1，411）= 6.91，p = 0.009*，Partial Eta Squared = 0.017］上存在显著差异。女生的词汇量（M = 65.71，SD = 0.63）显著高于男生（M = 63.13，SD = 0.75）。这个发现和 Gu（2002）的研究结果一致。这一结果可能由以下原因造成。首先，正如 Gu（2002）所指出的，在中国人们普遍认为女生在语言学习上应该更加成功，因此她们可能会有更高的英语学习动机；其次，一些研究（如：Nyikos 1990）发现，女生似乎比男生有更出色的记忆能力；最后，本文作者（2015）发现这些女生（相同受试者）用到的词汇策略频率高于男生。以往研究（如：Gu & Johnson 1996）指出词汇策略使用的频率和词汇知识水平有显著的正相关性，所以本研究结果可能是因为女生使用词汇策略频率高于男生。

文理科学生在接受性词汇量［F（1，411）= 7.81，p = 0.005*，Partial Eta Squared = 0.019］和接受性词汇深度上［F（1，411）= 8.67，p = 0.003*，Partial Eta Squared = 0.021］均存在显著差异。理工科学生接受性词汇量（M = 66.07，SD = 9.64）显著高于文科学生（M = 63.37，SD = 9.96）。同时，前者的接受性词汇深度（M = 100.86，SD = 14.23）显著高于后者（M = 96.25，SD = 17.23）。这一结论和 Gu（2002）的研究结果大致相似。本研究和 Gu（2002）同时发现理工科学生的词汇量高于文科学生，然而在 Gu（2002）的研究中这个差异在数据统计上并不显著。导致本研究结论的原因可能是理工科和文科学生在词汇策略使用上的差异。本文作者（2015）发现理工科学生比文科学生更加倾向于在语境中学习单词，比如使用更多的自主学习策略（self-initiated strategies），推测策略（inferencing strategies）和语言产出策略（production-based strategies）。

最后，不同英语水平上的学生在接受性词汇量［$F(2, 410) = 20.95$，$p = 0.000^{**}$，Partial Eta Squared = 0.093］和接受性词汇深度［$F(2, 410) = 21.89$，$p = 0.000^{**}$，Partial Eta Squared = 0.096］上均存在显著差异。

表5　接受性词汇广度和接受性词汇深度两个因变量分别在学生性别、专业和英语水平上差异的多因素方差分析结果

自变量	因变量	Type III SS	*df*	*MS*	*F*	*p*	Partial Eta Squared
性别	VST	665.91	1	665.91	6.91	0.009*	0.017
	WAT	311.97	1	311.97	1.21	0.271	0.003
专业	VST	751.21	1	751.21	7.81	0.005*	0.019
	WAT	2190.27	1	2190.27	8.67	0.003*	0.021
英语水平	VST	3737.50	2	1868.75	20.95	0.000**	0.093
	WAT	10229.18	2	5114.59	21.89	0.000**	0.096

* $p<0.025$，** $p<0.001$

我们采用图基事后检验法（the post-hoc comparisons using Tukey HSD test）（$p<0.025$）来检测显著性差异具体存在于哪些水平组学生之间。结果表明学生接受性词汇量和接受性词汇深度在每两两水平组之间均存在显著性差异。高水平组学生的接受性词汇量（$M = 71.83$，$SD = 10.44$）显著高于中水平组（$M = 64.29$，$SD = 9.17$）和低水平组学生（$M = 59.44$，$SD = 10.24$）。同时，高水平组学生的接受性词汇深度（$M = 109.44$，$SD = 16.21$）显著高于中水平组（$M = 98.15$，$SD = 14.65$）和低水平组学生（$M = 88.56$，$SD = 18.46$）。中水平组学生的接受性词汇量和接受性词汇深度均显著高于低水平组学生。这些研究结果和以往研究结果部分一致，比如 Qian（1999）发现接受性词汇量和接受性词汇深度与英语阅读能力密切相关。Gu & Johnson（1996）发现接受性词汇量和英语水平密切相关。

另外，我们采用一组单向多因素方差分析来探索学生产出性词汇深度在性别、专业和英语水平因素上的差异。产出性词汇深度指示值为因变量；性别、专业和英语水平为自变量。在做单向多因素方差分析之前，我们对初步假设进行了检验。词汇具体性和意象性两个因变量相关系数过高（0.929），超过了0.80，违背了多重共线性假设（multicollinearity），所以两个因变量必须删除一个。同时，词汇意象性和其他两个变量（词汇多义性和熟悉度）的相关系数较低，略微违背了因变量之间需要有适度的相关性的前提假设，所以词汇意象性被排除在数据分析外。

表6表明学生产出性词汇深度仅在其英语水平因素上存在显著性差异 [F（16，806）= 4.52，p = 0.000**；Wilks'Lambda = 0.84；Partial Eta Squared = 0.082]，而在学生专业和性别因素上差异不显著。

表6　学生的产出性词汇深度在其性别、专业和英语水平上差异的多因素方差分析结果

自变量	Wilks'Lambda	F	Hypothesis df	Error df	p	Partial Eta Squared
英语水平	0.84	4.52b	16	806	0.000**	0.082
专业	0.99	0.50b	8	404	0.855	0.010
性别	0.98	1.09b	8	404	0.373	0.021

** p<0.001

表7是八个因变量单独的分析结果。Bonferroni adjusted alpha level 设置为0.006，三个水平组学生的产出性词汇深度在词汇多样性（F = 23.86，p = 0.000**，Partial Eta Squared = 0.104）、词频（F = 13.63，p = 0.000**，Partial Eta Squared = 0.062）、词汇熟悉度（F = 12.46，p = 0.000**，Partial Eta Squared = 0.057）和词汇意义性（F = 5.38，p = 0.005*，Partial Eta Squared = 0.026）上存在显著差异。

图基事后检验法（p<0.006）结果表明在词汇多样性、词频和词汇熟悉度指示值上，高水平组学生和中低水平组学生均存在显著差异。在词汇意义性指示值上，高水平组仅与低水平组学生之间存在显著差异。这些研究结果表明，高水平学生比中低水平学生使用的单词更加多样化，并且倾向于使用较多的低频词。另外高水平学生使用的单词和其他单词的关联性（词汇意义性）低于低水平学生。这些研究结果和 Crossley *et al.*（2011）的研究结果一致。

表 7　学生产出性词汇深度单个指示值在英语水平因素上差异的多因素方差分析结果

自变量	因变量	Type III Sum of Squares	*df*	*MS*	*F*	*p*	Partial Eta Squared
英语水平	词汇多样性	14425.32	2	7212.66	23.86	0.000**	0.104
	词频	0.30	2	0.15	13.63	0.000**	0.062
	上位关系	0.03	2	0.02	0.35	0.708	0.002
	多义关系	0.20	2	0.10	0.39	0.679	0.002
	语义相似性	0.06	2	0.03	4.50	0.012	0.021
	词汇意义性	2244.65	2	1122.33	5.38	0.005*	0.026
	词汇具体性	2200.30	2	1100.15	3.15	0.044	0.015
	词汇熟悉度	600.29	2	300.14	12.46	0.000**	0.057

* $p<0.006$，** $p<0.001$

5　结语

本研究探讨了中国大陆非英语专业英语学习者的词汇广度和深度现状。学生的词汇量结果高于其他相关研究，但是这些学生在接触英文原版学习资料时仍然会遇到困难。因此，教师可以选择一些和学生水平相符的简化英文读物或者听力材料。另外，学生的接受性词汇深度（WAT）结果和相关研究相比存在差距。基于该问题，教师可以在课堂上多设计一些有关提高学生词汇深度的教学活动。关于产出性词汇深度，学生倾向于在英语写作中使用一些低频词，然后在词汇多样性方面有所不足。基于这方面不足，教师可以告知学生词汇多样性在英语写作中的重要性，并且提供相应的培训来提高学生这方面能力。最后，基于本研究关于词汇广度和深度在学生专业、性别以及英语水平上的差异分析，教师需要努力提高男生英语学习动机，并且鼓励他们像女生一样多使用一些词汇学习策略；文科学生需要更加重视词汇学习，并且可以像理工科学生一样多尝试在语境中学习单词；中低水平学生需要在词汇广度和深度两方面同时提高自己，比如提高英语写作中用词的多样化以及注意词频使用。

本研究存在一些不足之处。首先，受试者大部分选自中国重点大学非英语专业二、三年级的学生，因此受试群体并不能完全代表中国非英语专业外语学习者；其次，本研究采用学生 CET-4 成绩作为划分他们英语水平的标准，然而这个测试只包括听力，阅读和写作三部分（只有部分学生有参加口语考试的机会）。因此，CET-4 成绩并不能完全代表学生的英语水平；最后，由于受到目前词汇深度测试发展限制，本研究对学生词汇深度结果主要进行了与相关研究的横向对比分析，其分析只能大致反映学生词汇深度现状问题。

参考文献

Alderson, J. C., C. Clapham & D. Wall. 1995. *Language Test Construction and Evaluation*. Cambridge: Cambridge University Press.

Author, 2015. A Study of Vocabulary Knowledge and Vocabulary Learning Strategies of Chinese EFL Learners. Ph. D. Dissertation. Macquarie University.

Baayen, R. H., R. Piepenbrock & L. Gulikers. 1995. *The CELEX Lexical Database (CD-ROM)*. Philadelphia, PA: University of Pennsylvania, Linguistic Data Consortium.

Bauer, L. & I. S. P. Nation. 1993. Word families. *International Journal of Lexicography* 6: 253-279.

Beglar, D. 2010. A Rasch-based validation of the Vocabulary Size Test. *Language Testing* 27: 101-118.

Crossley, S. A., T. Salsbury & D. S. McNamara. 2009. Measuring L2 lexical growth using hypernymic relationships. *Language Learning* 59: 307-334.

Crossley, S. A., T. Salsbury & D. S. McNamara. 2011. Predicting the proficiency level of language learners using lexical indices. *Language Testing* 29: 243-263.

Crossley, S. A., T. Salsbury, D. S. McNamara & S. Jarvis. 2010. Predicting lexical proficiency in language learner texts using computational indices. *Language Testing* 28: 1-20

Dale, E. 1965. Vocabulary measurement: Techniques and major findings. *Elementary English* 42: 895-901.

D'Anna, C. A., E. B. Zechmeister & J. W. Hall. 1991. Toward a meaningful definition of vocabulary size. *Journal of Literacy Research* 23: 109-122.

González, M. C. 2013. The Intricate Relationship between Measures of Vocabulary Size and Lexical Diversity as Evidenced in Non - native and Native Speaker Academic Compositions. Ph. D. Dissertation. University of Central Florida Orlando.

Goulden, R., I. S. P. Nation & J. Read. 1990. How large can a receptive vocabulary be? *Applied Linguistics* 11: 341-363.

Graesser, A. C., D. S. McNamara, M. M. Louwerse & Z. Cai. 2004. Coh-Metrix: Analysis of text on cohesion and language. *Behavior Research Methods, Instruments, and Computers* 36: 193-202.

Gu, Y. 2002. Gender, academic major, and vocabulary learning strategies of Chinese EFL learners. *RELC Journal* 33: 35-54.

Hirsh, D. & I. S. P. Nation. 1992. What vocabulary size is needed to read unsimplified texts for pleasure? *Reading in a Foreign Language* 8: 689.

Hu, M. & I. S. P. Nation. 2000. Vocabulary density and reading comprehension. *Reading in a Foreign Language* 13: 403-430.

Ishii, T. & N. Schmitt. 2009. Developing an integrated diagnostic test of vocabulary size and depth. *RELC Journal* 40: 5-22.

Laufer, B. 2001. Quantitative evaluation of vocabulary: How it can be done and what it is good for. In C. Elder, A. Brown, E. Grove, K. Hill, N. Iwashita, T. Lumley, T. McNamara & K. O'Loughlin (eds.). *Experimenting with Uncertainty*. Cambridge: Cambridge University Press. 241-250.

Meara, P. 1982. *Word associations in a foreign language. Nottingham Linguistic Circular* 11: 29-38.

Meara, P. 1996a. The dimensions of lexical competence. In G. Brown, K. Malmkjaer & J. Williams (eds.). *Performance and Competence in Second Language Acquisition*. Cambridge: Cambridge University Press. 35-53.

Meara, P. 1996b. The vocabulary knowledge framework. Retrieved 14/Oct., 2012, from http://www.lognostics.co.uk/vlibrary/index.htm.

Meara, P. & G. Jones. 1988. Vocabulary size as a placement indicator. In P. Grunwell (ed.). *Applied Linguistics in Society*. London: CILT. 80-87.

Meara, P. & J. L. Milton. 2003. *X_ Lex: the Swansea Vocabulary Levels Test*. Newbury: Express Publishing.

Nassaji, H. 2006. The relationship between depth of vocabulary knowledge and L2 learners' lexical inferencing strategy use and success. *The Modern Language Journal* 90: 387-401.

Nation, I. S. P. 1986. *Vocabulary Lists: Words, Affixes, and Stems*. English Language Institute, Victoria University of Wellington.

Nation, I. S. P. 1990. *Teaching and Learning Vocabulary*. New York: Newbury House Publishers.

Nation, I. S. P. 2001. *Learning Vocabulary in Another Language*. Cambridge: Cambridge University Press.

Nation, I. S. P. 2006. How large a vocabulary is needed for reading and listening? *Cana-*

dian Modern Language Review/La Revue canadienne des langues vivantes, 63: 59-82.

Nation, I. S. P. & D. Beglar. 2007. A vocabulary size test. *The Language Teacher* 31: 9-13.

Nation, I. S. P. & R. Waring. 1997. Vocabulary size, text coverage and word lists. In N. Schmitt & M. McCarthy (eds.). *Vocabulary: Description, Acquisition and Pedagogy*. Cambridge: Cambridge University Press. 6-19.

Nguyen, L. T. C. & P. Nation. 2011. A bilingual vocabulary size test of English for Vietnamese learners. *RELC Journal* 42: 86-99.

Nyikos, M. 1990. Sex - related differences in adult language learning: Socialization and memory factors. *The Modern Language Journal* 74: 273-287.

Paribakht, T. S. & M. B. Wesche. 1993. Reading comprehension and second language development in a comprehension-based ESL program. *TESL Canada Journal* 11: 9-29.

Qian, D. D. 1999. Assessing the roles of depth and breadth of vocabulary knowledge in reading comprehension. *Canadian Modern Language Review/La Revue canadienne des langues vivantes* 56: 282-308.

Qian, D. D. 2002. Investigating the relationship between vocabulary knowledge and academic reading performance: An assessment perspective. *Language Learning* 52: 513-536.

Read, J. 1993. The development of a new measure of L2 vocabulary knowledge. *Language Testing* 10: 355-371.

Read, J. 1998. Validating a test to measure depth of vocabulary knowledge. In A. J. Kunnan (ed.). *Validation in Language Assessment: Selected Papers from the 17th Language Testing Research Colloquium*, Long Beach. Mahwah, New Jersey: Lawrence Erlbaum. 41-60.

Richards, J. C. 1976. The role of vocabulary teaching. *TESOL Quarterly* 10: 77-89.

Schmitt, N. 1998. Tracking the incremental acquisition of second language vocabulary: A longitudinal study. *Language Learning* 48: 281-317.

Schmitt, N. 2010. *Researching Vocabulary: A Vocabulary Research Manual.* Basingstoke, England: Palgrave Macmillan.

Schmitt, N. & P. Meara. 1997. Researching vocabulary through a word knowledge framework. *Studies in Second Language Acquisition* 19: 17-36.

Schmitt, N., D. Schmitt & C. Clapham. 2001. Developing and exploring the behaviour of two new versions of the Vocabulary Levels Test. *Language Testing* 18: 55-88.

Schmitt, N. & C. B. Zimmerman. 2002. Derivative word forms: What do learners know? *TESOL Quarterly* 36: 145-171.

Thorndike, E. L. & I. Lorge. 1944. *The Teacher's Word Book of 30,000 Words*. New York: Teacher's College, Columbia University.

Wesche, M. B. & T. S. Paribakht. 1996. Assessing second language vocabulary knowledge: Depth versus breadth. *Canadian Modern Language Review* 53: 13-40.

崔艳嫣、王同顺:《接受性词汇量、产出性词汇量与词汇深度知识的发展路径及其相关性研究》,《现代外语》2006 年第 4 期。

邓昭春:《英语词汇量调查问题探讨——兼评一份全国词汇量调查表》,《外语教学与研究》2001 年第 1 期。

李晓:《词汇量、词汇深度知识与语言综合能力关系研究》,《外语教学与研究》2007 年第 5 期。

刘绍龙:《论二语词汇深度习得及发展特征——关于词义与词缀习得的实证调查》,《外语教学与研究》2001 年第 6 期。

吕长竑:《词汇量与语言综合能力、词汇深度知识之关系》,《外语教学与研究》2004 年第 2 期。

谭晓晨:《中国英语学习者产出性词汇发展研究》,《外语教学与研究》2006 年第 3 期。

席仲恩:《英语专业学生的词汇发展状况调查》,《外语教学》1998 年第 2 期。

吴旭东、陈晓庆:《中国英语学生课堂环境下词汇能力的发展》,《现代外语》2000 年第 4 期。

周大军、文渤燕:《理工科学生英语词汇量状况全程调查》,《外语教学与研究》2000 年第 5 期。

A Study of Vocabulary Breadth and Depth: The Status Quoand Individual Differences

Abstract: This study examines the level of vocabulary knowledge (VK) of 419 Chinese non-English major sophomores atfour universities in Central and West China. VST and WAT were adopted to measure the students' breadth and depth of receptive VK respectively. Besides, 419 English essays were analyzed with Coh-Metrix to measure productive VK multi-dimensionally (i. e. word concreteness, word imagibility) . Findings showed that 1) their average vocabulary size was 6,494 English word families; 2) theirdepth of VK was less satisfactory than their vocabulary size; 3) there were significant differences in the participants' vocabulary size in relation to gender, discipline and proficiency; 4) concerning the participants' receptive depth of VK, the significant differences lay between different discipline and English proficiency groups, and 5) the productive depth of VK was found significantly different among three proficiency groups.

Key words: vocabulary breadth; vocabulary depth; individual differences